The Collected Short Plays of
THORNTON WILDER

The COLLECTED SHORT PLAYS *of* THORNTON WILDER

VOLUME II

Edited by A. Tappan Wilder

THEATRE COMMUNICATIONS GROUP

The Collected Short Plays of Thornton Wilder: Volume II is published by Theatre
Communications Group, Inc., 355 Lexington Ave., New York, NY 10017–0217.

Published by arrangement with The Barbara Hogenson Agency.

Because of space constraints the copyright information continues on page 279.

Wilder, Thornton, 1897–1975.
The collected short plays of Thornton Wilder.—1st ed.
ISBN 1-55936-149-2 (cloth)   ISBN 1-55936-148-4 (paper)
I. Title.
PS3545.I345A6   1998
812'.52—dc21   97-7734
CIP

Book design and typography by Lisa Govan
Cover design by Carol Devine Carson
Cover and frontispiece photographs courtesy of The Thornton Wilder
Archive, Collection of American Literature, Beinecke Rare Book and
Manuscript Library, Yale University

First Edition, June 1998

To Amos and Jenney
and to the memory of
their great-aunt
Isabel Wilder

CONTENTS

Contents

PART II

THE UNERRING INSTINCT

PART III

"THE EMPORIUM"

PREFACE

by A. Tappan Wilder

THIS SECOND VOLUME of *The Collected Short Plays of Thornton Wilder*, inspired by the Wilder Centenary, focuses on the author at work. Its content offers what we hope is a lively encounter with his less familiar drama written from his teen years up into his sixties. We hope this volume also illuminates something of the sources and methods of Thornton Wilder's artistry, indeed his struggles with creating art.

In broad strokes the material includes: a group of early and long-out-of-print "three-minute" playlets designed to be read rather than produced; a "five-minute" confection appearing here for the first time; a short play, once widely disseminated by an organization not ordinarily associated with greenrooms; two fragments from an uncompleted major play; and a complete but rarely produced major drama. All but the confection have published pedigrees, but are found in books either long out of print or not widely known in theatrical circles much less to a broader readership.

As windows to the author at work, this volume also contains the re-publication of several youthful pieces related to Wilder's drama: his own observations about writing and youth; a formal essay about playwriting, written in the same period as *Our Town* and *The Skin of Our Teeth*; and selections from Wilder's *Journals*, the author's most intimate companion in the creative process.

Isabel Wilder (1900–1995), the author's sister and longtime personal agent and confidant, contributed a foreword to the English edition of *The Alcestiad*, Wilder's little-known major play. We have reprinted it here because it deserves to be understood as an official part of the record of this drama.

With the exception of certain short plays in the Wilder cycles on "The Seven Deadly Sins" and "The Seven Ages of Man," the writing in this book spans almost the entirety of Wilder's half-century as a published dramatist. That story begins with the playlets, a disciplined venture in writing which Wilder launched as a teenager. In a September 12, 1916 letter to a family member, Thornton's father, ever nervous about his son's long-term (read "practical" and "remunerative") prospects, described Thornton writing just such a piece:

> He wrote a playlet the other day in ten minutes. I quietly observed him writing as rapidly as he could; no changes. That seemed to me tremendous. He certainly has genius. He lacks the power to tie down to anything he doesn't relish, and so is barred from high achievements, I fear. And yet, genius has laws of its own.

I take pleasure in acknowledging for this volume the same commitment and wise counsel that Terry Nemeth and Steven Samuels at TCG Books; Barbara Hogenson, the Wilder Literary Agent; and Robin Wilder demonstrated in Volume I. The press's editorial front line has been managed by Kathy Sova, whose patience and good sense make all things possible. Donald Gallup, who inspired this enterprise in the first place, contributed proofreading and a share of the notes and bibliography. For more about the background of this project and his role in it, readers should refer to Volume I, published by TCG in 1997, a book dedicated to Mr. Gallup.

A. R. Gurney has blessed this book—an odd duck of a Wilder book without such familiar fare as *Our Town*, *The Long Christmas Dinner*, *The Matchmaker*, *The Skin of Our Teeth*—with a wonderfully thoughtful introduction. I am honored to have the chance to thank him for helping Thornton Wilder's works continue to speak to readers and theatregoers as their author enters his second century.

In many ways, Wilder was never happier than when he was in command of a classroom. All of us involved with this book will have no greater satisfaction than if what Thornton Wilder wrote and *how* he went about writing not only entertains (as art can and should), but also helps (instructs) those who also cannot deny the urge to put their own words on paper.

A. Tappan Wilder
Literary Executor
May 1998

INTRODUCTION

by A. R. Gurney

HERE ARE VARIOUS SKETCHES, playlets, unproduced drafts, miscellaneous one-acts, selected essays, along with a complete full-length drama, by one of America's most cherished writers. Much of this material was written before and after the several notable plays and novels for which Wilder is duly famous, and is best viewed as the efforts of a major artist to find his voice when he was young or to reassert it toward the end of his career. What is so impressive are the clear signs of talent in even the most problematic pieces in this collection. For example, the many short plays from *The Angel That Troubled the Waters and Other Plays* (Coward-McCann, 1928), were not seriously intended for professional production, yet most of them contain surprisingly beautiful flourishes of writing and bright flashes of winsome humor. *The Alcestiad*, on the other hand, was obviously written to be produced, and indeed was so, at the Edinburgh Festival in 1955. Yet in spite of its disappointing subsequent stage history and somewhat erudite tone, it remains an ambitious and moving attempt to articulate Wilder's obsession with the gap between the human and the divine. Also included here are two scenes from a never completed work, "The Emporium," which point toward a fascinating central concept and make us wish that the playwright had developed and completed this work. Wilder's remarks on the theatre and drama are always compelling, and his essays here are particularly so. The remaining material, like all of Wilder's work, could never have been written by anyone else and so is valuable for this reason alone.

This collection, then, is especially useful in helping us arrive at a more general understanding of Thornton Wilder's vision. After all, he is a difficult writer to pin down, partly because of the wide variety and diversity in everything he wrote, and partly because of the strangely elusive nature of his theme. Not only could he shift from fiction to drama without skipping a beat, but he seems equally at home in Classical Greece, Imperial Rome, Eighteenth Century Peru, and Midwestern America. Even within a particular work, he is capable of startling shifts in tone. *Our Town* begins as a seemingly sentimental account of small-town life in New Hampshire, but as the Stage Manager has been reminding audiences all over the world for sixty years, the play turns out to be a tough-minded, starkly powerful meditation on death and human existence. *The Skin of Our Teeth* is a quasi-Joycean account of human survival and self-destructiveness framed in terms of a hackneyed, stagey farce. Even *The Alcestiad*, for all the high seriousness of its form and style, veers suddenly into broad comedy when it brings on Teiresias, emissary of the gods, as a senile clown.

Restless and eclectic, constantly experimenting with form and style, Wilder wrote opera libretti, a screenplay for Hitchcock, a number of astute essays, innumerable letters to some of the most distinguished writers and intellectuals of his day, all the while finding time to serve as an Army Air Force Intelligence Officer during World War II, and establishing himself as a popular and distinguished lecturer at several major universities and in innumerable bars and restaurants. (I myself met him in New Haven in the fifties where I was a student of drama, and I can testify personally to the range of his mind and the charm of his manner.) Is it possible for us to isolate any central theme underlying such protean activity? Is there any way of wrestling him to the ground?

The material anthologized here, because much of it is so simply articulated and straightforwardly presented, may illuminate his thinking more clearly than do those more celebrated works which are complicated by the usual ambiguities of art. Certainly this volume serves to remind us that Wilder is a fundamentally religious man. He says so himself in his introduction to *The Angel That Troubled the Waters and Other Plays*: "Almost all the plays in this book are religious," even though "there has seldom been an age when such a vein was less welcome or less understood." Some of the playlets work with specifically Christian imagery, but it would be wrong to say that he restricts himself to this particular orthodoxy. In fact, sometimes he strives to undercut it, as when "Our Lord" tells Malchus in one of the short plays that the Bible "... isn't always true about me, either." Yet most of these early works concern themselves with eschatological ideas, and these will continue to pervade everything he wrote when he hit his stride.

Several critics have suggested that Wilder's work is informed by a kind of vague pseudo-Christian Platonism, but even this might be too reductive a categorization. It makes more sense to say that he is religious in a general way, in that he is constantly implying a higher order, a world beyond this world, a "something" which seems to be "pushing and contriving" human events so that mankind might reach a higher plane of existence. This vision is articulated with particular power in *Our Town*, but it seeps through most of his other work as well. Time and again he suggests that behind all the trivialities and absurdities and agonies of everyday life there must be a valid meaning, which at least poets and saints are able to perceive dimly and darkly, and toward which they can point us, in a limited way. The title of his underestimated novel, *Heaven's My Destination*, might stand as a simplified statement of Wilder's vision, especially if we define heaven as a kind of weaning away of our earthy identities and concerns, as suggested in *And the Sea Shall Give Up Its Dead* in this volume, or later in *Our Town*.

Furthermore, like other writers who subscribe to a sense of order beyond what is immediately apparent or apprehensible, Wilder tends to focus on what we might call the clash or interplay between what he calls in *Nascuntur Poetae* . . . "the trivial and the divine." Certainly the intersection between two planes of existence has always been a good subject for drama. Sophocles' tragedies have to do with the human struggle to circumvent an Olympic order which may be cruel and undeserved, but is nonetheless relentless and unalterable. Shakespeare's plays resonate with cosmic repercussions when his heroes and villains are viewed as breaking or reinforcing what the Elizabethans saw as a Great Chain of Being ordained by God. Even Shaw, with his commitment to Creative Evolution and a Life Force, sees his characters struggling to confirm or deny the irresistible pressures of an evolutionary destiny operating on them in spite of themselves. Wilder's commitment to an Absolute, however clouded or unspecific, falls very much within this tradition. Like Shaw's supermen, or Shakespeare's kings, or Sophocles' tragic heroes, Wilder's Emily Webb, or Mr. Antrobus, or Alcestis all find themselves negotiating the middle ground between the world of familiar life and a more ultimate power acting on them from somewhere beyond. Wilder and Shaw both ask us to live more "intelligently," as Wilder says in *The Alcestiad*, or Shaw says in almost everything he wrote, so that we are more able to decode the signals which life presents to us. They want people to "realize life while they live it," as Emily says in *Our Town*.

In fact, one might go further in comparing Wilder to Shaw. Both playwrights are in some ways still men of the nineteenth century, in that they hold a firm and ultimately optimistic belief that life has a coherent, and finally benevolent, meaning. Comic though their perspectives may be, the world is neither absurd nor arbitrary to either of them. Both insist that there is a different dimension of experience which life is striving for and which is very much worth realizing. Shaw believes in seizing it through thoughtful intelligence and daring action, and even in his *Back to Methuselah*, attempts to dramatize what happens when we finally get there. Wilder is more passive and ambivalent, yearning for a sense of greater awareness of larger things even as he becomes increasingly reluctant to describe it. "Love is the bridge," he says early in his career, when he attempts to explain why five individuals fell to their seemingly random deaths at the collapse of the bridge of San Luis Rey. Yet this "answer" may now seem, to him and to us, a little reductive and disappointing. His sketches from the incomplete "Emporium" seem to point toward an unknowable, almost Kafka-esque entity presiding over everyday events. In any case, Wilder concludes his novel *The Eighth Day*, written toward the end of his career, by suggesting that while there is a "pattern" in the carpet of human events, there are innumerable and even conflicting ways of perceiving it. Still, for both these playwrights, as well as for their classical predecessors, there is a reality of existence beyond the workaday world which, if more clearly perceived, would inform life with coherence and meaning.

With such religious impulses at the heart of his work, one can understand why Wilder, like his distinguished predecessors, gravitated so naturally to the stage. Drama grew out of religion, and plays are still, in many ways, ritual enactments performed in front of the community to reinforce our sense of our common selves in terms of some larger backdrop. Behind the actors is the plot, and behind most good plots is a sense of moral order which the audience apprehends almost intuitively. When we watch a play, as opposed to when we read a book, we can more easily sense the pressures of a larger, communal vision impacted in the events of the plot and reinforced by the common responses of the audience around us. In most plays, the audience knows more than the characters do, and it is this sense of dramatic irony which brings about the tragic shudders or infectious laughter which give drama its particular power. Because plays tend to work this way, writers who want to suggest that larger forces are operating behind the ostensibly random events of daily life are naturally drawn to the stage.

Furthermore, since drama is, however specific, a crude, confined and intractable medium for articulating such expansive ideas, its very limitations also seem to have attracted Wilder. He delights in calling the audience's attention to the artificial and crude machinery of the theatre, and gains some of his most powerful effects by reminding us that events onstage are a hopelessly inadequate approximation of what they might ultimately mean. The short plays in this volume show Wilder discovering how he can play with the medium in these terms. In *The Flight into Egypt*, for example, Hepzibah, the donkey carrying Mary and the infant Jesus, is an embodiment of the crudeness of enacting an animal on stage, as well as a statement about the sluggishness of material form as it responds recalcitrantly to the inexorable will of God. Later on the playwright will call for the stepladders to serve as second-story windows in *Our Town* or the backstage crew to stand in for planets in *The Skin of Our Teeth* to underscore how the momentous may be couched in the ordinary. Certainly, as he says many times in his comments on the theatre, Wilder is impatient with what we might call realistic drama, because it makes what he would call the false claim of asking us to subscribe to the reality of what we see. Since so much of his work insists upon a greater truth beyond the immediate, one can understand why he'd view stage realism as a kind of heresy.

In fact, it is Wilder's awareness of the continual tension between the seriousness and largeness of his themes and the prosaic limitations of the medium in which they are conveyed that gives his work its special distinction. In his introductory remarks to *The Alcestiad*, he says he is attempting to dramatize what Kierkegaard calls "the incommensurability of things human and divine" as the mortal Alcestis and the divine Apollo strive to communicate with each other, and it is this agonizing strain which occupies so much of his other work. One can understand why Wilder was drawn to Hitchcock's *Shadow of a Doubt*, where a serial killer hides himself in a conventional family in the sunny, self-congratulatory streets of a small town in California. The ordinary is a crude and sometimes misleading mask for the extraordinary in Wilder, but they work together in strange and mysterious ways. Indeed, in those works of his where there is *not* this contrast, where subject and style too closely reflect each other, such as *The Woman of Andros* or *The Alcestiad*, he tends to slip into the precious and artificial. He is best when he can create a daring distance between the magnitude of his theme and the ordinariness of the events which dramatize it.

There is a famous moment in *Our Town* when George Gibbs's sister Rebecca tells him about her friend's receiving a letter which locates Grover's Corners in ". . . the Solar System; the Universe; the Mind of God—that's what it said on the envelope." Rebecca goes on to say: "And the postman brought it just the same." "What do you know!" says George, amazed. Wilder ends his first act on this note, which so feelingly hits home. It is a wonderfully concrete image of the interplay between the divine and the ordinary, and a human response which is both perplexed and astonished. The grand scope of his cosmic vision is modified by the specificity of the postman making his daily rounds. Many of the plays included in this volume show him struggling to find other ways to express this compelling vision.

A. R. Gurney
New York City
May 1998

The Angel That Troubled the Waters and Other Plays

THREE-MINUTE PLAYS
FOR THREE PERSONS

and

The Marriage We Deplore

ENORMOUSLY DISCIPLINED, experimental and industrious with his writing from an early age, Thornton Wilder could claim more than thirty publishing credits in mostly undergraduate journals by the time he graduated from college in 1920. This body of work encompassed essays, poetry, short pieces of fiction, dramatic criticism, a full-length play and, prominently in terms of numbers and thus training in playwriting, a number of three-minute playlets.

The unprecedented success of *The Bridge of San Luis Rey* after 1927 triggered the appearance in October 1928 of sixteen playlets in a volume entitled *The Angel That Troubled the Waters and Other Plays* (Coward-McCann, New York, 1928). Of the total number, twelve were written during his college years and four written especially for *The Angel* publication, his first book of published drama. The publishers were understandably not shy about tying *The Angel* to *The Bridge*, a novel then selling at the rate of some ten thousand copies a week. The dust jacket copy read:

> [These plays] should prove of exceptional interest as showing the development of a talent which has astonished the critical world.

While written to be read, Wilder's "Three-Minute Plays" have, in fact, had a notable if largely undocumented history of informal readings and performances in churches, schools and as curtain raisers. In 1978, in a true first—described as "Producing the Unproducible"—the public television station in Madison, Wisconsin, successfully "produced" four of these playlets in a half-hour show titled "Wilder, Wilder." In England and Germany several have also been fashioned into mini-operas.

■ ▭ ■

The Marriage We Deplore, the short play found on page 77, is an example of juvenilia from the same period as *The Angel* playlets, although scaled to last five minutes rather than three. It appears here for the first time.

FOREWORD

by Thornton Wilder

Wilder wrote this Foreword to *The Angel That Troubled the Waters and Other Plays* in June 1928, soon after receiving the Pulitzer Prize for *The Bridge of San Luis Rey*. At the time, to devote more time to writing, he was about to step out of his life as a French teacher and as the dormitory master of Davis House at the Lawrenceville School in New Jersey.

IT IS A DISCOURAGING business to be an author at sixteen years of age. Such an author is all aspiration and no fulfillment. He is drunk on an imaginary kinship with the writers he most admires, and yet his poor overblotted notebooks show nothing to prove to others, or to himself, that the claim is justified. The shortest walk in the country is sufficient to start in his mind the theme, the plan and the title, especially the title, of a long book; and the shortest hour when he has returned to his desk is sufficient to deflate his ambition. Such fragments as he is finally able to commit to paper are a mass of echoes, awkward relative clauses and conflicting styles. In life and in literature mere sincerity is not sufficient, and in both realms the greater the capacity

the longer the awkward age. Yet strange lights cross that
confusion, authoritative moments that all the practice of
later maturity cannot explain and cannot recapture. He is
visited by great depressions and wild exhilarations, but
whether his depressions proceed from his limitations in the
art of living or his limitations in the art of writing he cannot tell. An artist is one who knows how life should be lived
at its best and is always aware of how badly he is doing it.
An artist is one who knows he is failing in living and feeds
his remorse by making something fair, and a layman is one
who suspects he is failing in living but is consoled by his
successes in golf, or in love, or in business.

Authors of fifteen and sixteen years of age spend their
time drawing up title pages and adjusting the tables of contents of works they have neither the perseverance nor the
ability to execute. They compass easily all the parts of a
book that are inessential. They compose dignified prefaces,
discover happy quotations from the Latin and the French,
and turn graceful dedications. This book is what is left of
one of these projects.

The title was to have been *Three-Minute Plays for Three
Persons*. I have lately found one of my early tables of contents for it, written in the flyleaves of a First Year Algebra.
Quadratics in those days could be supported only with the
help of a rich marginal commentary. Usually these aids to
education took the shape of a carefully planned repertory
for two theatres, a large and a small. Here my longer plays
were to alternate with *The Wild Duck* and *Measure for
Measure* and were cast with such a roll of great names as
neither money nor loyalty could assemble. The chapter on
Combinations and Permutations ended short by several
inches, and left me sufficient space to draw up a catalog of
all the compositions I had heard of that were the work
of Charles Martin Loeffler. This list of *Three-Minute Plays*
was drawn up in Berkeley, California, in the spring of
1915. It contains several that have since been rejected, two
that are in the present volume, *Brother Fire* and *Proserpina*

and the Devil, and the names of many that were unwritten then and that still, through the charm of their titles, ask to be written.

Since then I have composed some forty of these plays, for I had discovered a literary form that satisfied my passion for compression. Since the time when I began to read I had become aware of the needless repetition, the complacency in most writing. Who does not know the empty opening paragraphs, the deft but uninstructive transitions, and the closing paragraphs that summarize a work and which are unnecessary to an alert reader?

Moreover, their brevity flatters my inability to sustain a long flight, and the inertia that barely permits me to write at all. And finally, when I became a teacher, here was the length that could be compassed after the lights of the House were out and the sheaf of absurd French exercises corrected and indignantly marked with red crayon. In time the three minutes and the three persons became a habit, and no idea was too grandiose—as the reader will see—for me to try and invest it in this strange discipline.

There were other plans for this book. There was to have been a series of Footnotes to Biographies, suggested by Herbert Eulenberg's *Schattenbilder*, represented here by the Mozart [*Mozart and the Gray Steward*], the Ibsen [*Centaurs*], and the St. Francis play [*Brother Fire*]. There were hopes of a still more difficult series. Dürer's two sets of woodcuts illustrating the Passion were to serve as model for a series of plays that would be meditations on the last days of Our Lord. Two of them are in this book [*Now the Servant's Name Was Malchus, Hast Thou Considered My Servant Job?*]. There was to have been a series illustrating the history of the stage, and again, two of them are in this book [*Fanny Otcott, Centaurs*]. How different the practice of writing would be if one did not permit oneself to be pretentious. Some hands have no choice: they would rather fail with an oratorio than succeed with a ballad.

During the years that these plays were being written I

was reading widely, and these pages are full of allusions to it. The art of literature springs from two curiosities, a curiosity about human beings pushed to such an extreme that it resembles love, and a love of a few masterpieces of literature so absorbing that it has all the richest elements of curiosity. I use the word *curiosity* in the French sense of a tireless awareness of things. (It is too late to arrest the deterioration of our greatest English words. We live in an age where *pity* and *charity* have taken on the color of condescension; where *humility* seems to mean an acknowledgment of failure; where *simplicity* is foolishness and *curiosity* is interference. Today *hope,* and *faith* itself, imply a deliberate self-deception.) The training for literature must be acquired by the artist alone, through the passionate assimilation of a few masterpieces written from a spirit somewhat like his own, and of a few masterpieces written from a spirit not at all like his own. I read all Newman, and then I read all Swift. The technical processes of literature should be acquired almost unconsciously on the tide of a great enthusiasm, even syntax, even sentence construction; I should like to hope, even spelling. I am thinking of some words of Renan commenting in the *Souvenirs d'Enfance et de Jeunesse* upon his education:

> *Pour moi, (je) crois que la meilleure manière de former des jeunes gens de talent est de ne jamais leur parler de talent ni de style, mais de les instruire et d'exciter fortement leur esprit sur les questions philosophiques, religieuses, politiques, sociales, scientifiques, historiques; en un mot, de procéder par l'enseignement du fond des choses, et non par l'enseignement d'une creuse rhétorique.*

The last four plays here [*Mozart and the Gray Steward, Hast Thou Considered My Servant Job?, The Flight into Egypt, The Angel That Troubled the Waters*] have been written within a year and a half. Almost all the plays in this book are religious, but religious in that dilute fashion that is a believer's concession to a contemporary standard of good manners. But these four plant their flag as boldly as they may. It is the kind of work that I would most like to do well, in spite of the fact that there has seldom been an age in literature when such a vein was less welcome and less understood. I hope, through many mistakes, to discover the spirit that is not unequal to the elevation of the great religious themes, yet which does not fall into a repellent didacticism. Didacticism is an attempt at the coercion of another's free mind, even though one knows that in these matters beyond logic, beauty is the only persuasion. Here the schoolmaster enters again. He sees all that is fairest in the Christian tradition made repugnant to the new generations by reason of the diction in which it is expressed. The intermittent sincerity of generations of clergymen and teachers has rendered embarrassing and even ridiculous all the terms of the spiritual life. Nothing succeeds in dampening the aspirations of the young today—who dares use the word "aspiration" without enclosing it, knowingly, in quotation marks?—like the names they hear given to them. The revival of religion is almost a matter of rhetoric. The work is difficult, perhaps impossible (perhaps all religions die out with the exhaustion of the language), but it at least reminds us that Our Lord asked us in His work to be not only as gentle as doves, but as wise as serpents.

Thornton Wilder
The Davis House
Lawrenceville, NJ
June 1928

Nascuntur Poetae ...

CHARACTERS

THE WOMAN IN THE CHLAMYS
THE BOY
THE WOMAN IN DEEP RED

SETTING

A painting of Piero di Cosimo.

We are gazing into some strange incomprehensible painting of Piero di Cosimo—a world of pale blues and greens, of abrupt peaks in agate and of walled cities, of flying red stags with hounds at their throats, and of lions in tears beside their crowns. On the roads are seen traveling companies, in no haste and often lost in contemplation of the sky. A boy sits on a rock in the foreground. He is listening to the words of a woman dressed in a chlamys that takes on the color of the objects about her.

THE WOMAN IN THE CHLAMYS: In a far valley, boy, sit those who in their lifetime have possessed some special gift of eye or ear or finger. There they sit apart, choosing their successors. And when on the winds toward birth the souls of those about to live are borne past them, they choose the brighter spirits that cry along that wind. And you were chosen.

THE BOY: For what gift, lady, did the choice fall? Am I to mould in clay, or paint? Shall I sing or mime, lady? What choice fell on me and from what master?

THE WOMAN IN THE CHLAMYS: It is enough to know that you were chosen.

THE BOY: What further remains to be done? You have poured on my eyes and ears and mouth the divine ointment; you have laid on my tongue the burning ember. Why do we delay?

THE WOMAN IN THE CHLAMYS: Be not so eager for life. Too soon you will be shaken by breath; too soon and too long you will be tossed in the tumult of the senses.

THE BOY: I am not afraid of life. I will astonish it. —Why are we delaying?

THE WOMAN IN THE CHLAMYS: My sister is coming now. Listen to her.

(The Woman in the Chlamys withdraws and gives place to her sister, whose feet stir not the shells upon the path. She wears a robe of deep and noble red and bears in her hands a long golden chain hung about with pendants. Her face is fixed in concentration and compassion, like the face of one taking part in a sacrifice of great moment.)

THE BOY: All is ready. What do you come to do?

THE WOMAN IN DEEP RED: My sister has given you the gifts of pride and of joy. But those are not all.

THE BOY: What gifts remain? I have been chosen. I am ready.

THE WOMAN IN DEEP RED: Those gifts are vain without these. He who carries much gold stumbles. I bring the dark and necessary gifts. This golden chain . . .

THE BOY *(With mounting fear)*: Your face is shadowed. Draw back; take back all the gifts, if I must accept these also.

THE WOMAN IN DEEP RED: Too late. Too late. You had no choice in this. You must bow your head.

THE BOY: I am trembling. My knees are hot with my tears.

THE WOMAN IN DEEP RED: Since only tears can give sight to the eyes. *(She drops the chain about his neck)*

THE BOY: Then am I permitted to know the meaning of these pendants?

THE WOMAN IN DEEP RED: This is a tongue of fire. It feeds upon the brain. It is a madness that in a better country has a better name.

THE BOY: These are mysteries. Give them no names.

THE WOMAN IN DEEP RED: This is a leaf of laurel from a tree not often plucked. You shall know pride and the shining of the eyes—of that I do not speak now.

THE BOY: And this, lady?

THE WOMAN IN DEEP RED: That is a staff and signifies the journey that awaits you your life long; for you are homeless.

THE BOY: And this . . . this is of crystal . . .

THE WOMAN IN DEEP RED: That is yours alone, and you shall smart for it. It is wonderful and terrible. Others shall know a certain peace, and shall live well enough in the limits of the life they know; but you shall be forever hindered. For you there shall be ever beyond the present a lost meaning and a more meaningful love.

THE BOY: Take back the chain. Take back your gifts. Take back life. For at its end what can there be that is worth such pain?

THE WOMAN IN DEEP RED *(Slowly drawing back into the shadow of the wood)*: Farewell, child of the muses, playfellow in the bird-haunted groves. The life of man awaits you, the light laughter and the misery in the same day, in the selfsame hour the trivial and the divine. You are to give it a voice. Among the bewildered and the stammering thousands you are to give it a voice and to mark its meaning. Farewell, child of the muses, playfellow in the bird-haunted . . .

(The Woman in the Chlamys returns.)

THE WOMAN IN THE CHLAMYS: You must go now. Listen to that wind. It is the great fan of time that whirls on the soul for a season.

THE BOY: Stay a moment. I am not yet brave.

(She leads him into a grotto and the young soul and his chain are lost in the profound shade.)

END OF PLAY

Proserpina and the Devil

A PLAY FOR MARIONETTES

CHARACTERS

THE MANAGER
THE FIRST MANIPULATOR
THE SECOND MANIPULATOR
THE PUPPETS: Proserpina, Demeter, Hermes and Devil

SETTING

A puppet show, Venice, 1640 A.D.

THE MANAGER *(Winningly)*: Citizens and little citizens! We are going to give you a delicious foretaste of our great performance this afternoon, to which the whole world is coming. This is a pantomime about how a beautiful girl named Proserpina was snatched away by the Devil, and how her mother searched for her over all the hills of the world, and how at last she was able to bring her back to the earth for six months out of every year.

THE FIRST MANIPULATOR *(Behind the scenes)*: Let go them strings.

THE MANAGER: At our great performance this afternoon this same play will be given *with words*; and besides it the story of the brave Melusina and her wanderings when she was driven out of Parma.

THE SECOND MANIPULATOR *(His voice rising in anger)*: You don't have to show me!

THE MANAGER: On with the play! —But don't forget to bring your rich aunts this afternoon.

> *(To the Manipulators)* Hurry through with it. I'm off for a cup of wine.

(The curtain rises with indecent haste and shows the under-world. The rivers Styx and Acheron have been replaced by a circular piece of cloth, sulphur-colored, with waves delicately embroidered about the margin. This is the Lake of Wrath and in it are seen floating arms and legs—all that are left, alas, of great puppets, Abraham, Penelope and Jephtha's daughter, Midas and Harlequin. Beside the lake Proserpina is straying, robed in bluish black as one anticipating grief. Pluto—now a medieval Satan—is stealthily approaching her. Suddenly Proserpina throws up her arms, runs to him and buries her face in his scarlet bosom. Noah's Ark—mutely protesting against the part it must play, with all its Christianized animals within it, of Charon's barge—is lowered from the proscenium and the curtain falls.)

THE FIRST MANIPULATOR *(Sotto voce)*: Beard of Medusa! You made her run in the wrong direction: The hussy courted death. Didn't I tell you he was to chase her three times around the lake?

THE SECOND MANIPULATOR *(Sulkily)*: I don't care. A person can't tell which is his right hand and which is his left in this place.

THE FIRST MANIPULATOR: Here, you let me take her; you take the Devil. —Got the orange?

(When the puppets are next seen Proserpina is exhibiting grief in pantomime. Her lord with affectionate gestures urges her to eat of a yellow pomegranate. Sadly she puts it to her mouth. With an odd recollection of the Garden of Eden, she tempts him into eating the remaining half. They go out cheerlessly.)

All right for that. Now I'll take the mother and the Devil. You take the other fellow and the daughter.

(Demeter, a handsome Italian matron in a wide gown of brocade, enters with her arms outstretched. At her elbow Hermes, the Archangel Gabriel, guides her through the Lake of Perdition. Proserpina and her husband return and throw up their hands in amazement. Again the frantic girl runs in the wrong direction and casts herself into the arms of Satan. Demeter tries to draw her away, but a matter of pins and hooks-and-eyes prevents her rescue.)

Oh, you Gazoon! You lack-eyed Silenus! Your hands are nothing but feet.

THE SECOND MANIPULATOR: The Devil take your show and you with it.

(The altercation behind the scenes grows out of bounds and one blow knocks down the stage. The Archangel falls upon the pavement and is cherished by gamins unto the third generation; the Devil rolls into the lake; Proserpina is struck by a falling cloud, and lies motionless on her face; Demeter by reason of the stiffness of her brocade stands upright, viewing with staring eyes the ills of her daughter.)

END OF PLAY

Fanny Otcott

CHARACTERS

MRS. OTCOTT, an actress
SAMPSON, a servant
ATCHESON, an old friend of Mrs. Otcott's

SETTING

Outside Mrs. Otcott's home.

Mrs. Otcott, that great actress in the tradition of the Siddons, the Oldfield, Bracegirdle, O'Neill, is spending a quiet month in Wales. We do not see the cottage, we do not even see the mountains, but there is a stretch of lawn on whose gentle slope there stands an ancient round tower overgrown with ivy. In the shadow of this Arthurian monument, Mrs. Otcott has placed a table whereon she is sorting old engravings, playbills, letters, contracts, ribbons—in short, her past. She is still the handsome, humorous, Irish soul from whom every item out of the old trunks exacts its exclamation, its gesture, its renewed indignation or pleasure. She is attended by a blackamoor boy in livery, half asleep against a flowerpot.

MRS. OTCOTT: Sampson! Tay!

SAMPSON *(Springing up)*: Yes, ma'am. Wid or widout a streak o' cream?

MRS. OTCOTT: Widout. And Sampson, tell Pence I am not at home. Not even to the one in the yellow curls, or to the good black beard. And if they seem to know that I am at home, tell them . . . that I have gone up the tower, or that I have the vapors.

SAMPSON: You wants tea widout, and tell Mrs. Pence you don't want to see none of de gentlemen from de village inn—dat you has de vapors.

MRS. OTCOTT: There! Do you see that, Sampson? I wore that the night the king dined with me on the stage.

SAMPSON *(His eyes as big as soup plates)*: King . . . James!

MRS. OTCOTT *(Shuddering)*: No, stupid—Charles. —Go away! This afternoon I shall devote to another woman, to another and a different woman, and yet to myself, to myself, to myself.

SAMPSON: I'll tell Mrs. Pence.

(He goes out. Mrs. Otcott picks up a packet of letters. One look, tosses them away, then rises muttering; goes and stamps on them and laughs. She returns to pick up a play-bill and reads the heading with glistening eyes: "Fanny Otcott as Faizella in the Princess of Cathay. *First time." She strides about lost in thought. She almost walks into a gentleman who has entered through the hedge. He is wearing a black hat and cape, and has a serious worn face.)*

ATCHESON: Your servant, Mrs. Otcott.

MRS. OTCOTT *(Thunderstruck)*: Why, *no*! Yes! By the garter, it is George Atcheson. Oh! Oh! Oh!

ATCHESON: I do not disturb you, Mrs. Otcott? I . . . I came to discuss a thing that is very serious to me.

MRS. OTCOTT *(Suddenly very pleased)*: Everything is—sit down, my friend. You always were very serious. That's why you made such a bad Hamlet. Delay your serious talk, George, and tell me about the women you have loved since you loved me, and confess that I finally made them all unendurable to you.

ATCHESON: You misunderstand me, Mrs. Otcott . . .

MRS. OTCOTT *(Loudly)*: Fanny.

ATCHESON: Ah . . . Fanny?

MRS. OTCOTT: All you need is a little coaxing. Well, George, a woman drove you on to the stage when you were preparing for the church, and a woman drove you off, and it was my greatest service to the stage. Look, George, you remember me as Faizella in the *Princess of Cathay.* I never did better than that. Great Rufus, you played opposite me in it. Look!

ATCHESON: Perhaps you remember . . . I lost consciousness . . .

MRS. OTCOTT: Ah yes! The pale divinity student fainted. Oh! George, you were the first of my lovers. No, it wasn't love, perhaps, but it was beautiful. It was like hawthorn buds and meadowlarks and Mr. Handel's Water Music. And since, I have never ceased searching for love. Perhaps love strikes the first time or never at all. Then I was too much in love with my work. And, oh, George, how young we were! But you were very dear to me in the old garret, and I'm sorry to see you're growing stout, for it's one more reminder that I shall probably live and die without having known the lightning of love.

(She sits down with a great flow of silken draperies and shakes her head at him ruefully.)

ATCHESON: I have come to discuss our . . . our association . . .

MRS. OTCOTT: Thunder and hell! Don't you call that an association!

ATCHESON: . . . but my view of it is very different.

(Her shoe commences to mark time nervously on the turf.)

After my retirement from the stage I resumed my theological studies, and I am now Bishop of Westholmstead.

(The shoe is now motionless.)

None of my friends know of that . . . that experience in my life, but it has always remained as a bitter . . . as a distressing spot in my conscience.

MRS. OTCOTT *(After a pause, very rapidly)*: I see, you want to make a clean breast of the perilous stuff. You want to make a public confession, probably. You are married?

ATCHESON: Yes.

MRS. OTCOTT: You have several sons probably?

ATCHESON: Yes.

MRS. OTCOTT: And you lie awake nights, saying: "Hypocrisy, hypocrisy."

(Pause) Well, make your confession. But why consult me?

ATCHESON: I have followed your course, madam, and seen the growing admiration your art commands in court— I might almost say in the church.

MRS. OTCOTT: You do not suppose that that revelation would cast any deeper shadow on the good name of Fanny Otcott, such as it is. Remember, George, the months you call sinful. It wasn't love, perhaps, but it was grace and poetry. The heavens rained odors on us. It was as childlike and harmless as paintings on fans. I was a girl tragedienne reciting verses endlessly before a mirror and you were a young student who for the first time had seen a young girl braid her hair and sing at her work. Since then you have learned long names from books and heard a great many sneers from women as old as myself. You have borrowed your ideas from those who have never begun to live and who dare not.

ATCHESON *(His head in his hands and his elbows on his knees)*: I do not know what to think. Your reasoning is full of perils.

MRS. OTCOTT: Go away and tell your congregations what you please. I feel as though you were communicating to my mind some of those pitiable remorses that have weakened you. I have sinned, but I have not that year on my conscience. It is that year and my playing of Faizella that will bring troops of angels to welcome me to Paradise. Go away and tell your congregations what you please.

ATCHESON: You give me no help in the matter, Mrs. Otcott.

MRS. OTCOTT: Go away. In the name of Heaven, go!

(Crooked with doubt and hesitation, the Bishop of Westholmstead goes out through the hedge. For a few moments Mrs. Otcott sits on the table, swinging one foot and muttering savagely in an imaginary conversation.

Reenter Sampson with a tray.)

SAMPSON: Three gentlemen waited on you from de village inn, but Mrs. Pence sent dem away. She said you was up de tower, ma'am.

MRS. OTCOTT *(Showily)*: Go call them back, Sampson. Tell them I have come down from de tower. Bring up the best box of wine—the one with my picture painted on it. I shall be young again.

END OF PLAY

Brother Fire

CHARACTERS

ANNUNZIATA, a peasant woman
ISOLA, her daughter, about eight
BROTHER FRANCIS, their friend

SETTING

A hut in the mountains of northern Italy.

Annunziata is preparing the evening meal over the fire. Isola is playing beside her.

ANNUNZIATA: Now, now! Not so near. One of these days you'll be falling into the fire, and there'll be nothing left to tell us about you but your shoes. Put them on and get out the bowls for supper.
ISOLA: I like to play with the fire.

ANNUNZIATA: What a thing to say!

ISOLA: I'd like to let my hair into it, gently, gently, gently, gently.

ANNUNZIATA: Don't you hear me tell you it's a wicked thing?

ISOLA: Brother Francis says it's our brother, and one of the best things in the world.

ANNUNZIATA: Tchk, Tchk! —What makes the starling sing in his cage all of a sudden?

ISOLA: It's Brother Francis himself looking at us.

ANNUNZIATA: Tell him to come in and have some supper.

ISOLA: Come in, my mother says, and have some supper.

(Brother Francis appears at the door. He blesses the house.)

BROTHER FRANCIS: I can very well go on to my own supper and need not lighten your kettle.

ANNUNZIATA: Come in, Brother Francis. What you take will not even make a new ring around the kettle. Besides, I see you have been up to the top of the mountain again. You are cold and wet. Come and sit by the fire.

BROTHER FRANCIS: Yes, I have been up to the very top since yesterday, among the rocks and the birds in the rocks. Brother Wind was there and Sister Rain was there, but Brother Fire was not.

ANNUNZIATA: Now you sit by him, Isola, while I get some more wood; but don't ask him any questions. Now, Brother, put this fur skin across your knees.

(She goes out.)

ISOLA: What did you do, Brother Francis?

BROTHER FRANCIS: I watched and waited to see what they would let me see. For a long while there was nothing; then they nodded to one another, meaning that it was permitted to me. I watched seven stars closely. Suddenly they turned and fled inwards, and I saw the Queen of

Heaven leading forth her company before all the shipwrecked seamen of this world. —However, do not tell
thy mother, for she believes in no one's miracles but her
own.

ISOLA: My mother says the fire is a wicked thing.

BROTHER FRANCIS *(Turning)*: What, Sister Annunziata,
how can you say that? —Why, what would cook your
broth, what would keep you warm? And when you
return from the mountaintops, what else shines out
from all the friendly windows of the world? Look at its
flames, how they lean towards us!

ISOLA: It says: Give me something to eat. Give me something to eat.

BROTHER FRANCIS *(Excitedly)*: Yes, yes. Its warmth is a kind
of hunger. I have a love for all things in fur, feathers and
scales, but I have not less a love for the fire that warms us.

(He edges the cloak into the fire) Look how it reaches
for it. Wicked? Wicked? Never.

ISOLA: But, Brother Francis, it will . . . it will . . .

*(The flames suddenly seize the cloak. Francis rises, wrapped
in fire.)*

Brother Francis, you are on fire! Mother, Mother!

*(She rushes from the hut and returns with her mother.
Annunziata snatches the fur from Brother Francis and
throws it into the hearth.)*

BROTHER FRANCIS *(Still standing ecstatically with lifted
hands)*: Eat, Brother Fire. I knew you wanted this. I
knew that you loved me too.

(He looks about him; then ruefully to Annunziata)
Sister, you have spoiled his supper.

ANNUNZIATA *(With somber and averted face)*: I do not know
what you mean. Here is your bowl of broth. Sit down
and eat it.

BROTHER FRANCIS: Sister, do not be angry with me.

ANNUNZIATA *(Breaking out)*: Come now, should we kill everything, the animals for their furs, yes, and one another, to feed them to the fire? Is it not enough that it takes our good pine tree by our road? There, that is logic, Brother Francis.

BROTHER FRANCIS: Bring me not logic, sister. She is the least of the handmaids of Love. I am often troubled when she speaks.

ANNUNZIATA: Must we give what makes us often warm for that which makes us warm only for a moment?

BROTHER FRANCIS *(Waving his wooden spoon about humorously)*: My mind is strangely light tonight, like the flames that play about the relics of Saint James. I could wander again through the whole night.

ANNUNZIATA: Where is your mother that she should watch over you? Had I not these other duties I should leave everything and watch over you myself.

BROTHER FRANCIS: She is in Paradise with a golden crook, leading the flames that died of hunger in this wicked world. She leads them to pasture on drifts of dried leaves. Look, Isola, I know that there is flame to burn all evil in the Lake of the Damned. I do not speak of that now, but I know also that fire is at all times useful to the great Blessed. It surrounds them and they dwell in it. And even now . . .

(And so on.)

END OF PLAY

The Penny That Beauty Spent

CHARACTERS

CLAIRE-LOUISE, "LA GRACILE," a dancer
QUINTE, her husband
THE JEWELER

SETTING

A jeweler's shop in Paris.

The little heartbreak takes place in a rococo jeweler's shop. The shop is elegantly small and elegantly polished. The few jewels and the few pieces of brocade are tossed from surface to surface in a world of glass, from the chandelier to the mirrors and from the mirrors to the cases. It is royalty's own place of purchase, and the great egotistical head is present in bust and in miniature and on the backs of spoons. The old jeweler, enigmatic and smiling, is suddenly called to the door by a great clatter. A girl enters borne on the shoulders of a boy little older than herself. La Gracile is thin and pinch-faced, but long penury has only made her the more elfin. Illness is already writing its progress in the eyes and on the brow of Quinte. But they are deliciously happy and full of their secrets. Quinte lifts her onto the counter and draws back.

LA GRACILE: While you are with me I need never touch the ground. You can carry me from cushion to cushion.

QUINTE: And on your gravestone will be inscribed: "Here lies an exquisite dancer, she who never touched the ground."

LA GRACILE: And beside mine yours will read: "Here lies her husband, the soul of her life, the sole of her shoes."

THE JEWELER: Mademoiselle is in pain? The feet of mademoiselle are in pain?

LA GRACILE *(After she has recovered, with Quinte, from the whirlwind of intimate amusement that this preposterous idea has caused them)*: No. I am the new dancer. I am La Gracile. Except when I dance I wear nothing on my feet but little velvet pockets. So when I am not wearing my practice slippers, my husband carries me about.

THE JEWELER: Oh, you are La Gracile. We have already heard of your great success last night. The king is delighted with you.

LA GRACILE *(Shrilly, clapping her hands)*: Yes, yes, yes. I was a great success. Even the king's favorite, Madame d'Hautillon, was jealous. She tried to stand on my foot. They call me the moth of Versailles.

THE JEWELER: And now the king has sent you here to choose a present for yourself.

LA GRACILE: How did you know?

THE JEWELER: The king sends to me for a gift every young lady who pleases him. Madame d'Hautillon was here last.

LA GRACILE *(Chattering on)*: I want nothing myself. It is to be for Quinte. A chronometer, please, that strikes every hour with a gavotte and midnight with a saraband.

QUINTE: Nothing for me, Claire-Louise. When my cough returns it will shake every ornament off me, the buttons from my coat, the rings from my thin fingers. You must have something in pearls.

LA GRACILE: Silly Quinte, I want nothing.

QUINTE: But I suppose . . . You must wear something for the king.

LA GRACILE *(Suddenly under a passing cloud of melancholy, resting her cheek on his hair, plaintively)*: I do not want a great showy pin on my breast. I want only a little white daisy from our beloved Brittany, from Grandmother's field that had too many stones.

QUINTE: Tell her what you have, Monsieur Jeweler.

THE JEWELER: Mademoiselle will look at this chain? Its art is secret. It is painted gold, the work of aged nuns in Hamburg.

QUINTE: Oh look, Claire-Louise, this flower for your hair. Many topazes were splintered to powder on the wheel before this perfect one.

THE JEWELER: Etiquette forbids, mademoiselle, your buying that; it happens to be the very thing that Madame d'Hautillon bought for herself.

LA GRACILE *(Arousing herself, imperiously)*: Have you a little fat chronometer with many jewels in it?

THE JEWELER *(Proffering a tray)*: The best in Paris.

LA GRACILE *(Giving one to Quinte)*: That is for you, Quinte, from myself and from the dull king. Like my thoughts, it will rest on your heart, but long after it is sold as wire and rust my love will go on in the land where clocks do not mark off one sad moment from another.

QUINTE *(With tears)*: Claire-Louise, it can be of no pleasure to me. In a while it will only please me because it is a little cool in my hot hand.

LA GRACILE *(Softly, in pain)*: Courage, dearest Quinte, courage.

THE JEWELER *(Interrupting formally)*: Remember, mademoiselle, that etiquette demands that you will choose a present that His Majesty will admire on you.

LA GRACILE *(Stormily)*: I shall choose what I please.

THE JEWELER *(Insinuatingly)*: Your life is only to please the king. He has chosen you. By sending you here he is telling you that.

LA GRACILE: You are mistaken . . . But I am only a poor thin dancer that . . . that has worked too hard. Besides, this is my husband.

THE JEWELER *(Smiling)*: No, mademoiselle, he is not your husband.

(La Gracile jumps down and walks away weeping bitterly, her little feet-sacks flopping against the polished floor. She suddenly turns with blazing eyes.)

LA GRACILE: I shall run away to Brittany . . . I shall scratch his eyes out.

(The Jeweler smiles at this foolish notion and leans across the counter, holding toward her a great jewel-encrusted buckle.)

LA GRACILE *(Wildly)*: Even though all Versailles kill me with steel pins, Quinte shall have the watch.

(But he has fallen among the gilt chairs.)

END OF PLAY

The Angel on the Ship

CHARACTERS

VAN, the under-cook
MINNA, the captain's wife
SAM, a crew member

SETTING

The foredeck of the *Nancy Bray*, lying disabled in mid-ocean.

The figurehead of the Nancy Bray *has been torn from its place and nailed to the forepost, facing the stern—back to back, as it were, with its former position. It is the half-length of an angel bearing wreaths; she is highly colored and buxom, and has flowing yellow hair. On the deck lie three persons in the last stages of rags and exhaustion: Minna, the remnant of a stout, coarse woman; Van, a little, sharp youth; and a fat, old sleepy Jamaica Sam.*

VAN *(Driving the last nail into the figurehead)*: There she is. She's the new Gawd of the Atlantic. It's only a she-Gawd, but that's a good enough Gawd for a sailor.

MINNA *(Seated on the deck)*: Us'll call her Lily. That's a name like a god's.

SAM: Youm be quick. Youm say your prayers quick.

MINNA *(Blubbering)*: Her can't hear us. Her's just the old figgerhead we had thirty years.

VAN: Her's an angel. Her knows everything.

(He throws himself on his knees and lays his forehead on the boards. In a hoarse whisper:)

That's the joss way. We all got t'do it.

(The others do likewise.)

SAM: Us'll pray in turns. Us must be quick. There ain't no more water to drink, and there ain't no more sails left to carry us on. Us'll have to be quick. Youm begin, Van. Youms a great lad with the words.

VAN *(With real fanaticism)*: Great Gawd Lily, on the ship *Nancy Bray*, all's lost with us if you don't bring us rain to drink. All the secret water I saved aside is drunk up, and we got to go over the side with the rest if you don't bring us rain today—or tomorrow. Youm allus been the angel on the front of this yere ship *Nancy Bray*, and you ain't goin' to leave us rot now. I finished my prayer, great Gawd Lily. Amen.

MINNA: Great God Lily, I'm the captain's wife that's sailed behind you for twenty years. Many's the time, great God Lily, that I shined your face so you'd look spick and span and we sailing into London in the morning, or into heathen lands. You knows everything, and you knows what I did to my husband and that I didn't let him have none of the secret water that me and Van saved up, and that when he died he knew it and cursed me and Van to hell. But youms forgiven everything and send us some rain or by-and-by we'll die and there'll be no one here prayin' to you. This is the end of my prayin', great God Lily.

VAN *(Whispers)*: Say Amen.

MINNA: Amen, great God Lily.

SAM: I ain't goin' to pray. I'm just a dog that's been on the sea since I was born. I don' know no land eddication.

MINNA: We all got to pray for some rain.

VAN: You got t'say your word, too.

SAM: God forgive me, great God Lily, I'm old Jamaica Sam that don't never go ashore. Amen. I'd be drowned, too, only for Van and the captain's wife, who gave me some of the secret water, so that if they died I could roll 'em over the side and not leave 'em on the clean deck. Amen. Youms known my whole life, great God Lily, and how I stole the *Portagee*'s red bag, only it was almost empty, and . . . and that other thing. Send a lot of rain and a ship to save us. Amen.

VAN *(Crawling up beneath the figure and throwing himself full length; hysterically)*: You've gone and forgiven me everything. Sure you have. I didn't kill the captain. The secret water was mine. Save us now, great Gawd Lily, and bring me back to my uncle in Amsterdam and make him leave me his three coal barges.

MINNA *(Rocking herself)*: We'm lost. She'll save Sam, but I've done what the gods don't like. They'm after me. They've got me now.

(Suddenly staring off the deck) Van! Van! Them's a ship coming to us. Van, look!

(She falls back crying.)

VAN: Them's comin'!

SAM *(Trying to jump up and down)*: It's the *Maria Theresa Third*, comin' right at us.

VAN *(His eye falls on the angel)*: What'll they say to the figgerhead here?

SAM *(Sententiously)*: But that's the great God Lily. Her's
saved us. You ain't goin' to do anything to her?

VAN *(Starting to beat the angel forward with his hammer)*:
They'll call us heathen, bowin' down to wood and
stone. Get the rope, Sam. We'll put her back.

MINNA *(Frightened)*: But I can't never forget her and her
great starey eyes. Her I've prayed to.

END OF PLAY

The Message and Jehanne

CHARLES, the goldsmith
TULLIO, the apprentice
LADY JEHANNE, a beauty

SETTING

A goldsmith's shop in Renaissance Paris.

The tops of the shop windows are just above the level of the street, and through them we see the procession of shoes, any one of them a novel or a play or a poem. In the workshop one finds not only medals and salad forks for prelates, but unexpected things, a viola d'amore and folios ruled for music.

Tullio enters from the street and confronts his master, Charles of Benicet. Tullio stands with his back to the door and lets his breath out slowly, as one who has just accomplished a great work.

CHARLES *(Rubbing his hands)*: So you delivered the rings?

TULLIO: Yes, master.

CHARLES: And what did my little brown Jacquenetta say?

TULLIO: She twice read the verse you had written in the ring. Then she looked at me. Then she looked at the ring. "It is too cold," she said.

CHARLES: Too cold?

TULLIO: She said: "But . . . but I suppose it's what must go inside a ring!" Then she kissed the ring and bade me tell you she loved it.

CHARLES *(Arrested and puzzled)*: Too cold, the verse! —But I'll make her another. We forget how they love us. And the other ring? Did you deliver the Graf's ring to the Lady Jehanne herself?

TULLIO: Yes, master. Into her very own hand. Her house is very old and in a bad part of the city. As I crossed the court and stood in the hall a great German, with fierce eyebrows, came in from the street with me.

CHARLES: Yes, that's the one she's to marry.

TULLIO: He asked me loudly what I had there. And I said, a box for the Lady Jehanne, and that it was for her hand alone, and I ran to the landing on the stairs. Then she came out herself. He cried out upon her: What gift was she receiving? And was it from a certain English student at Padua? And she said: "No, Baron, it is the wedding ring you have sent me." And when I gave it to her she went in, very white, and without speaking to him. Then I went to Jacquenetta's with the other ring, and she gave me some supper.

CHARLES: Too cold, the verse! Start putting up the shutters; I must go and see her.

(It has been growing darker. Suddenly a pair of shoes, a poem these, descends from the crowd, and Tullio opens the door to a knock. A beautiful lady gives Christian greeting, and a seat is made for her among the littered chairs. She sits in silence until Tullio has lighted the candles and retired.)

JEHANNE: You are Charles of Benicet, master in precious metals?

CHARLES: *Carolus Benizentius auro argentoque magister*, and composer of music to God and to such men whose ears He chooses to open.

JEHANNE: You are a composer too?

CHARLES: They are callings like two sisters who have ever their arms about the other's neck. When I have made a wedding ring I compose a motet thereto. The boy who calls to see if the candlesticks are done takes back with him a Mass.

JEHANNE *(Without a breath)*: Oh!

CHARLES: Can I serve you with music or with metals?

JEHANNE: You have served me today. I am the Lady Jehanne.

CHARLES: Ah, yes! The ring was unsatisfactory? I can make another tonight. I shall set about it at once.

JEHANNE: No, master. The ring is very beautiful.

CHARLES *(After a pause, pretending to be embarrassed)*: I am overjoyed that it pleases you.

JEHANNE *(Suddenly)*: The verses that you put in the rings— where do you find *them*?

CHARLES: Unless there is a special request, my lady, I put in nothing but the traditional legend: *fidelitas carior vita*.

JEHANNE *(Without reproach)*: But there are liberties you allow yourself? Master, what meant you when you wrote within my ring?

CHARLES: My lady!

JEHANNE *(Giving him the ring)*: Graf Klaus addresses me thus.

CHARLES *(Reading around the inside of the ring)*: "As the hermit his twilight, the countryman his holiday, the worshiper his peace, so do I love thee." It was the wrong ring that was delivered to you, my lady.

JEHANNE: It has broken my will. I am in flight for Padua. My family are truly become nothing but sparrows and God will feed them.

END OF PLAY

Childe Roland to the Dark Tower Came

The sun has set over the great marsh, leaving a yellow-brown Flemish light upon the scene. In the midst of the mire and among the tufts of iron-grass stands an old round tower. Its lower narrow door is of green bronze, scarred with many assaults. Above the door are two small windows, behind which a gleam seems to come and go.

In the half-light that hangs over the plain a man in armor stumbles through the bog to the single step before the door. He is many times wounded; his blood flows freely to the ground. The knight blows his horn; the landscape collects itself to listen.

CHILDE ROLAND: I die . . . Open the door to me.

(The landscape laughs, then falls suddenly silent. Presently its subterranean waters are again heard sucking at buried tree trunks.)

I have seen your lights here from a long way off . . . You cannot hide from me now.

(The marsh becomes animated and fully interested in the stranger. One of the windows brightens slightly and a girl looks out. Her voice and manner are strangely detached and impersonal, as though she had been called away from some absorbing interest, and was eager to return to it.)

Oh, you are here! Quick, descend to me. All my wounds are flowing. I am dying of thirst.

THE GIRL: Who are you to issue commands against this tower? Some emperor, surely.

CHILDE ROLAND: My name is written with many another upon the sword of Charlemagne: That is enough.

THE GIRL: You are some king, perhaps—driven into the wilderness by your not too loving subjects?

CHILDE ROLAND: No king, but a friend and soldier of kings.

THE GIRL: Oh! This is some wise counselor. If you are so wise we will quickly open the door to you.

CHILDE ROLAND: Not wise, but often listened to in grave matters, having a voice equal with many others.

THE GIRL *(Utterly untouched, lightly to someone within)*: I do believe this is some sweet singer. Let us bind on our slippers right quickly and put red wine to his lips, for poets are ever our delight.

CHILDE ROLAND: I am no singer, but one loving the string and the voice at all times. Open the door! For the wind is cold on the marsh, and the first terrible stars are stepping into their chains. Open the door, for my veins are emptied on your sill.

THE GIRL (*Leaning far out, while her red hair falls almost to his shoulders*): Beat upon the door, Sir Knight. Many things are gained by force.

CHILDE ROLAND: My hands are strengthless . . . I am fallen on my knees . . . Pity me!

(*The Girl laughs pleasantly to her companion within.*)

Reach over the stars to me, Mary, Mother of God. To you I was committed in my first year, and have renewed yearly my promises. Send from thy golden mind and thy voiceless might the issue out of this difficulty.

(*A second girl, dark and thoughtful, appears at the other window.*)

THE GIRL (*Intimately*): He is praying now.

THE DARK GIRL: He is a little boy. His thoughts this last hour are returning to his earliest year.

THE GIRL: Is it not beautiful that a knight should think of a little child?

THE DARK GIRL: What brought you here, Knight-at-Arms?

CHILDE ROLAND: The battle passed suddenly into the west. This tower was all I could see. And here I brought my wounds.

THE GIRL (*Softly*): You see he is still able to reason; he reasons very well.

THE DARK GIRL: What led you to think that we could help you?

CHILDE ROLAND: I know your name! All my life I have heard of this tower. They say that on the outside you are dark and unlovely, but that within every hero stands with his fellows and the great queens step proudly on the stair.

THE DARK GIRL: And do you believe this?

CHILDE ROLAND *(After a pause)*: Yes.

> *(With sudden fury)* Open the door! There is a place for me within. Open the door, Death!

THE GIRL *(Drawing up her hair languidly)*: He is irresistible, this great man.

CHILDE ROLAND: Oliver! Oliver! Charlemagne! I hear your voices. It is I, Roland, without, in the dark marsh. My body I cast away for you. My breath I returned to the sky in your defense. Open the door! . . .

(The marsh is a little put out by all this strong feeling. It lies quiet. The door slowly opens upon a hall full of drifting violet mists, some of which escape and fade over the marsh. The Girl with the red hair is seen walking away in the hall, her mocking face looking back over her shoulder. The Dark Girl, robed in gray, leans across the threshold extending a chalice to the knight's lips.)

THE DARK GIRL: Take courage, high heart. How slow you have been to believe well of us. You gave us such little thought while living that we have made this little delay at your death.

END OF PLAY

Centaurs

CHARACTERS

SHELLEY, the poet
HILDA WANGEL, a character in Ibsen
IBSEN, the playwright

SETTING

A theatre.

The usual chattering audience of our theatres is waiting for the curtains to part on a performance of Ibsen's The Master Builder. *Presently the lights are lowered to a colored darkness, and the warm glow of the footlights begins again the ancient magic. The orchestra draws its bows soothingly to a gradual close and files out gropingly into the rabbit hutch prepared for it, leaving perhaps a sentimental viola player staring upward into the darkness. Suddenly the curtains are parted by an earnest*

young man, who stares into the shadowy audience and starts,
with some difficulty, to address it.

SHELLEY: My name is Shelley. I . . . I am told that some of
you may have heard of me, may even know my poems—
or some of my poems. I cannot imagine what they may
seem like to you who live in this world that . . . that is,
I have just seen your streets for the first time—your
machines, your buildings, and especially the machines
with which you talk to one another. My poems must
seem very strange in a world of such things.

(Awkward pause) Well, I wanted to say something
about this play, but I don't know how to put it into
words for you. You see, I feel that, in part, I wrote this
play.

(With sudden relief calling back through the curtains)
Hilda! Will you help me a moment?

HILDA WANGEL'S VOICE: Yes, I'm coming.

SHELLEY *(Constrainedly, to the audience)*: A friend of mine.

(Hilda appears in her mountaineering costume of the first
act, carrying an alpenstock. Vigorously, to the audience:)

HILDA: He promised to do this by himself, but he has gotten
into difficulties. Have you told them that you wrote it?

SHELLEY: I tried to. It didn't sound reasonable.

HILDA: Well, you were able to explain it to me. Help me to
persuade Papa to come out here.

(She disappears.)

SHELLEY: Henrik, for my sake.

HILDA'S VOICE: There, did you hear that? For his sake, he
said. Miss Fosli, will you kindly push forward the wicker
settee from the last act? Thank you. *(A wicker settee sud-*
denly appears)
Now, Papa.

(Hilda reappears leading the dramatist. Ibsen is smiling sternly through his spectacles and through his fringe of up-curling white whiskers.)

Now sit down and Shelley will begin again.

IBSEN: Hurry, young man. My beautiful play is ready to begin. The kingdom is on the table, the nurseries are empty, and this house is full of unconverted people.

HILDA *(Touching his shoe with the tip of her alpenstock)*: Hush, Papa. Let him go about it in his own way. Have you told them about the poem you were about to write when you died?

SHELLEY: No.

(To the audience) Ladies and Gentlemen, on the day I died—drowned in the Mediterranean—I was full of a poem to be called *The Death of a Centaur*, that I did not have time to put on paper.

HILDA: You forgot to say that it was a very good poem.

SHELLEY: I couldn't say that.

HILDA: You said it to me.

(Turning to the audience) You should know that this young man had come to a time when everything he wrote was valuable. He was as sure to write great poems as a good apple tree is to give good apples.

SHELLEY: Perhaps it would have been one of the better ones. At all events, it was never written . . .

IBSEN *(Rising excitedly and stamping his feet as though they had snow on them)*: And I claim that I wrote it. The poem hung for a while above the Mediterranean, and then drifted up toward the Tyrol, and I caught it and wrote it down. And it is *The Master Builder*.

HILDA: Now you must sit down, Papa, and keep calm. We must reason this out calmly. In the first place, both are certainly about centaurs. What do you say, Shelley?

SHELLEY: Well, it is not a strange idea, or a new one, that the stuff of which masterpieces are made drifts about the world waiting to be clothed with words. It is a truth that Plato would have understood that the mere language, the words of a masterpiece, are the least of its offerings. Nay, in the world we have come into now, the languages of the planet have no value; but the impulse, the idea of "Comus" is a miracle, even in heaven. Let you remember this when you regret the work that has been lost through this war that has been laid upon your treasurable young men. The work they might have done is still with you, and will yet find its way into your lives and into your children's lives.

IBSEN: Enough, enough! You will be revealing all the mysteries soon. Enough has been said to prove that *The Death of a Centaur* and *The Master Builder* are the same poem. Get in with you, children. The play is ready to start. Solness sits with his head in his hands, and the harps are in the air.

(He goes behind the curtains. Shelley lingers a moment; a shadow has fallen across his face.)

HILDA *(Laying her hand on his arm)*: What is the matter?
SHELLEY: That reminded me . . . of another poem . . . I did not write down.

END OF PLAY

Leviathan

CHARACTERS

BRIGOMEÏDÉ, a mermaid
THE PRINCE, a shipwrecked young man
LEVIATHAN, a sea serpent

SETTING

The mid-Mediterranean.

*Sunrise after a night of storm, with the sea swaying prodigiously.
A great Venetian argosy has been wrecked overnight; ships and
men have disappeared, leaving only the cargo spread out upon
the waters. Momently new treasures from the ships' holds float
upward and, reaching the surface, are swept hither and thither
for miles—Persian rugs; great lengths of brocade; boxes of
spice, made from tropical leaves and bound with dried vine; and
an apparently interminable swathe of gray silk unwinding from
its ivory standard.*

In the foreground a mermaid is feeling her way among the stuffs with considerable distaste. To one used to the shadowed harmonies of deep-sea color these crimsons and oranges have no attraction. Brigomeïdé has the green wiry hair of her kind, entangled with the friendly snail; the iridescent shoulders of all sea-women, and the gray thin mouth.

Suddenly she comes upon the Prince. The royal divan has been swept from the decks, and while the huge pillows are gradually soaking up the water and floating away, their Prince lies on them unconscious. For a moment the mermaid watches him open-mouthed. She steals nearer and, holding on to the tassels of seed-pearls, leans cautiously over and scans his face long and wonderingly. She sighs faintly, splashes a little in discontent, and then gazes upon him again with a frown of concentration.

BRIGOMEÏDÉ: It's breathing. He has not lost—what they call—the soul. I wonder where he keeps it. It is the great difference between us; we sea-people have no soul. I wonder where he keeps it! I have heard that it can be seen at times, in the eyes. Perhaps if I borrowed it from him while he slept he would never miss it. No—I will ask him for it.

(She claps her hands suddenly to awake him, falling back, at the same time, into the water. The young man does not stir. She grows angry. She strikes the water sharply with the palms of her hands. By quick degrees a circling wind rises; great fantastic waves rear themselves, robed in silk; they break over the divan and the Prince stirs. Immediately Brigomeïdé strokes the water to a stillness, and fixes her attention on the young man.)

THE PRINCE: My father, take not your hand away. My brothers, why have you ceased talking? Where am I? —All is lost! *Ave Maris Stella!*
BRIGOMEÏDÉ *(Watching him intently)*: How could you sleep so—during the storm?

THE PRINCE: You—you are out of a dream. You are out of
my fever. Yes, yes—the storm—you—all this is but
the painting of my fever. I shall awake in Venice with
the lute player fallen asleep by the window. I will call to
him now and he will wake me up: Amedeo! —Lute
player! Shake me out of this dream!

*(The silence that follows is filled with the crackling noise as
the pith fillings of the heavier cushions become saturated.)*

BRIGOMEÏDÉ *(Harshly)*: Who is it you are calling to? There
is no one here, but you and me only.

THE PRINCE: Amedeo! —He does not answer: this is real. But
you, you are dream; you are illusion. *Ave Maris Stella!*

BRIGOMEÏDÉ *(Indignantly)*: I am not dream. I am not illusion. I am royal among all sea-women. —I am of the
Third Order: On the three great tide days I am permitted to bind my hair with Thetis-Agrandis and wear in
my ears the higher Muria.

THE PRINCE: You are out of an old ballad, taught me as a
boy, and you have come back to me in the last hour on
the tide of fever. In a moment my dream will have
passed on from you.

BRIGOMEÏDÉ *(Vehemently)*: You think I am only dream
because . . . you have heard it said . . . we sea-folk have
no souls.

THE PRINCE: Soul nor body.

BRIGOMEÏDÉ *(More softly)*: Tell me where it is you keep
your soul. Have you it always with you?

THE PRINCE *(As a great pillow floats away from under his
hand)*: *Flos undarum!* Save me! Deliver me! Hear my
prayer!

BRIGOMEÏDÉ: Who are you speaking to? Did I not tell you
there was no one here but you and me only?

THE PRINCE: You! Tell me where is shore. You can swim
for days. Draw me to some island. I will give you great
riches . . . all you desire.

BRIGOMEÏDÉ: Give me your soul. All my days I have longed for two things, black hair and a soul. I have not lacked anything else. I will draw you to your home if you will give me your soul.

THE PRINCE *(Violently)*: It cannot be given away. No one has seen it; it cannot be felt with the hands; seen or tasted.

BRIGOMEÏDÉ: And yet they say it is the greatest thing in the world; that without it life is a cold procession of hours; that it gives all sight to the eyes, and all hearing to the ears . . . you are mocking me! I see in your face that you have it now!

THE PRINCE: Yes, and am about to lose it.

BRIGOMEÏDÉ: Give it to me, and I will bring up from the bottom of the sea your father and your brothers. I will return to you all the pearls that have fallen here, and draw you softly into the narrows of Venice.

THE PRINCE *(As the water closes over him)*: Amedeo! —Lute player!

(Brigomeïdé turns away contemptuously.)

BRIGOMEÏDÉ: It is something you cannot touch or see. What could I do with it so?

(The Prince rises, dead, entangled in scarves. Brigomeïdé stares into his face long and earnestly.)

It is true! There is something gone . . . that lay about his eyes, that troubled his mouth. The soul, perhaps.

(She claps her hands. From a great distance a sea serpent swims hugely toward her. He is caught in the trailing lengths of gray brocade.)

Gog-etar! There is no longer anything precious in this man. You may divide him among your young.

LEVIATHAN: It is terrible here, lady. These spices have made the streams unendurable. By tomorrow morning the waters will be tainted as far as Africa. Already my young are ill, lady. They lie motionless in the mud, dear lady. It is terrible to see them so . . .

BRIGOMEÏDÉ: I do not want to hear your troubles. Take this man away.

LEVIATHAN: Thanks, gracious lady. Perhaps these hateful essences will have made him endurable . . .

BRIGOMEÏDÉ: Cease!

(He drags the Prince away. The frustrated Brigomeïdé starts to comb the shell out of her hair, singing. Suddenly she breaks her song and adds musingly:)

Perhaps it is better, although your body has passed to Leviathan, still to have another part of you somewhere about the world.

END OF PLAY

And the Sea Shall Give Up Its Dead

CHARACTERS

A WOMAN
A STOUT LITTLE MAN
A TALL THIN DREAMY MAN

SETTING

Atlantic abyss.

The clangor of Judgment Day's last trumpet dies away in the remotest pockets of space, and time comes to an end like a frayed ribbon. In the nave of creation the diaphanous amphitheatre is already building for the trial of all flesh. Several miles below the surface of the North Atlantic, the spirits of the drowned rise through the water like bubbles in a neglected wineglass.

A WOMAN *(To the gray weeds of whose soul still cling the vestiges of color, some stained purples and some wasted reds)*:

At last I could struggle no longer. My head and lungs were under intense discomfort by reason of the water with which they were filled. I said to myself: "Only think, Gertruda, you have actually arrived at the moment of death!" Even then I was unwilling to believe it, though my lungs were on the point of bursting. One is never really able to believe that one will die. It is especially difficult for sovereigns who seldom, if ever, confront inevitable situations. Perhaps you know that I am Gertruda XXII, Empress of Newfoundland from 2638 to 2698?

A STOUT LITTLE MAN: Your Imperial Highness's experience is much like mine. I lived about five hundred years before Your Imperial Highness. I had always dreaded the moment of extinction, yet mine was less painful than a headache.

THE EMPRESS: We know now that the real pain comes to us in the ages that have passed since then. Have you too been swinging in mid-ocean, tangled in a cocoon of seaweed, slowly liberating your mind from the prides and prejudices and trivialities of a lifetime? That is what is painful.

A STOUT LITTLE MAN: I was a Jew and very proud of my race. Living under what I took to be the aspersions of my neighbors I had nourished the arrogant delusion that I was notable. It has taken me five hundred years of painful reflection to disembarrass myself of this notion. I was a theatrical producer, and thought myself important to my time—wise, witty and kindly. Each of these ideas I have shed with a hundred times the pain of losing a limb. Now I am reconciled to the fact that I am naked, a fool, a child.

THE EMPRESS: In my life I believed fiercely that everything of which I said MY had some peculiar excellence. It was impossible to imagine a citizen proud of any country save Newfoundland, or a woman vain of any hair save the golden. I had a passion for genealogies and antiquities, and felt that such things merely looked forward to myself. Now these many years I have been wrapped in barnacles, divorcing my soul from all that it once loved. Even my love for my son and my son's love for me have vanished through sheer inconsequence. All this is the second death, and the one to be dreaded. I was afraid that when I had shed away my royalty and my beauty and my administrative talent and my pure descent and my astonishing memory for names—I was afraid that there would be nothing left. But, fortunately, underneath all this litter I have found a tiny morsel of . . . but dare we say the Name? —But what was yours?

A STOUT LITTLE MAN: Horatio Nissem.

THE EMPRESS: Speak to that man who is rising through the water beside you.

HORATIO NISSEM: Who are you, and what particular follies have you laid aside?

A TALL THIN DREAMY MAN: I was a priest of the gospel and a terrible time I have had taking leave of my sins. I tremble to think how but a few moments ago I still retained a longing for stupidities. Yes, sir, for the planets. I felt sure that they had personalities, and I looked forward after my death to hearing their songs. Now I know that sun and moon and stars have fallen like dust into the lap of their maker. I told myself, also, that after death I should sit through eternity overhearing the conversation of Coleridge and Augustine and Our Lord—there I should embrace my loved ones and my enemies; there I should hear vindicated before the devils the great doctrines of Infant Baptism and Sacramental Confession. Only now have I been delivered from these follies. As I swayed in the meteoric slime I begged God to punish me for certain sins of my youth, moments I well remembered of rage and pride and shame. But these seemed of no importance to him: he seemed rather to be erasing from my mind the notion that my sins were of any consequence. I see now that even the idea that I was capable of sinning was a self-flattery and an impertinence. My name was Father Cosroe: now my name is Worm.

THE EMPRESS: We still cling obstinately to our identity, as though there were something valuable in it. This very moment I feel relics of pleasure in the fact that I am myself and no one else. Yet in a moment, if there is a moment, we shall all be reduced to our quintessential matter, and you, Mr. Nissem, will be exactly indistinguishable from me. God Himself will not be able to tell the Empress of Newfoundland from the Reverend Doctor Cosroe.

HORATIO NISSEM (*In mounting terror*): I am afraid. I refuse to give myself up.

THE EMPRESS: Do not cry out, fool. You have awakened all my rebellious nature. O God, do not take away my identity! I do not ask for my title or my features; do not take away my myself!

HORATIO NISSEM: Do you hear? I refuse to give myself up. O God, let me not be mistaken for a Gentile.

FATHER COSROE: Your screaming has aroused my madness. Let me keep my particular mind, O God, my own curious mind, with all I have put into it!

(*The three panic-stricken souls reach the surface of the sea. The extensive business of Domesday is over in a twinkling, and the souls divested of all identification have tumbled, like falling stars, into the blaze of unicity. Soon nothing exists in space but the great unwinking eye, meditating a new creation.*)

END OF PLAY

Now the Servant's Name Was Malchus

CHARACTERS

THE ANGEL GABRIEL, secretary and soldier
OUR LORD
MALCHUS, of the Bible

SETTING

The house of the lord.

In his father's house are many mansions, and it is from the windows of one of them that he stands looking out upon the clockwork of the skies. With the precision that is possible only to things dead in themselves, the stars weave incessantly their interlocking measures. At intervals the blackest pockets of space give birth to a nebula, whirling in new anguish, but for the most part the sky offers only its vast stars, eased in the first gradations of their cooling, and fulfilling happily and with a faint humming sound the long loops of their appointment.

To him comes Gabriel.

GABRIEL: There are some unusually urgent petitions here . . . There's this colonel on a raft in the Bengal Sea. —Here again is the widow and her two daughters in Moscow. A lady in Rome. *(He lays some papers on the table)* Besides, there is someone outside who wishes to speak to you. He says he knew you on earth. I think he has something to complain of, even here.

OUR LORD: Let him wait a moment.

(There is loud rapping at the door.)

GABRIEL: There he is again.

OUR LORD: Then let him in.

(Gabriel admits Malchus and goes out.)

MALCHUS: Please, sir, excuse me being so hasty, but I had to speak to you about something.

OUR LORD: You are displeased with Heaven?

MALCHUS: Oh no, sir—except for one thing.

OUR LORD: We will talk about it in a minute. Come by the window and look. Can you tell me which of those stars is mine?

MALCHUS: Lord, all are yours, surely.

OUR LORD: No, only one is mine, for only one bears living things upon it. And where there is no life I have no power. All the stars save one are lifeless; not even a blade of grass pushes through their powder or their flame. But one of them is so crowded with event that Heaven itself is scarcely able to attend to its needs. —But you are not interested?

MALCHUS: Oh, sir, it was so long ago that I was there that I cannot be expected to . . . Even my children's children have long since left it. I cannot be very interested. Since

I am so happy here—except for one thing. But I should like to see it again. Which is it, sir?

OUR LORD: There, see! See where it floats for a moment out of a green mist. If your ears were accustomed to it as mine are, you would hear what I hear: the sigh as it turns. Now, what is it you want of me?

MALCHUS: Well, as you know, I was the High Priest's servant in the garden when you were taken. Sir, it's hardly worth mentioning.

OUR LORD: No, no. Speak out.

MALCHUS: And one of your fellows took out his sword and cut off my ear.

OUR LORD: Yes.

MALCHUS: It's . . . it's hardly worth mentioning. Most of the time, Lord, we're very happy up here and nothing disturbs us at our games. But whenever someone on earth thinks about us we are aware of it, pleasantly or unpleasantly. A sort of something crosses our mind. And because I'm in your book someone is always reading about me and thinking about me for a moment, and in the middle of my games I feel it. Especially at this season, when your death is celebrated, no moment goes by without this happening. And what they think is, that I'm ridiculous.

OUR LORD: I see. And you want your name to be erased from the book?

MALCHUS *(Eagerly)*: Yes, sir. I thought you could just make the pages become blank at that place.

OUR LORD: Now that you have come here everything that you wish is granted to you. You know that.

MALCHUS: Yes, sir; thank you, sir.

OUR LORD: But stay a minute. At this season, Malchus, a number of people are thinking of me, too.

MALCHUS: Yes, Lord, but as good, as great . . .

OUR LORD: But, Malchus, I am ridiculous too.

MALCHUS: Oh, no, no!

OUR LORD: Ridiculous because I suffered from the delusion that after my death I could be useful to men.

MALCHUS: They don't say that!

OUR LORD: And that my mind lay under a malady that many a doctor could cure. And that I have deceived and cheated millions and millions of souls who in their extremity called on me for the aid I had promised. They did not know that I died like any other man and their prayers mounted into vain air, for I no longer exist. My promises were so vast that I am either divine or ridiculous.

>   *(Pause)* Malchus, will you stay and be ridiculous with me?

MALCHUS: Yes, sir, I'll stay. I'm glad to stay. Though in a way I haven't any right to be there. I wasn't even the High Priest's servant; I only held his horse every now and then. And . . . and I used to steal a little—only you've forgiven me that. Sure, I'm glad to stay.

OUR LORD: Thank you, Malchus.

MALCHUS *(Smiling)*: It isn't even true in the book. It was my left ear and not my right.

OUR LORD: Yes, the book isn't always true about me, either.

MALCHUS: Excuse my troubling you, sir. Good day.

OUR LORD: Good day, Malchus.

(Malchus goes out. Gabriel enters discreetly and lays down some more papers.)

GABRIEL *(In a low voice)*: The raft has capsized, sir, on the Bengal Sea, and the colonel will be here at once. The women in Moscow . . .

END OF PLAY

Mozart and the Gray Steward

CHARACTERS

CONSTANZE, Mozart's wife
MOZART, the composer
THE GRAY STEWARD, a mysterious visitor

SETTING

Mozart's quarters in Vienna.

Mozart is seated at a table in a mean room orchestrating The Magic Flute. *Leaves of ruled paper are strewn about the floor. His wife enters in great excitement.*

CONSTANZE: There's someone come to see you, someone important. Pray God, it's a commission from court.
MOZART *(Unmoved)*: Not while Salieri's alive.

CONSTANZE: Put on your slippers, dear. It's someone dressed all in gray, with a gray mask over his eyes, and he's come in a great coach with its coat of arms all covered up with gray cloth. Pray God, it's a commission from court for a *Te Deum* or something.

(She tidies up the room in six gestures.)

MOZART: Not while Salieri's alive.

CONSTANZE: But, now, do be nice, 'Gangl, please. We must have some money, my treasure. Just listen to him and say "yes" and "thank you," and then you and I'll talk it over after he's gone.
　　(She holds his coat) Come, put this on. Step into your slippers.

MOZART *(Sighing)*: I'm not well. I'm at home. I'm at work. There's not a single visitor in the whole world that could interest me. Bring him in.

CONSTANZE *(Adjusting his stock)*: Now don't be proud. Just accept.

(She hurries out and presently reenters preceding the visitor. The visitor is dressed from head to foot in gray silk. His bright eyes look out through the holes in a narrow gray silk mask. He holds to his nose a gray perfumed handkerchief. One would say: an elegant undertaker.)

THE GRAY STEWARD: Kappelmeister Mozart, *servus.* Gracious lady, *servus.*

MOZART: *Servus.*

THE GRAY STEWARD: Revered and noble master, wherever music reigns, wherever genius is valued, the name of Wolfgang Amadeus Mozart is . . .

MOZART: Sir, I have always been confused by compliments and beg you to spare me that mortification by proceeding at once to the cause of your visit . . . the . . . the honor of your visit.

THE GRAY STEWARD: Revered master, before I lay my business before you, may I receive your promise that—whether you accept my commission or not—you both will . . .

MOZART: I promise you our secrecy, unless our silence would prove dishonorable to me or injurious to someone else. Pray continue.

THE GRAY STEWARD: Know then, gracious and revered genius, that I come from a prince who combines all the qualities of birth, station, generosity and wisdom.

MOZART: Ha! A European secret.

THE GRAY STEWARD: His Excellency moreover has just sustained a bitter misfortune. He has lately lost his wife and consort, a lady who was the admiration of her court and the sole light of her bereaved husband's life. Therefore, His Excellency, my master, commissions you to compose a Requiem Mass in honor of this lady. He asks you to pour into it the height of your invention and that wealth of melody and harmony that have made you the glory of our era. And for this music he asks leave to pay you the sum of four hundred crowns—two hundred now, and the second two hundred crowns when you deliver the first four numbers.

MOZART: Well, Constanze, I must not be proud.

THE GRAY STEWARD: There is but one proviso.

MOZART: Yes, I heard it. The work must represent the height of my invention.

THE GRAY STEWARD: That was an easy assumption, master. The proviso is this: You shall let His Excellency have this music as an anonymous work, and you shall never by any sign, by so much as the nod of your head, acknowledge that the work is yours.

MOZART: And His Excellency is not aware that the pages I may compose at the height of my invention may be their own sufficient signature?

THE GRAY STEWARD: That may be. Naturally my master will see to it that no other composer will ever be able to claim the work as his.

MOZART: Quick, give me your paper and I will sign it. Leave your two hundred crowns with my wife at the foot of the stairs. Come back in August and you will have the first four numbers. *Servus. Servus.*

THE GRAY STEWARD *(Backing out)*: *Servus,* master. *Servus,* madame.

(Constanze returns in a moment and looks anxiously toward her husband.)

CONSTANZE: A visit from Heaven, 'Gangl. Now you can go into the country. Now you can drink all the Bohemian water in the world.

MOZART *(Bitterly)*: Good. And just at a time when I was contemplating a Requiem Mass. But for *myself.* However, I must not be proud.

CONSTANZE *(Trying to divert him)*: Who can these people be? Try and think.

MOZART: Oh, there's no mystery about that. It's the Count Von Walsegg. He composes himself. But for the most part he buys string quartets from us; he erases the signatures and has them played in his castle. The courtiers flatter him and pretend that they have guessed him to be the composer. He does not deny it. He tries to appear confused. And now he has succeeded in composing a Requiem. But that will reduce my pride.

CONSTANZE: You know he will only be laughed at. The music will speak for itself. Heaven wanted to give us four hundred crowns—

MOZART: —And Heaven went about it humorously.

CONSTANZE: What was his wife like?

MOZART: Her impudences smelt to Heaven. She dressed like a page and called herself Cherubin. Her red cheeks and her black teeth and her sixty years are in my mind now.

CONSTANZE *(After a pause)*: We'll give back the money. You can write the music, without writing it for them.

MOZART: No, I like this game. I like it for its very falseness.

What does it matter who signs such music or to whom it is addressed?

(He flings himself upon the sofa and turns his face to the wall.)

For whom do we write music?—for musicians? Salieri! for patrons? Von Walsegg! for the public? The Countess Von Walsegg! —I shall write this Requiem, but it shall be for myself, since I am dying.

CONSTANZE: My beloved, don't talk so! Go to sleep. *(She spreads a shawl over his body)* How can you say such things? Imagine even thinking such a thing! You will live many years and write countless beautiful pages. We will return the money and refuse the commission. Then the matter will be closed. Now go to sleep, my treasure.

(She goes out, quietly closing the door behind her. Mozart, at the mercy of his youth, his illness and his genius, is shaken by a violent fit of weeping. The sobs gradually subside and he falls asleep. In his dream the Gray Steward returns.)

THE GRAY STEWARD: Mozart! Turn and look at me. You know who I am.

MOZART *(Not turning)*: You are the steward of the Count Von Walsegg. Go tell him to write his own music. I will not stain my pen to celebrate his lady, so let the foul bury the foul.

THE GRAY STEWARD: Lie then against the wall, and learn that it is Death itself that commissions . . .

MOZART: Death is not so fastidious. Death carries no perfumed handkerchief.

THE GRAY STEWARD: Lie then against the wall. Know first that all the combinations of circumstance can suffer two interpretations, the apparent and the real.

MOZART: Then speak, sycophant, I know the apparent one. What other reading can this humiliation bear?

THE GRAY STEWARD: It is Death itself that commands you this Requiem. You are to give a voice to all those millions sleeping, who have no one but you to speak for them. There lie the captains and the thieves, the queens and the drudges, while the evening of their earthly remembrance shuts in, and from that great field rises an eternal *miserere nobis.* Only through the intercession of great love, and of great art, which is love, can that despairing cry be eased. Was that not sufficient cause for this commission to be anonymous?

MOZART *(Drops trembling on one knee beside the couch)*: Forgive me.

THE GRAY STEWARD: And it was for this that the pretext and mover was chosen from among the weakest and vainest of humans. Death has her now, and all her folly has passed into the dignity and grandeur of her state. Where is your pride now? Here are her slippers and her trinkets. Press them against your lips. Again! Again! Know henceforth that only he who has kissed the leper can enter the kingdom of art.

MOZART: I have sinned, yet grant me one thing. Grant that I may live to finish the Requiem.

THE GRAY STEWARD: No! No!

(And it remains unfinished.)

END OF PLAY

Hast Thou Considered
My Servant Job?

CHARACTERS

SATAN
CHRIST
JUDAS

SETTING

Another place.

*Now it came to pass on the day when the sons of God came to
present themselves before Satan that Christ also came among
them. And*

SATAN *(Said unto Christ)*: *Whence comest thou?*
CHRIST *(Answered Satan and said)*: *From going to and fro in
    the earth, and from walking up and down in it.*

(And)

SATAN *(Said unto Christ)*: *Hast thou considered my servant Judas? For there is none like him in the earth, an evil and a faithless man, one that feareth me and turneth away from God.*

(Then)

CHRIST *(Answered Satan and said)*: *Doth Judas fear thee for naught? Hast thou not made a hedge about him, and about his house, and about all that he hath on every side? But draw back thy hand now and he will renounce thee to thy face.*

(And)

SATAN *(Said unto Christ)*: *Behold, all that he hath is in thy power.*

(So Christ went forth from the presence of Satan.
He descended to the earth. Thirty-three years are but a moment before Satan and before God, and at the end of this moment Christ ascends again to his own place. He passes on this journey before the presence of the adversary.)

SATAN: You are alone! Where is my son Judas whom I gave into your hands?
CHRIST: He follows me.
SATAN: I know what you have done. And the earth rejected you? The earth rejected you! All hell murmurs in astonishment. But where is Judas, my son and my joy?
CHRIST: Even now he is coming.
SATAN: Even Heaven, when I reigned there, was not so tedious as this waiting. Know, Prince, that I am too

proud to show all my astonishment at your defeat. But now that you are swallowing your last humiliation, now that your failure has shut the mouths of the angels, I may confess that for a while I feared you. There is a fretfulness in the hearts of men. Many are inconstant, even to me. Alas, every man is not a Judas. I knew even from the beginning that you would be able, for a season, to win their hearts with your mild eloquence. I feared that you would turn to your own uses this fretfulness that visits them. But my fears were useless. Even Judas, even when my power was withdrawn from him, even Judas betrayed you. Am I not right in this?

CHRIST: You are.

SATAN: You admitted him into your chosen company. Is it permitted to me to ask for how much he betrayed you?

CHRIST: For thirty pieces of silver.

SATAN *(After a pause)*: Am I permitted to ask to what role he was assigned in your company?

CHRIST: He held its money bags.

SATAN *(Dazed)*: Does Heaven understand human nature as little as that? Surely the greater part of your closest companions stayed beside you to the end?

CHRIST: One stayed beside me.

SATAN: I have overestimated my enemy. Learn again, Prince, that if I were permitted to return to the earth in my own person, not for thirty years, but for thirty hours, I would seal all men to me and all the temptations in Heaven's gift could not persuade one to betray me. For I build not on intermittent dreams and timid aspirations, but on the unshakable passions of greed and lust and self-love. At last this is made clear: Judas, Judas, all the triumphs of Hell await you. Already above the eternal pavements of black marble the banquet is laid. Listen, how my nations are stirring in new hope and in new joy. Such music has not been lifted above my lakes and my mountains since the day I placed the apple of knowledge between the teeth of Adam.

(Suddenly the thirty pieces of silver are cast upward from the revolted hand of Judas. They hurtle through the skies, flinging their enormous shadows across the stars and continue falling forever through the vast funnel of space.

Presently Judas rises, the black stains about his throat and the rope of suicide.)

What have they done to you, my beloved son? What last poor revenge have they attempted upon you? Come to me. Here there is comfort. Here all this violence can be repaired. The futile spite of Heaven cannot reach you here. But why do you not speak to me? My son, my treasure!

(Judas remains with lowered eyes.)

CHRIST: Speak to him then, my beloved son.
JUDAS *(Still with lowered eyes, softly, to Satan)*: Accursed be thou, from eternity to eternity.

(These two mount upward to their due place and Satan remains to this day, uncomprehending, upon the pavement of hell.)

END OF PLAY

The Flight into Egypt

CHARACTERS

HEPZIBAH, a donkey
OUR LADY, Mary
ST. JOSEPH, her husband

SETTING

The Holy Land. Egypt.

From time to time there are auctions of the fittings that made up the old dime museums, and at such an auction you should be able to pick up a revolving cyclorama of the Holy Land and Egypt, which is the scenery for this piece. Turn down the gaslights, for it is night in Palestine, and introduce a lady and a child on a donkey. They are accompanied by an old man on foot. The donkey's name is Hepzibah.

HEPZIBAH *(For the tenth time)*: I'm tired.

OUR LADY: I know, I know.

HEPZIBAH: I'm willing to carry you as far and as fast as I can, but within reason.

ST. JOSEPH: If you didn't talk so much you'd have more strength for the journey.

HEPZIBAH: It's not my lungs that are tired, it's my legs. When I talk I don't notice how tired I am.

OUR LADY: Do as you think best, Hepzibah, but do keep moving. I can still hear Herod's soldiers behind us.

(Noise of ironmongery in the wings, right.)

HEPZIBAH: Well, I'm doing my best.

(Silence. The Tigris passes on the cyclorama.)

We must talk or I'll have to halt. We talked over the Romans and the whole political situation, and I must say again that I and every thinking person can only view such a situation with alarm, with real alarm. We talked over the village, and I don't think there's anything more to say about that. Did I remember to tell you that Issachbar's daughter's engagement had been broken?

OUR LADY: Yes.

HEPZIBAH: Well, there's always ideas. I hope I can say honestly that I am at home in ideas of all sorts. For instance, back in the yard I'm the leader of a group. Among the girls. Very interesting religious discussions, I can tell you. Very helpful.

(As some more iron is heard falling in Judaea, the Euphrates passes.)

ST. JOSEPH: Can't you hurry a bit?

HEPZIBAH: I always say to the girls: Girls, even in faith we are supposed to use our reason. No one is intended to swallow hook, line and sinker, as the saying is. Now take these children that Herod is killing. Why were they born, since they must die so soon? Can anyone answer that? Or put it another way: Why is the little boy in your arms being saved while the others must perish?

ST. JOSEPH: Is it necessary to stop?

HEPZIBAH: I was stopping for emphasis. —Mind you, it's not that I doubt. Honest discussion does not imply doubt necessarily. —What was that noise?

OUR LADY: I beg of you to make all the haste you can. The noise you hear is that of Herod's soldiers. My child will be slain while you argue about Faith. I beg of you, Hepzibah, to save him while you can.

HEPZIBAH: I assure you I'm doing the best I can, and I think I'm moving along smartly. I didn't mean that noise, anyway; it was a noise ahead. Of course, your child is dearer to you than others, but *theologically speaking*, there's no possible reason why you should escape safely into Egypt while the others should be put to the sword, as the Authorized Version has it. When the Messiah comes these things will be made clear, but until then I intend to exercise my reasoning faculty. My theory is this . . .

OUR LADY: Hepzibah, we shall really have to beat you if you stop so often. Hepzibah, don't you remember me? Don't you remember how you fell on your knees in the stable? Don't you remember my child?

HEPZIBAH: What? What! Of course!

OUR LADY: Yes, Hepzibah.

HEPZIBAH: Let me stop just a moment and look around. No, I don't dare stop. Why didn't I recognize you before! Really, my lady, you should have spoken more sharply to me. I didn't know I could run like this; it's a pleasure. Lord, what a donkey I was to be arguing about reason while my Lord was in danger.

(A pyramid flies by.)

Do you see the lights of the town yet? That's the Sphinx at the right, madam, yes, 3655 B.C. Well, well, it's a queer world where the survival of the Lord is dependent up on donkeys, but so it is. Why didn't you tell me before, my lady?

ST. JOSEPH: We thought you could carry us forward on your own merit.

HEPZIBAH: Oh, forgive me, madam; forgive me, sir. You don't hear any more soldiers now, I warrant you. Please don't direct me so far—excuse me—to the right, madam. That's the Nile, and there are crocodiles. My lady, may I ask one question now that we're safe?

OUR LADY: Yes, Hepzibah.

HEPZIBAH: It's this matter of faith and reason, madam. I'd love to carry back to our group of girls whatever you might say about it . . .

OUR LADY: Dear Hepzibah, perhaps some day. For the present just do as I do and bear your master on.

(More pyramids fly by; Memnon sings; the Nile moves dreamily past, and the inn is reached.)

END OF PLAY

The Angel That
Troubled the Waters

CHARACTERS

THE NEWCOMER, an invalid
THE MISTAKEN INVALID
THE ANGEL

SETTING

A great pool of water.

The pool: a vast gray hall with a hole in the ceiling open to the
sky. Broad stone steps lead up from the water on its four sides.
The water is continuously restless and throws blue reflections
upon the walls. The sick, the blind and the malformed are lying
on the steps. The long stretches of silence and despair are bro-
ken from time to time when one or another groans and turns in
his rags, or raises a fretful wail or a sudden cry of exasperation
at long-continued pain. A door leads out upon the porch where
the attendants of the sick are playing at dice, waiting for the call

to fling their masters into the water when the angel of healing stirs the pool. Beyond the porch there is a glimpse of the fierce sunlight and the empty streets of an oriental noonday.

Suddenly the Angel appears upon the top step. His face and robe shine with a color that is both silver and gold, and the wings of blue and green, tipped with rose, shimmer in the tremulous light. He walks slowly down among the shapeless sleepers and stands gazing into the water that already trembles in anticipation of its virtue.

A new invalid enters.

THE NEWCOMER: Come, long-expected love. Come, long-expected love. Let the sacred finger and the sacred breath stir up the pool. Here on the lowest step I wait with festering limbs, with my heart in pain. Free me, long-expected love, from this old burden. Since I cannot stay, since I must return into the city, come now, renewal, come, release.

(Another invalid wakes suddenly out of a nightmare, calling: "The Angel! The Angel has come. I am cured." He flings himself into the pool, splashing his companions. They come to life and gaze eagerly at the water. They hang over the brink and several slide in. Then a great cry of derision rises: "The fool! Fool! His nightmare again. Beat him! Drive him out into the porch." The mistaken invalid and his dupes drag themselves out of the water and lie dripping disconsolately upon the steps.)

THE MISTAKEN INVALID: I dreamt that an angel stood by me and that at last I should be free of this hateful place and its company. Better a mistake and this jeering than an opportunity lost.

(He sees the Newcomer beside him and turns on him plaintively) Aïe! You have no right to be here, at all events. You are able to walk about. You pass your days in the city. You come here only at great intervals, and it

may be that by some unlucky chance you might be the first one to see the sign. You would rush into the water and a cure would be wasted. You are yourself a physician. You have restored my own children. Go back to your work and leave these miracles to us who need them.

THE NEWCOMER *(Ignoring him; under his breath)*: My work grows faint. Heal me, long-expected love; heal me that I may continue. Renewal, release; let me begin again without this fault that bears me down.

THE MISTAKEN INVALID: I shall sit here without ever lifting my eyes from the surface of the pool. I shall be the next. Many times, even since I have been here, many times the angel has passed and has stirred the water, and hundreds have left the hall leaping and crying out with joy. I shall be the next.

(The Angel kneels down on the lowest step and meditatively holds his finger poised above the shuddering water.)

THE ANGEL: Joy and fulfilment, completion, content, rest and release have been promised.

THE NEWCOMER: Come, long-expected love.

THE ANGEL *(Without turning makes himself apparent to the Newcomer and addresses him)*: Draw back, physician, this moment is not for you.

THE NEWCOMER: Angelic visitor, I pray thee, listen to my prayer.

THE ANGEL: Healing is not for you.

THE NEWCOMER: Surely, surely, the angels are wise. Surely, O prince, you are not deceived by my apparent wholeness. Your eyes can see the nets in which my wings are caught; the sin into which all my endeavors sink half performed cannot be concealed from you.

THE ANGEL: I know.

THE NEWCOMER: It is no shame to boast to an angel of what I might yet do in love's service were I but freed from this bondage.

THE MISTAKEN INVALID: Surely the water is stirring strangely today! Surely I shall be whole!

THE ANGEL: I must make haste. Already the sky is afire with the gathering host, for it is the hour of the new song among us. The earth itself feels the preparation in the skies and attempts its hymns. Children born in this hour spend all their lives in a sharper longing for the perfection that awaits them.

THE NEWCOMER: Oh, in such an hour was I born, and doubly fearful to me is the flaw in my heart. Must I drag my shame, prince and singer, all my days more bowed than my neighbor?

THE ANGEL *(Stands a moment in silence)*: Without your wound where would your power be? It is your very remorse that makes your low voice tremble into the hearts of men. The very angels themselves cannot persuade the wretched and blundering children on earth as can one human being broken on the wheels of living. In love's service only the wounded soldiers can serve. Draw back.

(He swiftly kneels and draws his finger through the water. The pool is presently astir with running ripples. They increase and a divine wind strikes the gay surface. The waves are flung upon the steps. The Mistaken Invalid casts himself into the pool, and the whole company lurches, rolls or hobbles in. The servants rush in from the porch. Turmoil. Finally the no-longer Mistaken Invalid emerges and leaps joyfully up the steps. The rest, coughing and sighing, follow him. The Angel smiles for a moment and disappears.)

THE HEALED MAN: Look, my hand is new as a child's. Glory be to God! I have begun again.

(To the Newcomer) May you be the next, my brother. But come with me first, an hour only, to my home. My son is lost in dark thoughts. I—I do not understand

him, and only you have ever lifted his mood. Only an hour . . . my daughter, since her child has died, sits in the shadow. She will not listen to us . . .

END OF PLAY

The Marriage We Deplore

THIS PLAY, appearing here for the first time, is dated "June 10, [19]17," in author's hand, when Wilder was a Yale sophomore. In his drama, Wilder always worked most comfortably within self-imposed parameters of idea and structure. Here he plays with drawing room comedy, class structure and a "five-minute/five-person" design. The first two themes reoccur many times throughout his career, notably in *The Matchmaker* (1954), and in his last novel *Theophilus North* (1973).

The Marriage We Deplore

CHARACTERS

EVA, an aristocrat, fifty
CHARLES, her second husband
JULIA, Eva's daughter, twenty-five
GEORGE, Eva's son, Julia's brother
PHYLLIS, George's wife

SETTING

Living room of Mrs. Eva Hibbert-Havens, Boston.

At the rise of the curtain Eva Hibbert-Havens is seated, dressed for dinner, in a beautiful chair from which she does not rise until the close of the play. She is a stout aristocratic lady, assertive but illogical. In short, a Boston grande dame. She calls to her second husband who passes in the hall:

EVA: Charles! Come in, please.

CHARLES *(Offstage, reluctantly)*: I could wait in the den, dear, until they come.

EVA *(Firmly)*: Well, please sit down just for a minute.

(Charles Havens comes in. He is an absentminded, slightly apologetic man in a tuxedo.)

I haven't told Daughter yet just who the guests are. I told her to dress for dinner quietly and she'd find out later who they were.

CHARLES *(Indifferently)*: Surely it wouldn't hurt her to say that her brother is coming to dinner.

EVA *(Severely)*: Her brother, and her brother's wife.

CHARLES *(Mildly)*: Yes, her brother's wife. Her sister, so to speak.

EVA: Well, if I had told Daughter that! —And I want her to look especially well tonight. *(Forcefully)* To contrast with the rouge and tinsel of her "sister."

CHARLES *(In surprised protest)*: But George's wife won't wear rouge and tinsel.

EVA: How do we know what George's wife won't wear? Where did he find her, I'd like to know? In a station lunchroom, very likely. In a prize shooting gallery.

CHARLES *(Amusedly)*: In a circus, perhaps.

EVA *(With indignation)*: I mean that my son, George Hibbert *Junior*, of the Boston Hibberts, married miles beneath him.

CHARLES *(Absentmindedly)*: Was that her name?

EVA: As you say, he may have married a trapeze artiste.

CHARLES *(Prosaically)*: My dear, you're always reminding me that you married beneath you when you married me. Why blame George for doing what you have found fairly satisfactory?

EVA: I blame George because he is a young man with still some prestige to make. When I married you I had been for eight years the widow of the most distinguished citizen of Boston. I could have married someone much lower than my husband's assistant manager, and still faced the world.

CHARLES *(Gently)*: My dear, I was not your husband's assistant manager. I was his foreman.

EVA: Foreman, never. I used to see you sign his checks for him. I married my husband's sub-manager; George has married his landlady's furnace-shaker.

CHARLES *(Shaking his head)*: He has dragged the name of Hibbert in the coal bin.

(Enter Daughter in evening dress. A beautiful girl of twenty-five is Julia Hibbert-Havens. She is strong-minded and so has naturally found with such a mother that concealment is the best policy. We know her to be excitingly tricky, so we are able to appreciate that her demureness in the presence of her mother is a trifle exaggerated.)

JULIA: Well, Mother, who are these secret guests we're having tonight?

EVA: Who, indeed!

CHARLES: It's your brother George.

JULIA: And his bride?

EVA: Yes, his acquirement. He holds an indignation meeting against me for two years because I married your present father, and then he marries a Nobody and breaks the silence by inviting himself to dinner.

JULIA: Who was she?

EVA: No one seems to know; a boardinghouse girl; someone says, a waitress in a station lunchroom—

CHARLES: —You said so yourself.

EVA: Perhaps the proprietress of a shooting gallery—

CHARLES: —That was your guess.

EVA: Don't interrupt! And Charles heard that she was from a circus.

CHARLES: I didn't hear, I guessed.

EVA: Well, take your choice. Those are the rumors. George has married beneath him. It's a wonder the church allows it. Every debutante marries her chauffeur; her brother marries her lady's maid. It is a national danger. If everybody married beneath them where should we be, I'd like to know. It is the peril that lurks for democratic nations. It shows a nationwide admiration for the lower classes that is deplorable. That's what George said in his terrible letter after I had married a second time. Such names he called me! It was like Forbes-Robertson talking to his mother in *Hamlet.* *

CHARLES *(Vaguely)*: Ah . . . is there a situation like that in *Hamlet? (He wanders to the bookcase)*

EVA *(With alarm)*: No, there is not . . . not the slightest.

JULIA: What does it matter?

EVA *(Anxiously)*: Do let us be frank with one another. You don't realize how difficult this is for me. What are you doing, Charles? You're not listening to me.

CHARLES: Oh, yes I was. I was seeing if I could find *Hamlet.*

EVA: Julia, I want you to burn every copy of *Hamlet* there is in the house.

JULIA: It'll spoil the sets, Mother.

EVA: There are more important things than preserving sets.

JULIA: Not in Boston.

EVA: What was I saying, Charles?

CHARLES: You wanted us to be frank with one another. My dear, I've been frank. I understand perfectly that your son was angry with you when you married me. I wrote him that I did not pretend to be more than a plain ordinary man.

JULIA: Mother, it's you that are not being frank.

EVA *(Crying)*: Haven't I told you that she was a station restaurant waitress?

CHARLES *(Pained)*: Dear me! What an affliction!

---

*[Sir Johnston Forbes-Robertson was a British actor whose daughter and son-in-law, Dinah and Vincent Sheehan, were Wilder's close friends.]

JULIA: All the better. Then he's in a glass house; and won't dare to throw stones at you anymore.

EVA: It's not *that* I mind. I'd like to give him a good talking to, myself. It's because I'm in a glass house.

CHARLES *(Gently)*: My dear, seeing that this doesn't concern me, may I retire to my den until your son arrives? *(He is unnoticed)*

JULIA: Now there'll be peace in the family. No more mutual recriminations; everybody wears muzzles—in fact, they've married muzzles.

CHARLES: I daresay he's timorous about coming to see you now.

EVA *(Sharply)*: Not at all! There's always you as a precedent.

CHARLES *(Cowed)*: Dear me! So there is, so there is. There's the doorbell now.

EVA: Now don't anyone be tactless.

JULIA: Don't anyone mention boardinghouses or glass houses, or anything that might cause self-consciousness.

CHARLES: Am I to stay in the room all the time?

EVA: Yes; they are not to think I have any regrets. —I shall soon find out which rumor was correct.

(Enter George and his wife. George is an obstinate young man; Phyllis is an extraordinarily pretty young girl with large blue eyes. Her hair is arranged to resemble Billie Burke's; she is exquisitely dressed and has charming manners. It is the most difficult moment in her life.)

GEORGE *(Kissing his mother)*: How are you, Mother? Mother, this is my wife.

EVA *(Offering her cheek)*: You may, my dear. *(After Phyllis has kissed her)* We meet at last, so to speak.

PHYLLIS *(Blushing)*: Better late than never, as they say.

GEORGE *(To Charles, shaking hands stiffly)*: How do you do, Mr. Havens. Phyllis, this is my father.

PHYLLIS *(Faintly)*: I'm very happy to know you.

EVA: George, why don't you introduce your wife to Daughter?

JULIA: Oh, we have met, Mother.

EVA *(In astonishment)*: When was that?

JULIA: I have called on them several times.

EVA *(With evident displeasure)*: So *that's* how you spend your time in Atlantic City. And never say a word about it to me!

JULIA: I was saving it as a pleasant surprise.

EVA: You misjudged! —Were you ever in Boston before, Phyllis?

PHYLLIS: Unfortunately not. I have been kept pretty regularly to Atlantic City.

EVA *(Marveling)*: And yet Boston so close!

PHYLLIS: I have occasionally run up to New York for shopping.

EVA *(Urgently)*: Charles! My smelling salts—in the hall. *(He gets them)* But naturally from your position in the station you were able to see the trains depart for Boston.

PHYLLIS *(Agreeably)*: Oh, yes. There are trains.

EVA *(Nodding her head enigmatically)*: Hmm—yes . . . yes. Did you find it monotonous? —Standing over the counter, long hours . . . ?

PHYLLIS *(At sea)*: You mean, did we come by boat?

JULIA: No, dear, Mother means: Did you find the trip longer than you expected?

PHYLLIS *(To her)*: I like traveling.

EVA: I see! Naturally. How fortunate. There must be long waits while the tents are being nailed down. —Then there's the long, hot parade.

PHYLLIS *(To George)*: I'm afraid—I do not understand . . .

GEORGE: You mean, Mother—?

JULIA *(To the rescue)*: By parade, Mother means the board-walk at Atlantic City we all hear so much about.

PHYLLIS *(To Eva, brightly)*: Oh, no. It's a pleasure, I assure you. And on the hottest days there are the awnings—that's what you meant by "tents."

EVA: Yes, yes. But no doubt there are tents, too. Fortune tellers, and—

PHYLLIS: —A very few.—

EVA: —And among them, the shooting gallery.

PHYLLIS *(Seeking light)*: *The* shooting gallery?

EVA *(Boldly)*: The one you were interested in.

(At last Phyllis is completely perplexed.)

PHYLLIS *(In a pretty confusion)*: I'm afraid I'm very dull. But I've heard of the subtlety—the wit—of Boston conversation. I have always lived quietly with my mother in our little home on the North Shore. I've had little experience—

JULIA: —Don't apologize, Phyllis. Mother has a playful way you'll understand when you get to know her better.

EVA: I was not aware of it.

CHARLES *(Soothingly)*: Now Eva! You know you're famous for your wit.

GEORGE: It has developed then in the last year—amazingly.

EVA *(Retorting)*: Think of what I've had to bear.

GEORGE: I warned you in good time.

(Fortunately dinner is announced at this point.)

EVA *(Rising and repeating a formula used by all Boston hostesses at informal dinners to relatives)*: We live very simply, but of such as it is we try to obtain the best, and to that you are always welcome. *(She leads the way out with Charles)*

PHYLLIS *(Turning, at the front of the stage; plaintively)*: I don't understand your mother at all, George—
      (She sees Julia and runs to her) When are you to be married, Julia?

JULIA *(Smiling down at her happily)*: On Saturday afternoon at four o' the clock.

PHYLLIS: Why at four?

JULIA: Because they don't let the dear boy out of the factory until three; and he says he *must* brush his hair.

(They go on into dinner.)

END OF PLAY

PART
II

The Unerring Instinct

A PLAY IN ONE ACT

WILDER often said that the inscription on his gravestone should read: "Here lies a man who tried to be obliging." When his country or his profession called, more often than not he went, including service in two World Wars. When asked to lecture, preside, be present, he would try to fit the date in, especially if he admired the cause or the institution or the person behind the invitation. The impulse also carried over into the writing of "occasional plays," works done for an occasion—a birthday party, a club's centenary celebration (*Our Century: A Play in Three Scenes*, for the Century Association in New York City, 1947), a milestone in the life of a dormitory where he was living temporarily (*On the House*, in honor of the twentieth anniversary of Dunster House at Harvard College, 1950).

In the same vein but on a serious level, in late 1947, he wrote *The Unerring Instinct: A Play in One Act*, for the National Conference of Christians and Jews' "NCCJ Scripts for Brotherhood" program. Beginning in January 1948, the Conference distributed the play free to schools and dramatic clubs throughout the country. The Conference continued to promote it until at least the mid-1960s. Publicity described *The Unerring Instinct* this way:

> Story of a woman whose fears and sweeping judgments of people are swept away when she is shown how susceptible she is to nonsensical talk. For high school and adult groups.

Wilder enjoyed the NCCJ assignment (a piece that employs a signal system reminiscent of the warning device in Act II of *The Skin of Our Teeth*). "I have just finished a short play for the nationwide use of the Conference of Christians and Jews," he wrote family in late 1947. "Those I have read it to are enthusiastic . . . It is very funny and yet drastic and searching."

The Unerring Instinct

A PLAY IN ONE ACT

CHARACTERS

LEONORA THORPE, a pleasant woman of middle age
BELINDA WATSON, a younger woman, Leonora's sister-in-law
ARTHUR ROGERS

SETTING

Leonora's home.

No curtain and scenery are required. Three comfortable chairs and a small table. At the players' right is a table or board on which there are three colored lights: red, blue and green. They are worked on dimmers.

Leonora enters and coming to the front of the stage addresses the audience.

LEONORA: My name is Leonora Thorpe. I've been asked to come here to tell you about a practical joke I played on a friend of mine—on my sister-in-law, in fact. Some of you may think I was a little cruel. Perhaps I was. My sister-in-law, Belinda Watson, has always been full of fears about people and full of sweeping judgments about those she wants to meet and those she doesn't want to meet. On this occasion I lost my patience with her. I decided to plant a brand-new prejudice in her mind— just to show her how susceptible she was to nonsense.

While we act this out I've asked some electricians to operate these three colored lights. They will show you the various emotions that were going on inside Belinda Watson during this session.

(During the following explanation the lights are turned up as they are described.)

This light is red. It's for fear and it needs no explanation.

This blue light indicates despair—bewilderment, confusion and despair. It denotes that state which we all get into when it seems that thinking is too difficult; that thinking never gets us anywhere; that reason and justice are simply too complicated; that it's easier to give up and just attack.

So this last light is green—that's the last resort of fear and despair: that's malice and snarl and bite and attack.

This thing took place in a friend's house in the town where we all live. There'd been an auction for some benefit—Visiting Nurses or Boys' Clubs. Hundreds of people had been there. In fact, it was the first time that I'd felt that our whole community had gotten together in a friendly way and had really met one another. At the end of the afternoon I went out to the veranda to sit down and rest. I'd been one of the auctioneers.

(She sits down. Enter Belinda, fanning herself with an auction program.)

BELINDA: Well, dear, it's been a great success, a really great success. And I've shaken a great many hands that I hope I never shake again. I know they're very nice, I hope they're happy, I hope they eat three meals a day, but let them lead their lives and let me lead mine.

LEONORA: Now, Belinda, I'm too tired to listen to you protesting about how broad-minded you are.

BELINDA: Well, I am. You're always scolding me about what you call my prejudices. You're wrong. I'm the most broad-minded woman in this town. As far as I'm concerned: color, religion, rich or poor—makes no difference to me.

LEONORA: Good heavens, here we go again.

BELINDA: It's only when it comes to my children that I draw the line. I want every association that they make to be of the *very best*. I don't want them to get into any situation that might be embarrassing—*ever*.

LEONORA: I know. And for that you have that infallible instinct of yours to guide you as to who is or is not suitable for them. Let's not talk about it.

BELINDA: Well, after all, you're their aunt. You must see what I mean.

LEONORA *(Sitting up)*: Yes, I'm their aunt, aren't I?

BELINDA: And you've said a thousand times that they're perfectly beautiful children. And, of course, you have a certain responsibility to them, too. After all, little Leonora's named after you—she looks like you, she dotes on you.

(Leonora has risen. She walks about and is seen to be forming a decision. Standing behind Belinda's chair, she says:)

LEONORA: Belinda, I noticed something odd this afternoon. I wonder if you did.

BELINDA: Why . . . what?

LEONORA: Oh, George Smith and his brother and sister.

BELINDA: . . . Which ones? . . .

LEONORA: Belinda, do you happen to know many people named Smith?

BELINDA: No. —Yes, I know a few. Why do you ask?

LEONORA *(Sitting down)*: Well, dear, have you ever noticed anything *funny* about them?

BELINDA: Funny? How do you mean? *(The red light begins to glow)*

LEONORA: Oh, well, if you haven't, I'm sorry I mentioned it. After all, you have enough to worry you as it is—to bring up the children and everything.

BELINDA: What were you going to say, dear?

LEONORA: Forget it. —My, what an attractive dress that is. Have I ever seen that before?

BELINDA: Yes, it's new. —No, I mean it's an old thing I've had for years. But what were you going to say about the Smiths? —Now, Leonora, if there's anything I ought to know, I insist on your telling me.

LEONORA: Well, it's nothing really. Yet I feel that it's something everybody should at least know *about*. Have you ever really stopped to think about the name Smith?

BELINDA: No-o-o-o. What do you mean? *(A brief flare-up of the red light)*

LEONORA: Before the War, I read a paper by a famous German scholar—oh, a *very* great scholar—about the Schmidts in Germany. And of course, they're the same thing as our Smiths.

BELINDA: Yes?

LEONORA: Don't you see? They're all descended finally from blacksmiths and ironworkers, aren't they?

BELINDA: I suppose so.

LEONORA: Swinging great hammers all day.

BELINDA: You mean . . . ? Leonora, hundreds of years have gone by since . . .

LEONORA: So you *do* see? This professor studies thousands of them. You must have read it; it was in all the magazines. Naturally, they'd be very *strong willed* and ruthless, wouldn't they? Heartless, really.

BELINDA: Leonora! I never thought of that.

LEONORA: Pounding. Hammering. Driving nails into poor horses' feet all day. Twisting white-hot iron into the strangest shapes. Well—that's all I meant.

BELINDA: Goodness! But, Leonora . . . what should we do about it?

LEONORA: The only thing for us to do is to *know* it and to keep our wits about us.

BELINDA: To think that I never, never thought of that before!

LEONORA: Of course, there are *some* nice Smiths—

BELINDA *(Sudden strong burst of red light; sudden cry)*: But the principal of my boy's school is named Smith!! He *seemed* perfectly nice.

LEONORA: Oh, I don't deny it. But listen: a nice Smith is still a *Smith.* You keep your eyes open, dear—you'll see. Take another example—come nearer, dear, we mustn't talk so loud. Take that woman who sings on the radio—Rose Smith or Bessie Smith—what's her name?

BELINDA: Why, I always thought she was so nice and wholesome, so to speak. *(The blue light begins to glow. The red light off)*

LEONORA: Yes, but look at how *famous* she is! To arrive at a position like that, my dear, one must be . . . *strong willed,* believe me. Why, do you realize that Al Smith almost became president of the United States?

BELINDA: But, Leonora, the principal of my William's school is named Smith. *(A brief return of the red glow)*

LEONORA: Now you're beginning to misunderstand me. There are lots of perfectly nice Smiths.

BELINDA: Oh, dear, I'm almost sorry that you told me all this. It's so upsetting. *(Brief intensity of blue; then back to blue glow)* Really, one doesn't know what to do or to think these days.

LEONORA: The answer to that is this: Don't try to think, just know what you know, trust to that instinct of yours, and keep your eyes open. You'll see the Smiths behaving in very Smithy ways wherever you look.

BELINDA: Oh, I just thought of . . . Who could have been kinder and better than Dr. Buckingham Smith?

LEONORA: Oh, yes. The one who was so kind to your mother all through her illness?

BELINDA: He was an angel, a perfect angel. *(Strong blue light)* Oh, Leonora, it's so hard to . . . I mean, it's really hard . . .

LEONORA: Of course, it's *easiest* just to distrust them *all*.

BELINDA *(No lights on; pause; then thoughtfully)*: Do you know something? *(Green light begins full)* I never did really like that school.

LEONORA: Oh, Belinda, you've always been very enthusiastic about it.

BELINDA: No. From the first day I saw it I knew it wasn't right. Fortunately I have an instinct for such things . . . Of course, William admires this Mr. . . . . this Mr. Blacksmith.

LEONORA: Smith, dear, Smith.

BELINDA *(Green reduced to red glow)*: Whatever you call him. William admires him, but, of course, William's a mere child. Children don't sense these things. I'll speak to Wallace about it tonight.

LEONORA: About what, Belinda?

BELINDA *(Green light full for a moment; harshly)*: Why, about taking William out of that dreadful place, of course. I'll speak to him about it this very night.

(Enter Arthur, carrying a teacup.)

ARTHUR *(Remaining at back of stage)*: Oh, there you are, Leonora. Can I bring you ladies some tea?

(All colored lights off.)

LEONORA: No, Arthur, we've had some. Arthur, I want you to meet my sister-in-law, Belinda Watson.

ARTHUR: Happy to meet you, Mrs. Watson. —I'll be back in one minute.

(Exit Arthur.)

BELINDA *(Pleased)*: Why, who's that? He seems . . . very nice man . . .

LEONORA: That's . . . old friend of my husband's. That's Arthur . . . uh . . . I'm surprised you don't know him. That's Arthur Smythe.

BELINDA *(Quickly)*: What? Smythe?! How do you spell it?

LEONORA: S.M.Y.T.H.E. —Why?

BELINDA: Leonora!! *(Flare-up of red beside the green glow)* That's the same as Smith, isn't it?

LEONORA: Oh, that's all right. Everybody likes Arthur. I'm glad you're going to meet him.

BELINDA: Do you think it wise, dear? *(Red glow; green strong)* Really, I'd rather not.

LEONORA: Now, Belinda, you're getting hysterical. Arthur's an exceptional person. Wonderful war record. And besides, he's the best citizen in this town; your own husband says so. He should get all the credit for the new hospital wing.

BELINDA *(Add brief full strength of blue light)*: But, dear, he's one of those Smiths!

(Arthur reappears; he promptly drops his cup and saucer.)

ARTHUR: Confound it! Holy blazes! If I'm not the awkwardest pigheadedest—

BELINDA *(Brief red flare; pointing dramatically)*: —Look at that! Look at that!

(Arthur kneels down and dabs at the floor with his handkerchief. All lights off except a faint green glow.)

ARTHUR: Have I ruined this rug, Leonora?

LEONORA: Was there any cream in it?

ARTHUR: No.

LEONORA: Then it's all right. Come over and talk to us.

ARTHUR *(Crossing)*: Well, at last, I'm very glad to meet you, Mrs. Watson. I've been seeing your husband almost every day. In fact, I had lunch with him yesterday.

BELINDA *(Flare-up of red light, then out; very gracious)*: Did you? How nice!

ARTHUR: Yes, I was complaining to him that Amelia and I had never had the opportunity to meet you. I asked him: What's the matter with us?

(Red and green lights begin to flicker on and off at medium strength. Belinda laughs nervously.)

Anyway, I think you're coming to dinner with us next Thursday.

BELINDA *(Flickering continues; charming)*: Oh, I *wish* we could. Now, isn't that too bad! I'm so sorry, but we're engaged on Thursday.

ARTHUR: Sorry. However, we'll hound you until you do come.

(Belinda laughs prettily.)

I believe my daughter Helen has been doing her algebra with your daughter Leonora.

BELINDA *(Red and green up)*: Has she? Has she? Well, I've always believed—of course, I may be wrong!—that children should do their homework *alone*. I certainly hope that I shall have the pleasure of meeting Mrs. Black . . . I mean Mrs. . . . . I mean Mrs. Smythe some day; but my husband's been overworking lately—in fact, he's a perfect wreck—and we almost never go out in the evening.

ARTHUR: Oh . . . uh . . . what Mrs. Smythe is that?

LEONORA *(Quickly)*: Oh, I know you'll like each other enormously when you do meet. There's no doubt about it.

(Red and green flicker at half strength.)

ARTHUR: Mrs. Watson, your husband was telling me that your son William has been having a succession of colds all autumn. I suggested that just after Christmas he could go with my son Jim down to my mother's house in Florida.

BELINDA *(The blue light starts flickering with the other two)*: Oh . . . uh . . . uh . . . uh . . .

LEONORA: Oh, Belinda, it would do him a world of good. I've been there; it's a perfectly beautiful place. They could be out in the sun all day.

ARTHUR: Of course, I have purely selfish reasons for urging it, since my boy would have so much better a time with another boy along.

BELINDA *(All lights off, but a strong green; rises)*: Mr. Smythe, I thank you very much, really very much. But our family has made the rule never to be separated. We may be unusual in that; I don't know. But I couldn't let William . . . it's such a distance . . . Thank you very much.

ARTHUR: That's as you think best, of course—I must be going now. Leonora, I shall probably be telephoning your house tonight . . . to ask about the weather. I'm glad to have met you, Mrs. Watson. Perhaps Mrs. Rogers and I may hope to meet you—*some day.*

(Exit Arthur. All lights off.)

BELINDA: What did he say "Mrs. Rogers and I"?
LEONORA: What, dear?
BELINDA: Who's Mrs. Rogers? Why did he say "Mrs. Rogers and I"?
LEONORA: Why not? That's Arthur Rogers.

BELINDA: But you said his name was SMYTHE! Leonora!
—Arthur Rogers! Why, my husband thinks the world of
him. How could you say that he was one of those *Smiths?*

LEONORA: Belinda, sit down. I have something to tell you.

BELINDA: What an awful mistake! Leonora, I might have
hurt his feelings.

LEONORA: You didn't hurt his feelings; he merely thought
you peculiar.

BELINDA: Leonora!

LEONORA: Now listen to what I'm saying, Belinda.
Everything I've told you about the Smiths today is nonsense. Do you hear me?—perfect nonsense.

BELINDA *(Weeping)*: I shouldn't have listened to you.

LEONORA: Exactly! You shouldn't have believed me. You
have no infallible instinct at all. What you call your
instinct about people is merely made of listening to
nonsense like this.

BELINDA: Leonora, I don't know when I'll forgive you.
You've made a fool of me in front of a perfectly nice
man.

(Exit Belinda quickly. Leonora turns to the audience.)

LEONORA: Well, that's the story. I realize that what you all
want to know is whether Belinda profited by this lesson.
Maybe not. Only one Belinda in ten ever learns anything. It's my nieces and nephews that I'm interested in.

Before bidding you good-bye I wish to ask the forgiveness of all Smiths who were for a moment dispar-
aged in this play—of Kate Smith; of Mary Pickford,
born Smith; of Smith College; and of the Smithsonian
Institution.

But I have no apologies to make to those who
were—even for a moment—shaken in their good opinion of the Smiths.

Good night.

END OF PLAY

PART
III

"The Emporium"

I N 1948, THORNTON WILDER launched a major drama he titled "The Emporium," a work Donald Gallup (Wilder's literary executor for many decades) has described as "Wilder's attempt to write a play influenced by both Kierkegaard and Gertrude Stein, combining the atmosphere of Kafka's *The Castle* with a Horatio Alger theme." Despite efforts lasting into the mid-1950s, the play remained incomplete, although widely commented upon in the press. In 1948, for example, he told a Connecticut reporter that his new play is to be "a typical American success story and a *spine-chilling* melodrama . . . a combination of Horatio Alger and Kafka . . . and there'll be a little bit of me in it, too." In 1953, to a German reporter seeking Wilder's views of Oswald Spengler's work, *The Decline of the West*, the playwright responded in part:

> The mysterious divine plan is not accessible to us. Eternity will balance the ledger; we are only agents and sufferers. I am attempting to shape these thoughts in a parareligious form in my new drama "The Emporium." I have been working on it for three years now, but I am in no hurry. I follow the inner law of maturation without pressure.

The publication of Wilder's private journals in 1985 by Yale University Press, selected and edited by Donald Gallup, threw new light on the author's struggles with "The Emporium." As appendices to that volume, Mr. Gallup added two scenes from "The Emporium" that Wilder had declared "solid and good," as well as special portion of the author's journal entries dealing with the play. This material is republished here as an example of how the author used his journal as a tool for thinking and meditating about his work in progress.

"The Emporium"

A PLAY IN [] SCENES
AND A PROLOGUE

CHARACTERS

STAGE HANDS
MEMBER OF THE AUDIENCE
MR. FOSTER, superintendent of the orphanage
MRS. FOSTER, his wife
MR. CONOVER, a janitor
MRS. GRAHAM, a farmer's wife, played by the same actor as
    Mrs. Foster
JOHN, the Grahams' adopted son
MR. GRAHAM, a farmer, played by the same actor as Mr.
    Foster

SETTING

The Amanda Gregory Foster Orphanage. The Graham
Farm.

The curtain of the stage is not used in this play.

Members of the audience arriving early will see the stage in half light. The six screens and the furniture and properties will be seen stacked about it at random.

Two Stage Hands dressed in light blue jumpers, like garage mechanics, will enter ten minutes before the beginning and will remove these properties and set the stage for Scene One.

The six screens are about six-and-a-half by twelve. They are like the movable walls of a Japanese house and are on rollers. They are all slightly off white, one faintly bluish, another toward buff, or green, and so on.

There is a light chair on the left front of the stage (from the point of view of the actors), by the proscenium pillar.

A few minutes before the play begins the Member of the Audience enters from the wings at the left, looks about a little nervously and seats himself in this chair, turning it toward the center of the stage. He affects to be at ease, glances occasionally at the arriving audience, and studies his program. He is a modest but very earnest man of about fifty. He will be on the stage throughout the play and, except at the moments indicated, he will remain motionless, fixing an absorbed attention on the action before him.

A screen has been placed far front in the center of the stage, parallel with the footlights. The other screens are placed as though casually at the back of the stage though masking the entrances at the right and left. In front of the central screen is an old-fashioned "deacon's" chair. Beside it is a stand on which lies a vast Bible.

A bell starts ringing at the back of the auditorium.

SCENE ONE

The Amanda Gregory Foster Orphanage

Enter Mr. Foster, superintendent of the orphanage. He is an excitable man of late middle age dressed in an old, faded and unpressed cutaway. He looks like a deacon or a small-town undertaker.

He dashes out a few steps from the right and shakes his hand imperiously at the back of the auditorium, calling out loudly:

MR. FOSTER: Ring the bell, Mr. Conover. Ring it again. Ring it louder. I want every child in this orphanage to be in this auditorium in four minutes.

(He disappears as rapidly as he came.

Enter from the same entrance Mrs. Foster, a worn woman of her husband's age, dressed in faded blue gingham. She also calls to the back of the auditorium:)

MRS. FOSTER: Come in, children. Come in quietly. Take your places quietly, girls. —Boys, behave yourselves! —Girls here on my left, as usual. Mr. Conover, are they ringing the bell out in the vegetable garden, too? Thank you. —I wonder if the girls in the laundry can hear it, with all that machinery going.

Henry Smith Foster, is that you? Will you run over to the laundry and tell all the children that Mr. Foster wants them—all of them—here in the Assembly Hall.

Boys! Boys! —Don't play now. Just take your places quietly.

(Exit Mrs. Foster. A second alarm bell starts ringing in dissonance. Enter Mr. Foster.)

MR. FOSTER: That's right, Mr. Conover. Ring all the bells. George Washington Foster, are *you* there? Form them into lines, two by two. They're all pushing and crowding. Girls on this side *(Left)*; boys over here *(Right)*. All children over eleven down here in front. Very young children in the back. The blind children and the lame children in the last rows. Children eight to eleven up in the balconies.

(He shades his eyes and seems to be peering up to fourth, fifth, and sixth balconies. Then again to the back of the auditorium:)

Now what's all that group late for? Oh, you've been working in the dairy. Very well, take your places.

(Enter Mrs. Foster. She goes up to her husband and says in his ear:)

MRS. FOSTER: Now you mustn't get excited! You remember what the doctor said.

MR. FOSTER: Stragglers! Stragglers!

    Yes. —Edgar Allan Poe Foster! Late as usual. Always trying to be different.

MRS. FOSTER: Remember your asthma! Remember your ulcers! You only hurt yourself when you get so excited. Remember, this has happened before and it will very certainly happen again.

    (Suddenly in irritation to a girl apparently coming down the aisle) Sarah Bernhardt Foster! Stop making a show of yourself; sit down and take your place quietly among the other girls!

MR. FOSTER: I want you all to come to attention. James Jones Foster! —You may assist George Washington Foster in closing the doors.

(Impressive pause.)

Wards of the Amanda Gregory Foster Orphanage! Of William County, Western Pennsylvania! Another of our children has attempted to run away! That makes the twelfth since Christmas!

(He has a moment's convulsion of asthmatic coughing and sneezing into an enormous red-checked handkerchief. During this, his eyes fall on the Member of the Audience

seated on the stage at his left. He stares at him a moment, then dropping his characterization, he says:)

Who are you?

MEMBER OF THE AUDIENCE: I?

MR. FOSTER: Yes, you—who are you? What are you doing up here on the stage?

(To the audience) Excuse me a moment. There's— there's something wrong here.

(To the Member of the Audience) What are you doing— sitting up here on stage?

MEMBER OF THE AUDIENCE: Euh—the management sold me this seat—I told them I was a little hard of hearing.

MR. FOSTER: What? What's that? I can't hear you.

MEMBER OF THE AUDIENCE: The management sold me this seat. I won't be in the way. I told them I was a little hard of hearing and they sold me this seat here.

MR. FOSTER: You certainly will be in the way. I never heard of such a thing.

(He turns to Mrs. Foster) We can't go on with this man here.

MRS. FOSTER: Perhaps. Anyway, we'd better not stop now. We'll try to do something about it at the intermission.

MR. FOSTER: At the intermission. —I must say I never heard of such a thing. —Anyway, while you're here— draw your chair back against the wall. You're preventing those people from seeing the stage.

(The Member of the Audience draws his chair back.)

I hope you know enough not to distract the audience's attention in any way. It's important to us that you be as quiet as possible.

MEMBER OF THE AUDIENCE: Yes, oh, yes.

(Mr. Foster glares at him and resumes his role.)

MR. FOSTER: Wards of the Amanda Gregory Foster Orphanage! Of William County, Western Pennsylvania! Another of our children has attempted to run away. That makes the twelfth since Christmas. He will be found. He will be brought back to us any moment now. I have brought you together this morning to talk this over. You run away: to what? to whom? Last fall *you* ran away *(Fixing an orphan in the audience)*, George Gordon Byron Foster! You were brought back after a week, but what kind of week was it? You slept in railroad stations; you fed yourself out of refuse cans, or from what you could beg at the back door of restaurants. We asked you why you ran away and you said you wanted to live—to live, to live, impatience to *live*.

Joan Dark Foster, will you stop throwing yourself about in your seat! I shall not keep you long.

And you said you wanted to be free. Every lost dog and cat is free. The horse that has run away from the stable and wanders in the woods is free.

—Do I hear talking up there—in the fourth and fifth balconies? Surely you nine year olds can understand what I'm saying! The five year olds down here are quiet enough!

Gustav Froebel Foster! —Can't you keep order among the children up there?

(He waits a moment in stern silence.)

This orphanage was founded by a noble Christian woman, Amanda Gregory Foster, and here—for a time—you are taken care of. You have all been given the name of Foster, in memory of our foundress, and some of you have been given names of eminent—of great and useful—men and women. But you are all foundlings and orphans. These are facts. Do not exhaust your minds and hearts by trying to resist these things *which are.*

Prometheus Foster! Ludwig van Beethoven Foster! Sit down, both of you! Glaring and shaking your fists at me cannot change these matters one iota. What has to be, has to be.

But that is not the only thing which you must patiently accept in life. There is also much about each one of you which cannot be changed: your *self*. Your eyes and nose and mouth. Your color. Your height—when you have finally gained your growth. And your disposition. Some of you are timid. Some of you are proud. We know which ones of you are lazy and which of you are ambitious. In addition, each of you has a different store of health. Your sum of health—*yours*!

(Mrs. Foster rises quickly and points to audience, left.)

MRS. FOSTER: What's that? John Keats Foster has fainted.

MR. FOSTER: Lower his head between his knees, boys; he will come to himself.

MRS. FOSTER: Who's sitting beside him? Joseph Severn Foster and Percy Shelley Foster—carry him out into the open air, boys. You'd better take him to the Infirmary.

MR. FOSTER: And what's that noise I hear in the back row?

MRS. FOSTER: It's—it's the blind children. Where's Helen Keller Foster? —Oh, there you are! —Will you comfort the—? Yes.

(She returns to her seat.)

MR. FOSTER: There is no greater waste of time—and no greater enemy of character—than to wish that you were differently endowed and differently constituted. From these things you cannot run away.

Now one of our number, John Vere Foster, has again tried to change all this. For the third time he has tried to run away. Ah, there he is! Mr. Conover, will you bring John Vere Foster right down here, please. To the front row so that we can all see him.

(Mr. Conover, a shuffling old janitor, leads a boy, invisible to us, holding him by the ear, to a seat in the front row of the theatre aisle. Mr. Foster rises, steps forward, and fixes his eyes on the boy.)

Now, young man, will you tell us—tell all of us—why it is that you tried to run away?

(Pause.)

What! You're going to be stubborn and silent?

(Pause.)

You all have enough to eat. You have suitable clothing. The work is not difficult. Many of you enjoy your classes and we hear all of you playing very happily among yourselves in your recreation hours. Mrs. Foster and I make every effort to be just. There is very little punishment here and what there is is light. Many visitors tell us that this is the best orphanage in the country.

(Again he has an asthmatic convulsion.)

MRS. FOSTER: Take a glass of water. Sit down a moment and take a glass of water.

(He sits down, his shoulders heaving.
Mrs. Foster comes to the front of the stage and addresses John—more gently but unsentimentally:)

John, tell us—tell us why you have tried to run away. I can't hear you. Oh—you want to *belong.*
MR. FOSTER: What did he say? What did he say?
MEMBER OF THE AUDIENCE *(Helpfully)*: He said he wanted to belong.
MR. FOSTER: Oh—to belong.

Children! —I am going to give John Vere Foster his wishes. He wishes—as you all say you do—to live and to belong.

A farmer and his wife called on me this morning. They wish to adopt a boy. Mr. Graham seems to me to be a just man. We do not usually place you—you, children—in homes until you are sixteen. John is only fourteen, but he is strong for his age—and, as you see, he is *impatient*.

John, go to Mrs. Hoskins: she will give you a new pair of shoes and a new overcoat; and she will pack your box. You are leaving with your father and mother—Mr. and Mrs. Graham—on the railway train this afternoon.

Belong!—to belong!

All of you have one thing in common: you do not belong to parents; you do not belong to homes; you do not belong to yourselves. You all *belong*.

Thousands of children have passed through this school—thousands of schools. The names of many of them you find on tablets in the corridor. The names of many of them are forgotten. The very ink has faded on our school records.

The generations of men are like the generations of leaves on the trees. They fall into the earth and new leaves are grown the following spring. The world into which you have been born is one of eternal repetitions—already you can see that.

But there is something to which you *can* belong— you *do* belong: I am not yet empowered to tell you its name. It is something which is constantly striving to bring something new into these repetitions, to lift them, to color them, to—

It's not by running away—from place to place— that you will find something to belong to—or that you will make yourself free—

(Convulsions.)

You are looking in the wrong place. —You will find it when you least expect it.

(He is shaken with coughing. His wife speaks to the children:)

MRS. FOSTER: That will be all! Go back to your rooms *quietly,* children.

Benvenuto Cellini Foster, put away your slingshot! This is no time for play.

SCENE TWO

The Graham Farm

The screens have been arranged to suggest a large room—the kitchen of the Graham farmhouse. A gap between the two screens at the back indicates the door into the parlor.

Stage left: a kitchen table. The chair at its left faces right. Enter Mrs. Graham—played by the actress who has just played Mrs. Foster. She now seems gaunt and stony-faced. She has thrown a worn blue shawl over her shoulders. She carries a farm lantern. She comes to the front of the stage, opens an imaginary backdoor. She peers toward the back of the auditorium.

MRS. GRAHAM: John Graham, I want you should come in and eat your supper before Mr. Graham comes back from prayer meeting. I've just heated it up for the second time and I want you should eat it. It's eight o'clock. It's cold and it's black as pitch. But I've seen you down by the corncrib there. You finished chores a long time ago and there's nothing for you to be doing down at the barn, and a growing boy should eat his food hot. It's real good. It's hominy cooked in bacon, and greens, and it's real good. And I put some molasses in it.

(She puts her lantern down and hugs her shawl tighter around her.)

All right, I won't call you by your whole name; I'll just call you John. Now, John, I want you to come and eat your supper. I know you think Mr. Graham's unjust—I know that—but you ought to see that he *thinks* he's doing the right thing. In his mind he's just. When he does that—when he whips you, John; when he whips you on Wednesday nights—he thinks he's doing it for your own good.

And I've stewed up some of them crab apples that you picked yourself. I know what your argument is—and I can understand it—that, what with all the work you've done, you've got a right to take the horse and go into town nights, once in a while. It's not *that* that Mr. Graham minds so much, I think—maybe it's that when you're in town you talk with those men down in Kramer's livery stable—and learn swear words—and—he prays to God that you don't touch liquor and learn other things. That's the truth of the matter. Now, John, I'm catching my death of cold here, and twice I've heated up that good supper for you.

(She takes a step forward) What's more, if you'll come in now, I'll tell you something—*something about yourself* that I never told you before. Something real interesting that I learned when we called for you at that orphanage. It's about where you come from, where you were found. I see now that I should've told you this a long time ago, because you're a grown-up man now, almost, and it's right you should know everything important about yourself.

(John seems suddenly to rise up in the middle aisle of the auditorium, about six rows from the stage. He is about eighteen and wears faded blue overalls.)

JOHN *(Darkly)*: You got something really to say? You're not just fooling me?

MRS. GRAHAM: I'm not fooling you. You come in and eat your supper and I'll tell you.

JOHN: You can tell it to me here.

MRS. GRAHAM: No, I can't. I'm perishing of cold. I can scarcely talk the way my teeth are chattering.

JOHN: Is it *long*—what you got to tell me?

MRS. GRAHAM: Oh, yes, it's long. I guess it'll take a whole quarter-hour to tell it right. So you come inside.

JOHN: I swore I wasn't ever going into that house again. I ain't going into any house where they call me a thief. I haven't ever stolen anything from anybody. It's him that's stolen from me: he steals from me every hour of the day, that's what he does. Maybe fathers can make their sons work for them for four years without one cent of pay—but he's not my father and I'm not his son. He owes me a lot. I'll bet you he owes me a whole hunnert dollars. I'll bet that by now I own that whole horse and I can take it wherever I want to.

MRS. GRAHAM: I know that's your argument, John.

JOHN: You go fetch a coat or something and tell me right here what you've got to tell me—because I'm not going into that house another night to be whipped by him.

MRS. GRAHAM: Now, John, you know he's not coming back for a while yet, and you can tell when he's come by the bells on the horses, can't you? —Until he comes back, you come inside. Whatever you do then, I can't stop you.

JOHN: Well, I'll only just come inside the door. I won't go any farther than that.

MRS. GRAHAM: You don't have to come any farther than you want to—but scrape the snow off your shoes when you come in.

(She opens the imagined door and returns into the kitchen. After scraping his shoes, John follows her. She busies her-

*self at the stove. He takes his stand down left center, his
back to the audience, feet apart, proud and resentful.)*

JOHN: Don't you worry about where I'll go. —Mr. Stahl-
schneider's hired man gets five dollars a week. I guess
I'm worth two dollars a week—leastways, these last two
years I've been. I bet I've even been worth three dollars.
And Mr. Graham hasn't given me anything except that
blue suit—and even that he locks up between Sundays.

MRS. GRAHAM: Now, John Graham—if you're thinking of
running away, I can't stop you, but I've got fourteen dollars I saved making buttermilk. It's right there behind
the clock in a tobacco bag. If you must go, I'm glad you
should have it.

JOHN *(Loud)*: I don't want no presents. I want what's *mine*.
And my name's not John *Graham*. I haven't got any
name—only John.

MRS. GRAHAM: We tried to be a father and mother to you,
best we could.

JOHN: I don't want no father or mother. I'm glad I didn't
have any.

MRS. GRAHAM *(Handing him an imagined plate)*: Here's
your supper.

JOHN: Put it on the table. I don't think I'm going to eat it.
—You can say what you were going to say.

MRS. GRAHAM *(Putting the plate on the corner of the table, but
speaking with spirit)*: And I'm not going to say one living word until you take a mouthful of that good supper
while it's hot.

*(Silence. War of wills. Suddenly John goes to the table,
digs an unseen spoon into the dish and puts it in his mouth.
He then resumes his former vindictive position.)*

JOHN: Well, say it!

MRS. GRAHAM: When we went to that Amanda Gregory
Foster Orphanage to adopt you we had a talk with that

Mr. and Mrs. Foster that run it. We asked them if they knew anything about you and where you come from.

(Pause.)

I must say I can't tell this very good with you standing there and showing hate in every muscle.

JOHN: Well, what do you want me to say? I run away three times and I'd run away again.

(Their eyes meet. She points at the plate. He abruptly takes one more mouthful and replaces the plate on the table.)

MRS. GRAHAM: You were found in a baskit, John—about three months old. Now maybe you'll think what I'm going to tell you isn't important, but you'll be mistaken there. That baskit, and every stitch of clothes that baby had on—and the blankits and the rattle and the milk bottle and the nipple—all of it, all of it come from the Gillespie and Schwingemeister Emporium. *(Pause)* Now I hope you see what that means. There wasn't a thing there that was second-rate or skimped. Some-body thought a lot of you, John—thought enough of you to get you A-number-one fittings.

JOHN *(After a short pause)*: Now I've et and I'm going back to the barn.

MRS. GRAHAM: I got something more to tell you. You eat every mouthful on that plate.

  I guess you've heard of the G. and S. Emporium in Philadelphia, P.A.

(There is a sound of sleigh bells at the rear of the auditorium. Both listen in suspense.)

That's Deacon Riebenschneider's bells.

(They relax.)

JOHN: Course, I have.

MRS. GRAHAM: Well, it'd be a funny thing if you hadn't, because I've noticed that you're awful interested in stores. Goodness, when we take you into town, that's all you want to see—asking me a thousand questions. I never saw anybody so interested in anything like you're interested in stores.

Well, I should think that you'd be real proud—that all your baby fittings come from the G. and S.

JOHN: Well, I ain't proud of it.

MRS. GRAHAM: That just goes to show how ignorant you are. I guess you think that's a store like any other store. A store that buys a lot of things and then sells 'em; a store that don't do any more than that: just does the same thing over and over, buy-sell, buy-sell. I guess you think it's that kind of store.

JOHN: Have you ever—have you ever been in it?

MRS. GRAHAM: Have I ever been in it?

(Without looking at him. Brooding, with muted exaltation) There's a kind of well that goes up the middle of it—and balconies and balconies with little white colyums. And red carpets with roses on them. And at the corners of the aisles, there's big brass cuspidors. And over the salesladies' heads there's wires, and when they sell something, little iron boxes run along the wires with the change. And at one side there are these elevators that go up and down taking people where they want to go.

JOHN: It's—it's only one of these stores for rich people.

MRS. GRAHAM: That shows you know nothing about it, simply nothing about it.

(Again brooding) It'll never burn up—that's what they say. Never even been a little fire in it. Of course, they keep a whole fire-fighting outfit in it—but that's just for show. Of course, if you buy goods there and bring them home—*then* they'll burn. But not in the store they won't. Why, if Philadelphia, P.A., had a fire

like Chicago, Illinois, had—you go in the G. and S. and you'll be perfectly safe. That's what they say and I believe them.

JOHN: That's not reasonable.

MRS. GRAHAM: Reasonable? Ain't nothing reasonable about it. Why, there are millions of people in the world who think that the G. and S. is crazy. Why, my sister went in to buy a wedding dress and there was one there—all fine sewed. The most beautiful dress in the world. And it looked like it cost a hundred dollars and, of course, she couldn't pay that. But the lady sold it to her for eighteen dollars, that's a fact. Not a thing wrong with it. My sister's husband—well, one terrible thing after another happened; but it was a beautiful dress; and her daughter wore it at *her* wedding. Then on other days, little things, little everyday things cost a world of money. Nobody's ever been able to understand it— nobody. Some days the G. and S. insults the customers—there's no other way of putting it—and other days it loads you down. It's not reasonable—but it's the greatest store in the world.

JOHN: What's this other thing you were going to tell me?

MRS. GRAHAM: Before I tell you, I want you to promise me— that you won't raise your hand against Mr. Graham when he . . . when he thinks it's his duty to punish you. Mr. Graham don't seem to notice that you're getting bigger and stronger every month. Will you promise me that?

(John, silent a moment; then goes to back wall and takes the same pose facing the audience.)

JOHN: Say what you were going to say without making any bargains.

(Relents) Depends on what he does.

(Pause.)

Have you been in it often?

MRS. GRAHAM: Have I been in it often?!

(*Gravely she brings out a locket from the neck of her dress*) See that lockit? I got that lockit for three years' faithful service at the G. and S.

JOHN (*Fascinated, peers at it*): That says Gertrude Foster. You're name ain't Foster.

MRS. GRAHAM: 'Fore I married Mr. Graham it was.

JOHN (*Backing; outraged*): I *thought* you was like that Mrs. Foster that run the orphanage. Are you kin of hers? Are you—kin of hers?

MRS. GRAHAM: 'Course not. Lots of people named Foster in West Pennsylvania. Lots of 'em. —Now you eat these crab apples while I tell you what comes next. You eat 'em slow—get the nourishment out of them.

(*She gives him the plate and goes back to the stove. She is again lost in thought*) You can scarcely see to the top of it where there's painting—handpainting on the dome. And always, way up, very faint—there's music. Music wrote special for the Emporium. You never saw such a place.

JOHN (*Now spellbound*): And the superinten'ants and managers? Are they walking around? I mean Mr. Gillespie and Mr. Schwingemeister?

MRS. GRAHAM (*Sudden scorn*): Well, if you aren't the most ignorant boy in the world I don't know who is!! Mr. Gillespie! Mr. Schwingemeister, indeed! Why nobody's ever seen even Mr. Sordini—and he's on the fifth floor. Looks like you think the Emporium's like other stores. Huh! I wouldn't have called you in from the barn if your baby fittings come from an ordinary store. If you want to work in any ordinary store you can go to Craigie's—yes, sir, you can go to Craigie's Deepartmental Store, that's next door to the G. and S. In Craigie's you know where you are. You're paid regular—

(*Sleigh bells at back of auditorium. Same business.*)

That's Widow Ochshofer's.

JOHN: Don't they *pay* you at the Emporium?

MRS. GRAHAM: And you can see Mr. Craigie, every day, ten times a day. You're paid good and you're paid regular—and everything's perfectly clear. At six o'clock you can go home. Yes, sir, you can work there fifty years and any night you like you can go home and hang yourself. At Craigie's Deepartmental Store, the color's green. Everything green. What color is the Emporium color?

JOHN *(Weak)*: I don't know.

MRS. GRAHAM *(Whispers)*: What color do I always wear?

JOHN: Blue . . .

MRS. GRAHAM: Of *course* I do—and what color you got on?

JOHN: Blue!

MRS. GRAHAM: And what color was all over that baskit you was found in? Blue. *Now,* I'll tell you something about yourself. Where was your baskit found? On the steps of the City Hall? Or the hospital, like most babies? Or at the Public Liberry? No. You were found on the steps of the G. and S. itself. You kind of belong there—that's what I think. You're an Emporium man.

But that ain't all: you know what I think? I think that Amanda Gregory Foster Orphanage—I think that orphanage is run by the G. and S. —That's what I think. I think I've seen that Mr. and Mrs. Foster before—and I know *where* I saw 'em too.

JOHN *(Excitedly)*: You look like her. That's what I always thought—that you look like her.

MRS. GRAHAM *(Contemptuously)*: I don't look like her at all. But I've often said to myself: if anything happened to Mr. Graham—that's where I'd like to be. I'd like to be working at that orphanage, helping some way, working with all those children. Something like that.

(Sleigh bells. This is it.)

There he is. That's him.

JOHN *(Frozen)*: I'm going to stay right here.

MRS. GRAHAM: Now remember, John. You promised.

JOHN: I never made no promise in my life.

MRS. GRAHAM: I ironed your blue suit today. It's just inside that door. And if you think you've got to go—here it is. The buttermilk money. *(She goes quickly to the mantel and pushes an (imaginary) bag toward him)*

JOHN: I don't need no money.

MRS. GRAHAM: Take it. Hasn't anybody ever told you that this world is a terrible place—hasn't nobody ever told you that? *Take it!*

(She returns to her chair and sits down.

Enter Mr. Graham—fur cap; short green coat of blanket material. Strides down the auditorium aisle, on to the stage; without glancing right or left, goes out stage center. They stare motionless while he passes through the room.)

JOHN *(Whispering)*: What do you mean: the Emporium don't *pay* you? —It's no good, if it don't pay you when you work for it.

MR. GRAHAM'S VOICE *(From the parlor)*: John Graham, will you come into the parlor?

MRS. GRAHAM: Listen, now—I haven't told you the whole truth about it: how *hard* it is. And some days you just despair. Yes, some weeks it forgets to pay you. And some weeks it pays you too much—like there's been a mistake in the books. And that it takes every bit of you and don't hardly leave you any life to yourself. And that it doesn't thank you—and it almost never gives you a compliment for what you've done. Just the same— it's something you can feel that you can *belong* to. You go there! You'll see.

MR. GRAHAM'S VOICE: John!

(Mr. Graham appears at the parlor door. He is holding a large stick.)

John Graham, did you hear me? You will go into the parlor and lower your overalls. Mrs. Graham, you will go upstairs.

MRS. GRAHAM: Mr. Graham, I will stay right here.

MR. GRAHAM: Mrs. Graham, you will go upstairs.

MRS. GRAHAM: You and I, before God, adopted this boy for our own—together.

(She flinches.)

I'm going out on the porch, but I'm not going upstairs.

(Hugging her shawl about her, she goes out on the porch, and stands with pursed mouth.)

MR. GRAHAM: Did you hear me, John?

JOHN *(Rapidly)*: I'm coming in. But I tell you right now that you owe me a hunnert dollars and maybe more; and that any man that's hit by another man has a right to defend himself; and that that time the hook fell down on you from the top of the barn and you were sick a week—you thought it was me but it wasn't; and the only lie I ever told you was about when the old heifer got in the lower pasture (and that was in the second week I was here): so I guess everthing's square between us now.

(He goes out back, center. Mr. Graham is astonished by this speech.)

MR. GRAHAM: I don't know what you're talking about. Anybody'd think you'd gone crazy. Your smoking and your drinking have made you crazy—that's what's happened.

(He follows John off. His voice can be heard.)

We'll first kneel down and ask God's blessing.

(Mrs. Graham slowly reenters the kitchen; sits at the table. Sudden sounds of violence from the parlor. Stumbling. Breaking furniture.)

MR. GRAHAM'S VOICE: How *dare* you—you young—*devil*!

(Silence. Mrs. Graham does not move.)

Gertrude! Gertrude!

(John appears at the door, somber, and a little dazed. He is holding the stick. Mrs. Graham does not look at him.)

JOHN: I'll take my blue suit.
MR. GRAHAM *(Off)*: Gertrude!

(John becomes aware that he is holding the stick. He throws it back into the parlor. He returns to the parlor and reappears with his suit wrapped in a brown-paper parcel. He starts to leave via the audience; then pauses, drops the parcel and going to Mrs. Graham leans over her with his hands approaching her throat.)

JOHN: Give me that!
MRS. GRAHAM *(In terror, defending her throat)*: John! What you doin'? What you doin'?
JOHN: I'm taking that lockit.

(He breaks it and holds it before him.)

That's the only thing I ever stole.
MRS. GRAHAM: All right. You didn't steal it. I give it to you.
JOHN *(Looking about him)*: Of all the hundreds and thousands of farms I could'a been sent to—I was sent to this one!
MRS. GRAHAM *(Proudly)*: Anyway, in this one you got one thing: you heard about the Emporium firsthand.

JOHN: I'll bet it ain't much.

(He dashes down into the audience and leaves the auditorium by the aisle.)

MR. GRAHAM'S VOICE: Gertrude—get Dr. Krueger—go, get him—

(Mrs. Graham goes slowly out back.
    Sound of galloping horse at the back of the auditorium.)

MEMBER OF THE AUDIENCE *(Looks at the audience, smiles, rubs his hands)*: I guess that's the end of the scene.

NOTES TOWARD "THE EMPORIUM"

After stopping for several years, Wilder returned to work on "The Emporium" in the summer of 1953. The notes in this section contain, in Wilder's words a "series of notations toward a continuation of 'The Emporium,'" written between August 1953 and June 1954. Because Wilder did not, in fact, bind them into his journals (see the August 2, 1953 journal entry below), Mr. Gallup retained their identity by publishing them as an appendix in *The Journals of Thornton Wilder: 1939–1961.*

August 2, 1953
(Hors-Série)
MacDowell Colony
Peterborough, NH
"The Emporium"

As I take up "The Emporium" again, I shall begin a series of notes here. I may or may not bind them into the Journal later.

My difficulty with it was that it was going on a road all too moralizing and didactic: the choice of Hercules and the development "*par la femme l'idéalité entre dans la vie, et sans* *elle que serait l'homme?"** I'm not afraid of truisms; but I must believe in them vitally for myself, and I must present them tragicomically.

With that Orphanage and Farmhouse Scene the hero is certainly Everyman in Everyhome. Then I go into his Relation-to-Standards.

But what I've got now is too vast a portal for my Emporium-Craigie material; or rather, my Emporium-Craigie material is not being presented by me in a large enough way to permit it adequately to follow the Orphanage and Cleaning-Women Scenes.

August 6, 1953
Thursday
Later

Thinking about time I begin to wonder whether my gropings haven't been halfhearted merely because I've been seeing the boy's life story wrongly from the point of view of time. A myth must be staged as something already known. Its end must precede its beginning; or rather, its end is in its beginning and in every part of it. It loses its force the minute it is conceived as a story-in-succession, and unfolding-into-the-unknown; so break up, throw away any interest in it that may depend upon chronological progression.†

Shouldn't we look into the John story as into a pit, a gulf, a cistern? A myth is not a story read from left to right, from

---

*Kierkegaard: *Etapes sur le chemin de la vie*, Gallimard, 1948. (Chapter, "In vino veritas," page 54.)

†Perhaps I should say, for the record, that I arrived at this by a stage (yesterday) where I seemed to see the play as a succession of prologues: Prologue One: The Council of the Emporium founding an Orphanage; Prologue Two: The Orphanage; Prologue Three: The Farmhouse Scene; Prologue Four: The Emporium Council preparing to baffle, repudiate, invite, etc., the aspirant; Prologue Five: etc.

beginning to end, but a thing held full-in-view the whole time. Perhaps this is what Gertrude Stein meant by saying that the play henceforth is a landscape.

(1) So today my mind has been pressing on the possibility that I begin the play with the New-Year's-Eve-party-at-Craigie's story"* (or with some "vision" that has not yet occurred to me—John's reception into the Emporium or his death at its doors) and then work *both backward and forward*, and close the play with the Orphanage Scene.

August 7, 1953
Friday

How can I best show, without overt moralizing pressures, the weakness of the Craigie Store (the inadequacy of the Ethical) and the strength of the Emporium? Answer: by an indication of the latent fears in the former.

(2) Suppose at the new opening scene, the Annual Party, I have Ermengarde Craigie address the guests before her father's arrival: "Let me remind you of two things: you know my father's displeasure at any reference to *another* store in this city—let's us remember *not* to mention any other store. And secondly, since some of you are new here, I think I ought to tell you that my father has been in a very nervous condition—we're all so glad that he's getting better—and I don't want you to become alarmed if he seems—that is if he suddenly seems to be convinced that there's a flood or—or that the earth is turning to ice, or that Philadelphia's on fire. My father every now and then *imagines* these things." And when Mr. Craigie enters that's what he does: inveighs against the Emporium, and has a paroxysm lest the snow then falling will never cease. He's stored the cellars with food. Ethics does not offer any relief to the

---

*That scene I began to write Tuesday (rewrite; earlier draft lost or destroyed) and without conviction; *now* I could find a new spirit about it.

basic fear in men; though millions try to make themselves believe so.

This, then, can make writing the Emporium scenes easier: they are careless of fire and thieves. And when, in the reverse-movement of the new design for the play, we come to the scene on the Graham Farm, Mrs. Graham can be given ([in the theatre] at 10:35 [P.M.]) a truer, briefer, surer statement of the motto of the play and the character of the Emporium: that one can only belong to that that is not threatened with extinction.

And instead of my single Noh-theatre ideal spectator, won't I have five people over seventy—from the Veteran Department-Store Workers' Garden Home—one blind, two deaf—and who must sit on the stage?

And isn't it possible that I open the play at the Craigie Party; carry it to the moment when Mr. Hobmeyer as messenger from the Emporium brings a summons to our young hero; then break the scene off? The whole play then unrolls and we resume that scene where we left off and continue to our finale. So that this play is a one-act play with interpolated switchbacks (or what are they called?).

August 8, 1953
Saturday

Have been writing up the scene. Haven't I found a way of expressing the abyss under the Ethical by the system of alarm bells? The Just Man, *conscius recti*, cannot dissipate or liquidate his fears; he can only ignore them; or, as we say, rise above them. They lie in wait to assail him at those moments when weakness or some sudden blow of circumstance (mis-*chance*) robs him of the will-constructed resolution *not* to confront them. And the long-time contemplation of the totality of experience is itself the enemy of his serenity. Many a stoic has significant resolution to be unshaken by the ills within his own life; can he sustain it in the contemplation of the ills of all mankind? Again there is a transition from quantity to quality: to remain sincere in the presence of a few ills is stoicism; to remain serene in the face of a myriad demands faith.

August 9, 1953
Sunday

I have reached the point where Mr. Craigie offers John the store and his daughter's hand. If this is to be the first scene in the play I am in a world of difficulties. The audience which receives this at 8:45 [P.M.] is in the presence of mere story-telling. Its only interest can be in what-will-happen-next. My dimensions are not wide and poignant enough to generate in this audience a passion to know, also, what happened before. This, then, is either not the first scene, or it is not correctly written. The play should begin with a vast reversal or a coming-to-himself.

August 10, 1953
Monday

(3) Have begun a prologue(!): Mr. Hobmeyer addressing the crowd that's waiting to get into the Emporium's annual sale. Oh, the difficulty of it—to avoid the moralizing-didactic, to sound some large notes, and to establish the "crazy" aspect of the store.

August 12, 1953
Wednesday

Each time I rewrite the new opening scene, it is better. To be sure, it has no explicit mention of any central aspect of John's or Laurencia's stories; but I think that from today I am free to write the plot, freed that is from that other aspect of writing which is searching for an idea.

August 14, 1953
Friday

Now, again, I've been returning to the notion of chronological order—but this time inserting the Annual-Sale Scene after the Farmhouse Scene (taking the place of a scene I had several times written for that place: a scene in the Employment Office). The uneasiness I have about it comes from: (1) How many times in a play can you address the audience, each time identifying them with a different public? (Query: Did Shakespeare use his audience as the Roman mob in the scene of Caesar's funeral orations? anywhere else?) (2) Can the higher-lower aspects of the Emporium be indicated in this way, at this moment—do they detract from the "touches" to be added in the next scene: the Laurencia-Hobmeyer, Laurencia-John conversations after the store's closing-time? What I like is the introduction of John as an unseen questioner from the audience; and a possible first sketch of Laurencia in a relation to the waiting bargain-hunters. Let me now try this scene again, looking for ways to build up some real give-and-take between Hobmeyer-Bernice [the cleaning woman]-Laurencia.

It seems impossible to find a way to trouble the waters in this scene by injecting doubt as to whether the Emporium is senile or asleep or all but nonexistent.

August 18, 1953
Tuesday
Peterborough, NH

Vacillation. Insecurity in progress. But what it comes down to is that I cannot make any decision about form or anec-

dote until I discover the next characteristic of the Store—
the next image or merely fact or symbol—to feed the
curiosity of the audience, which is the true life of the play.
And the difficulty lies in the fact that I must present the
characteristic under the form of a department store's oper-
ation. And what I am looking for is something dealing with
the fact that the Absolute "sells" primarily to the individual
and is only individually perceived. And this I must do by
presenting the contrast of this method to the method
employed over at Craigie's. The classic way of presenting
this is, I suppose, Hans Christian Andersen's story of the
king who has no clothes. Each person sees the Emporium
and its goods differently; while Craigie and all its objects
are of equal valuation to all its customers.

Now this I have done pretty well but only partially in
John's outburst to Laurencia ("old-fashioned—can't find
the doors"): what I need further is a figure for the relation
between the customer and the goods.

(4) (Rejected tries: to some eyes they are moth-eaten and
rusty; some claim that when you take them home the colors
fade, or the objects break.) Remembering that I'm after the
idea of the suitability of each object to an individual pur-
chaser, shouldn't I search among motifs such as: the objects
(claim the disparagers) are unsuitable for daily life; that
they don't—in many ways—fit?*

Anyway, as I see it this motif—when I find it—should
follow the motif of the has-no-doors-is-stuffy-etc. Yet I
should be able to introduce it in the Mrs. Graham-John
Scene (though I groan when I think of anything that over-
burdens that scene with overt symbolic material; so early in
the play, it should catch up the spectator, mostly, as passionate human story). Now let me again go back and see if
I can weave this into the Bargain-Sale Scene.

---

*To remember: that Kafka records a moment in which K., seeing the
Castle for the first time, has the impression that it resembles the town
in which he was born—Kafka's Castle, however, is *also* the Law.

(5) For a while I have considered putting all this material (except: how can I get a job at the Emporium?) into the present "third scene" by having Bernice arriving for work, pulling a hatpin from her hat (arriving after Laurencia's discussion of the dome, the music, etc.). It is her duty to collect the complaints from the complaint boxes—to burn them. Mirthful or indignant, she reads several of them: ". . . that your wares are unsuitable for a modern American home. I regret I must transfer my patronage to Craigie's. I hope you will accept this letter in the spirit in which it is written . . ." "Never, I repeat, never shall I put my foot in your store again . . ." (this letter is twelve pages) "to be so insulted by clerks," etc.

Yet this has the overwhelming disadvantage that it brings Bernice upon the scene before her big appearance as a cleaning woman, and presents her colloquial side without intimating her sybillic quality. Besides, one could wish to do better than read aloud letters.

No, I must keep my meditations turning on the attributes of the Emporium itself—when I have those truly in hand the play will flow from them.

And to the idea of Belonging: and here I seem merely to flounder from one tiresome moralizing formula to another: you belong to what you make (or give), not to what you receive.

Later: Rewrote Laurencia resigning and first part of Laurencia-John. Raising the intensity on the realistic level; and the Bernice Scene. I think it's now all better and moving forward.

August 27, 1953

(6) One thing keeps worrying me: apart from what I shall do with the Member of the Audience on stage, I seem to see in my mind's eye that this Third Scene needs to be dressed

with more people. The First Scene: doesn't matter, it's an auditorium; Second Scene, comes sufficiently to life with the opening speech of Mrs. Graham; the Third opens with the liveliness of getting the customers out of the store; but we need some higher liveliness here and that could be accomplished by the (pretty soon) arrival of a third actor (that's why I tried also to introduce Bernice earlier—but that, in this last rewriting, I've disposed of). Certainly, it would be vivacious enough, if I could introduce a belated customer—an indignant insulted busybody, of the Craigie faction. To think over—but only if I can find legitimate working use for her later: just [as] I have two Seniors (Foster-Hobmeyer and Graham-Craigie) so would I be justified in having two Matrons?

(7) In this writing I have discarded the former Prologue (John-Gillespie and Dr. Abercrombie) with all its attendant business. Do I regret it? Will it ultimately find a place?

Now as to the Member of the Audience.

September 7, 1953

Twisting and turning. Rewriting scene after scene. Forever trying to focus and define the two great problems behind this play: what is the Emporium?; and how to bring into highlight the qualities it has in common with a department store while attenuating and veiling the qualities it *hasn't* in common.

(8) These last few days I have seen that it is unsuitable that I build the Second Part on a Laurencia-Gretchen story. The framework is too big for a "simple-life lone narrative" and the point that women are catalysts of the Absolute can be made clearly without lingering too long over our illustrative anecdote (*all* Emporium girls do not shipwreck their lives in its service; and this play must see to it that it is giving a report on all). So now I think that Laurencia *quia*

Laurencia has only one scene. The play approaches the form of a succession of one-act plays at the same time that it approaches the form of an oratorio or mysterium. So now I am attacking the Third Scene (first floor of the Emporium) as a one-act play. John has been "annoying" Laurencia for almost a year. What is its climax? That Laurencia denounces and repudiates John? Something more.

(9) *Later*:

HOBMEYER: Sometimes I think that *this*—all this that we see—isn't the Emporium at all.

JOHN *[Breathlessly]*: What? What do you mean?

HOBMEYER: All this selling—all this buying and selling.

JOHN: Well, it's a store, isn't it? The Emporium's a store.

HOBMEYER: Yes, but—maybe it's only a front. A front for something else that it's doing.

JOHN: Why, that's crazy. Of course, it's a store.

HOBMEYER: But you've noticed yourself that it's not interested in selling—not interested in the same way that Craigie's is.

JOHN *[Stopped for a moment]*: Then what is it interested in?

HOBMEYER: Come, it's time to lock the doors. Go down that corridor.

JOHN: Well, I know one thing: I'm never going to come here again. I don't want to work in a place that you don't know what it's doing. I'm going to stick to my job at Craigie's. At Craigie's you know where you [are].

HOBMEYER: You're perfectly right about that, boy. At Craigie's you know where you are.

So we have the scene at Craigie's party, culminating in John's mock-speech and repudiation—he will return to the Emporium.

November 26, 1953
Key West
Later

(10) Now we're putting back the Employment-Office [Scene] (of long ago) with the whole new emphasis throughout of: How do you get a job there?

November 30, 1953

Finished the scene on the Emporium floor—now the fourth. I think the shape is coming clearer. Some vestiges of *Kitsch*, alas.

December 2, 1953

Rewrote the former Prologue—now as a dream-sequence to open Part Two.
     Later: No, that won't do.

January 21, 1954
Deepwood Drive
Hamden, CT

(11) Have been writing the Employment-Office Scene (now Scene Three), incorporating from Notion (under 2, above) the visitors from the Retired Employees' etc. Now I think it's going right. Great violence on the stage—John's manhandling of the Employment Officer. I think that, at last, this is it. And now I have the stage dressed with these disparate on-watchers who themselves are dynamic feeders of the developing tensions. And more and more Scene Four takes its shape—getting nearer and nearer to *Das Schloss* from which I should not have departed in the first place.

And all this new spurt of activity has had its point of departure from reading (through a glass darkly) an article in the latest (*Drittes Heft*, 1953) *Die Neue Rundschau*: Theodor Adorno: "*Aufzeichnungen zu Kafka*"—all the more useful too in that I cannot fully follow such thick involved German.

January 23, 1954
Saturday

Now at last I think I'm advancing. The things that put me on the right track were seeing: (1) That the present Third Scene—the Employment Office—must all represent the terrible urgency of getting into the G. and S. —not only my hero's distrustful curiosity, but the whole world's urgency; and (2) That in the next scene Laurencia is but an episode-figure. She now has a different characterization: she is a limited little goose, but with streaks and intimations of belonging to the Great Sisterhood (young exemplar therefore of Mrs. Antrobus); now we see, with the help of the preceding scene, that John's passionate advances are a devouring urge to capture the Emporium-secret in her; and now I can *show* it without (or almost without) having to say it.

This probably means that I now discard the Boarding-House Scene (though Ruth [Gordon?] was so wild about it), unless some other use for it can be found other than developing a consecutive Laurencia-story. What I would love to do now is to introduce another girl—perhaps Ermengarde Craigie—who must be played by the same actress who has just played Laurencia—which device will be all the more lively and theatric now that we have made Laurencia an extreme-character part. And how greatly form and pattern will be enhanced if we have our Young Actress also appearing in several roles and only John himself throughout the play.

To be sure, I now know less than ever where I am going next, but I feel less anxious about that with each new addition of a solid brick in the pavement that is leading there, and I feel pretty sure now that these first four scenes are solid and permanent bricks.

January 24, 1954
Sunday

Now I've been able to move on to Scene Four, Laurencia an episode-girl in this scene alone. Allusions to the fact that John has been hanging around girls in the other departments, too. All the John-tone is new, too—now he is boastful. He will some day own and reform the G. and S.

Walked into town this evening: teased by a large audacity. Laurencia is an early stage, of course, in the life of Mrs. Foster—of the Mrs. Graham. How about showing that all these characters are stages in the lives of four characters? That Mr. Foster once kept an Employment Office for the G. and S.; that Mr. Dobbs (present—unsatisfactory—name for our Employment Officer) will move on to head the Orphanage. That Bertha [Bernice], the cleaning woman, was once a farmer's wife (name not given); that Laurencia will leave the G. and S. to marry a young farmer named Graham!! In which case, shall we say that she will change her name to Gertrude? That Mr. Hobmeyer will retire to take over an Employment-Agency job? —Yes, yes, yes, it would woefully confuse the audience—but when they get the point, isn't it a prodigious point to make? And what are we to make of the end of John's life? —Is he to be a successful or unsuccessful G. and S. man? If the latter, couldn't we thus indicate that he will be following the Hobmeyer-Dobbs-Foster plan?

There's a cyclic drama for you. And reinforcing that image that is now stirring: department stores with their endless buying and selling are like leaves replacing leaves on trees, are like people who have children who have children; but that the G. and S. has something else and something more.

January 26, 1954
Tuesday

Walked into town. Yes, yes, I think it can be done. Writing a letter Monday to [X], I tried to describe what I now see to be the direction of the play and my efforts to describe it to him continue to operate in my mind. It is about the Wheel of Being; the endless repetitions of the life-forms; but the Emporium is, precisely, the evidence of pressures from Elsewhere to introduce a qualitative change into the mechanical repetitions. The wheel therefore is one of the images of the play: Craigie's is the wheel of repetitions, and in the scene of Craigie's Anniversary Party I must put (droll) emphasis on the Niagara of intake and outgo. And now I must find ways of adumbrating this into the Orphan-age Scene: those children (the Orphanage is "associated" with, sponsored by G. and S.) are the effort to alter and "redeem" the wheel. This wheel-motif, therefore, will give me the atmosphere in which to play this other game: the repetition of lives in my characters: Laurencia will grow up to be Mrs. Graham, etc.

Now I come up against another "enlargement" of my scene: the Emporium Girls. Dare I venture again (as in the Orphanage Scene) the roll-call of great names: of great women who have been able to get their men into the Emporium? Oh, how I hate "symbols" and bookish allu-sions—but how in my plays I cannot escape them. Here it is doubly difficult, because the names are not so current in the average audience's field of allusion. I thought (on the walk) of such a passage as this:

HOBMEYER: Do you imagine for a moment that these girls can get you a job in the Emporium?
JOHN [*Sullenly*]: They are sure that they can.
HOBMEYER: Maybe it has happened once or twice. I don't say that it's impossible. In the Emporium we can never say that a thing is impossible—eh. For instance, do you

know that Eyetalian girl that works in the dress-fabrics department, Beatrice her name is—calls herself *Beatrice*—or those other two Eyetalian girls, Laura and Vittoria. Couldn't they perhaps bring a man to himself? And that way, somehow, get him a job here?

I shrink, but maybe I must do it. And follow it by a catalog:

HOBMEYER: Oh, we have some fine girls here: Monica and Aspasia, that Greek girl, and Teresa and Clara and Magdalene and [blank space] —oh, I won't say they couldn't bring a man into the G. and S. if he were ripe for it.

Digression: Several things about these developments have an almost comical effect upon me. I have been writing this piece on the theatre for Rosamond Gilder and the European anthology on décor (weeks behind on it, as usual) and toward the close I have been trying to describe what the play of the future might be like, and I have (in my notes—it may not appear in the final draft) described just such a play as this: the realism in the specific detail subtended by the largest arcs of time and place and custom. Secondly, I see that this play which took its point of departure from Kafka's *Castle* is drawing into itself more and more modalities of *Finnegans Wake*. Maybe this play will have originality, will be original. It has always been quite clear to me that the other two [*Our Town* and *The Skin of Our Teeth*] were not. The other two were *calqués*.* It may be possible that by now my possession of my time concepts, my human-situation concepts is so deep-digested and so all-permeating that

---

*I see the dictionary gives *calquer* as *copier servilement*. I don't mean that. I mean merely superimposed upon a variety of molds and prior achievements in theatrical art. They derive their air of originality from the facts that: (1) Very few persons knew (or profoundly knew) the great originals; and (2) The variety and disparateness of the models concealed the indebtedness; and (3) The indebtedness was one of admiration and love—which is seldom the case in such borrowings.

I may be permitted to write a really original play—original not in the sense that it is filled with novel devices, but that it makes people see for the first time things that hitherto they had known without being aware that they knew them.

February 9, 1954

It's all in a ferment. But I see that out of my Member of the Audience seated on the stage I must derive elements still lacking from my play: there must be fear and awe and— somewhere there must be melodrama. And yet every nerve of me revolts at introducing any more of those devices that erupt in the Second and Third Acts of *The Skin of Our Teeth*. Oh, Heaven help me not to have to make the *dramatis personae* emerge from their roles, or members of the audience, further, intrude themselves into the play. And yet! —when the play is about Everybody, isn't it legitimate and functional that Everybody should be drawn into the unfoldment of the play? So if I have to do it, Heaven help me to make it irresistibly real and spontaneous.

Now what is the active enemy of the Emporium? Not Craigie's, which merely rages impotently and enviously. There are two enemies: for those "in it" there is doubt; for those outside it (in addition to doubt), there is the thing that prevents them entering, the deference to the opinion of the market place, the inability to think alone. (I have just written that into Laurencia's Scene, groaning because I had to state it so explicitly.) So the Journey of John is the journey to self-as-authority; and the stadia are: (1) His outburst at the Employment Office; (2) His revolt and final acquiescence before the charges of Bertha [Bernice]; and (3) His consciousness that Craigie's is precisely the servile adherence to the market place and his release. But where can I get melodrama into that? And how introduce my sitters-on-the-stage? Well, I shall take a walk into town in an hour and see what the walk can bring me.

February 13, 1954

Well, nothing came of that walk into town. Then I went to New York.* Another lacuna in the play has been glaring me in the face: I haven't found any way to express what it is in the G. and S. that has been attracting John. So far I have merely stated it in the shape of that he is puzzled by it: and that's not enough. While I had the so-called dreamed episode, the former "Prologue," I could convey sufficiently to the audience that he belonged there by divine inheritance. Now, I have nothing but Mrs. Graham's assertion. So the elements I must bring up and coalesce are the magnet-pull, the *Schaudern*, and the audience seated on the stage.

I have been phantasizing long scenes in which the actress playing Bertha (*ossia* Bernice) recognizes among the actors-on-the-stage some old long-lost friend—or enemy. And some such thing may well develop, but the whole raison d'être of such an encounter must be that it illustrates an aspect of the Emporium; and also that it contributes to our matrix-form of repetitions. Say she recognizes Mrs. Frisbee (of the Veteran Department-Store Workers):

BERTHA: What are *you* doing here?! And what are *you* doing as an actress?

MRS. FRISBEE: They didn't tell me this was about the Gillespie-Schwingemeister. Oh, I won't stay a minute. I'm going right out to sit in the bus. The G. and S. killed my husband.

---

*It's well to name here what I have been reading and seeing that has contributed: more and more Hölderlin; Ezra Pound's translation of Sophocles' *Trachiniae* [*The Women of Trachis*], comparing it line by line, in laughing amazement with old [Richard C.] Jebb's; some ineffable passages of Balanchine's choreography of Mendelssohn's Scotch Symphony; and "tea" with Alma Mahler [-Werfel]—an Emporium girl, genre *viennois*, who flatters me to the last limits: *"Mein Herz hat' so geklopft, als wäre es einen König den ich erwartete."* As "tea" were champagne, caviar, and pâté de foie gras.

Then big fracas as she tries to draw all her companions out "to sit in the bus." All that could work—but oh! I cannot, must not, place it there, at the Cleaning-Women's Scene—can I? I'll draw up some sketches and see.

February 15, 1954

The sketches I then drew up are not final (doubly distressing, since they inevitably overemphasize the aspect of "theatrical tricks," tiresome *Wiederholung* of the non-actors' intrusion into the play, that I must render completely vital and organic or else discard), but they perhaps point the way.

To encourage myself, let me put the fairest possible face on what I am doing: my "instinct" urges me to do two things (two things at the same time—perhaps more than two—in the simultaneity of several operations is the health and reassurance of the measures), to break up and frustrate any interest in mere anecdote, in mere individual life story; and to make converge upon my action-idea as many and as diversified a series of pertinent elements-of-life as possible. One of the reasons that this play has been so long a-writing is, of course, that I have not been able to make fiercely clear to myself what the Emporium is—what I am saying; the other is that my will-to-work slackens, my faith fades, when the daily task (*i.e.*, the pages I am at work on) do not bristle, sparkle, dance, with representations of life's diversity, time's achroneity, and any idea's *Vielseitigkeit*. All that is what kept me interested in *The Ides of March*.* No view of life, then, is real to me save that it presents itself as kaleidoscopic—which does not mean essentially incoherent. (The

---

*Was that long a-borning? I don't know. That is the kind of thing I blandly, balmily forget. I kept no Journal then. My impression is that it went quite blithely on, interrupted only by my ever-reprehensible enjoyment in distractions and by the everpresent interruptions caused by the mismanagement of life's *corvées*.

very children's toys of that name show us always a beauti-
fully ordered though multi-fragmented pattern.)

In my plays, and last novel [*The Ides of March*], there is
this constant interruption. The more I seek to exhibit an
idea about life, the more I must make sure that the tumult
of sheer existences be introduced, pertinent and impertinent (perhaps it is my fault that I do not sufficiently introduce the confessedly absurdly impertinent, as Gertrude
Stein does), and the more I start out to give an instance of
some character's individual action, the more I lift it from the
specific-unique into the realm of the typical and the idea-
expressive. It is natural, therefore, that in a play I should not
rest content with the actors moving only in their fictional
play: my *dramatis personae* are characters in the fiction, *and*
representatives of an idea, but they are also men and women
engaged in an impersonation. More than that, the members
of the audience are not inert intelligences. Since my play is
about Everybody, everybody is in my play. Even in *The
Skin of Our Teeth* I went so far (in introducing the captain
of the ushers, etc.) as almost to introduce characters who
were not intent upon the play. *This* play is also about the
man and woman who are passing by the theatre, in the street
outside: why not introduce them?

So let me reassure myself that there is an organic, legitimate way to introduce these intrusions and interruptions,
and when I have found and expressed that way correctly I
shall be able to overcome my diffidence. And one sign that
I shall be getting it correctly will be laughter—the right
kind of laughter: the recognition that it is wildly dispropor-
tionate that these members of the audience seated on the
stage should be caught up into the fiction, but that that *dis-
proportion* is not in contradiction with the fact that they
move in a real relation to the drama.

Now to get down to specific instances: what precisely do
I want Mrs. Frisbee to carry in this scene? Why—as I said
in the previous entry—the magnet-pull, the fascination of
the Emporium. And this I can do—as I have done so

often—*in reverse*. She can warn the audience against the fascination. And if through her warnings, I can also intimate the *Schaudern*, so much the better. It has ruined her life and that of her husband.

Now let's go back and try that.

February 16, 1954

But what my play above all lacks is passion—which, in all the forms that passion could take, is here the *movement* of the passion of people seeking the "Right Way." I feel that it is present in the first scenes, but it slips away, somehow, between the scenes. The figure of John must be a hot-winging arrow that carries the whole play with it. And it seems to me that the reason I've lost it is that I haven't been clear in my head as to what obstacle it is that prevents his being invited to enter the Emporium. I shy away from facing this problem because every side-glance at it seems to lead toward moralizing *platement*: he lacks humility; he refuses to renounce worldly success, etc.

But we decided—didn't we?—that the qualification of the Emporium-worker was that he could "do a thing alone"—nay, that nothing worthwhile was done save unaided (whereby G[ertrude]. S[tein]. enters the play). There too all the pitfalls of eupeptic moralizing lurk, but less flagrantly; this introduces, rather, the pitfalls of the sentimental and pathetic. So that John can be represented as desiring the G. and S. and yet incapable of seeing that success, etc., are forms of dependency. Now it would seem that for this we need a *raisonneur* or *raisonneuse*, probably several.

Let me return now to the text and see what I can do.

Walked downtown.

Now it seems to me that we can follow this line: Scene One: Orphanage; Scene Two: The Graham Farm; Scene Three: First Floor of the Emporium; Scene Four: The

Employment Office; Scene Five: First Floor of the Emporium (terminating with John's dream).

Certainly very dangerous seems the plan for placing *two* scenes in the same Emporium corridor; but out of our dangers let us make us successes. In this way, I can make ever more *serré* the inner intensity of John's "hunt"—hunter and hunted. I want John (and the audience) to get into their consciousness that Laurencia-Hobmeyer dialogue about the vast traditions of the G. and S. before we see the scene at the Agency. I want a first stage of a flirtation with Laurencia, and I want a complete first picture of Hobmeyer kicking John out of the store. All this, too, will give me more space in which to develop all the other motifs which have been developing.

In this new layout, do I have the Cleaning-Women's Scene in the first or the second of the Emporium scenes? And can I give Mr. Hobmeyer four big scenes in a row: Hobmeyer-Dobbs (the Employment Officer)–Hobmeyer-Dr. Abercrombie? Or should I assign Mr. Dobbs (as a feeble member of the G. and S. community) to the actor who has just died offstage as Mr. Graham?

Both the Emporium scenes begin in the same way: floorwalker's injunction to the customers to leave the store.

Let's write at it all and see what happens. (I now can restore that first entrance of John into the store: "Fifth-rate store—air bad—no doors.")

February 18, 1954

Yes, it's going forward. I'm pretty sure it's on the right tack. And several of those boldest tricks with time seem to have found their way with naturalness into the text; and I've found a place to insert the figure of the Wheel. Of course, it's all just first draft still. The best sign that it is moving correctly is that it is beginning to indicate its further development; but more of that later.

What I want in it now is richness, not as ornament, but as expressive force. And one of these richnesses is more humor—precisely because it is so heaven-reaching a subject—hence, a disconcerting humor. I want [it] in Laurencia; her role is so important because it shows us that the G. and S. does not mean an intellectual élite. A few of my touches so far relate her to Sabina [in *The Skin of Our Teeth*], but she is not a Sabina, she is a Mrs. Antrobus at twenty-one. I don't want much more humor from the Ex-Department-Store Workers; they are in danger of being too funny as it is. Then, too, I want a sort of splendor in Scene Five—the material's all there, but I want it better: Laurencia's cry for more life; the love scene; the Cleaning Women; the dream. Oh, I must have John threaten not only to stay in the store all night, so as to glimpse the Higher-Ups (that I have already), but his threat "to go up to the offices on the fifth and sixth floor"—an echo of Kafka (K. to the Innkeeper's wife: "*Was fürchten Sie also? Sie fürchten doch nicht etwa . . . für Klamm?*"). Somehow I must get into that scene—at the climax; it is the close of Part One, preceding the only intermission—a big rebellion or reaction from the persons seated on the stage.

Now as to the impediment in John: my Mr. Hobmeyer must again serve as *raisonneur*. Here so hard not to bore us with the moralizing-didactic. It is John's craving for success, and his boasting; to which Hobmeyer points out—how? How avoid the most abysmal sententiousness? —the craving for success is a dependency. John's surprised answer. Can I somehow swing it up into the splendor? Can I give [it] to the cleaning woman as laughing derision?

How can my one lone cleaning woman give the impression I want? I wish I could have fifteen. At least, thank Heaven, I have the benefit of the stage-picture dressed with those members from the audience. Now to involve them. The first little man no longer demands the Prologue. What else does he do at his first appearance?

February 23, 1954

A succession of interruptions: dinners, guests, concerts. Not this time so distressing and harmful, because they have been confined to a few days—delimited and clearly terminated last evening, leaving few engagements before me now. (Though that other interruption, the real enemy, is there forever without intermission: correspondence, manuscripts submitted, etc. From that there's no surcease, and talking about it is no alleviation.) This time I return to this problem here, after the interruption, with renewed spirit.

What the play needs is a larger deeper happier immersion on my part in what it's all about. Today the emphasis is on *happier*, for the sign that all is going well in this portentous and often painful subject matter will be that it will be permeated with the comic.

Oh, the form isn't bold and splendid and revolutionary enough. That's why I'm so inhibited and tentative and scratchily groping.

Now let me put down some of the fancies that have been crossing my mind in this matter of form—not because they are the *eureka*, but because they give me imaginative practice in bold form-shattering invention.

(Before I put them down I want to add another thing: when I find the right form—the right statement for this cosmological comedy—wouldn't it be wonderful if I could do it without those names of celebrated orphans—those names of the painters and music-makers of the Emporium? To other people—but not to me—they bring in the smell of professor and historian. Not to me, because "culture" is in me a second nature. Hitherto it has always seemed to me that the "comic" aspect of their introduction into the play—the anachronistic game, for instance—saved them from the academic stink—but *even* I, as I have expressed it several times in the Journal, am aware that in those names, through those names, is felt the hated didactic formal-symbolic strain. After all, Kafka did it without names.)

So to return to formal liberation, enlargement:

(1) Maybe that first Member of the Audience seated on the stage—maybe he objects:

MEMBER OF THE AUDIENCE: This scene in the Orphanage—I heard that that scene was the last scene in the play. Why—excuse me—are you playing it *first* tonight?

MR. FOSTER: If you make interruptions you must go back and sit down in the audience. It's not important *what you've heard*. We on the stage are doing what we have been instructed to do.

MEMBER OF THE AUDIENCE: Well—but isn't it true that this scene in the Orphanage used to be last?

MR. FOSTER: This is very tiresome. We can't go on, if this is going to happen.

MRS. FOSTER *[To Mr. Foster]*: Since he's brought the matter where the whole audience can hear him, we might as well explain. *[She addresses the man]* We have been instructed—I mean, the author says—that the order of the scenes in this play should be changed every performance. Some nights this scene comes first and some nights it comes last. Some nights we begin at the Fourth Scene and go through the whole play and end at the Third Scene. Some nights we begin at the Sixth Scene and end at the Fifth Scene.

—Would I stop the *explication* there? Anyway, something like. There's an advance notice of the Wheel-motif.

(2) To resort, as I did in *The Skin of Our Teeth*, to a parodic (the dictionary also allows *parodical*) allusion to old-fashioned kinds of playwriting. To return more closely to what was the initial departure of this play, the Horatio-Alger novel—via the theatre contemporary to Horatio Alger. All this would involve throwing away the Orphanage Scene. I could here launch upon a long essay to show that one of the livelier expressions of our time (of collapse

of old modes, of bewildered helplessness before new frights and new grandeurs) is the mock-heroic and the parody.

Now let these notations (and here is the benefit of the Journal) start a train of opening up and encouraging the imagination to all but anarchical freedoms—whatever the cost of time and effort.

June 17, 1954

(That was almost six months ago . . . Here I am back with some new impulses toward "The Emporium"—and at a moment when so many other *corvées* and projects surround me—nevertheless:)

It's the Hero I haven't got right—the Hero and the Girl. Since the play, by very reason of its mode of staging, to say nothing of the vast implications of the theme, the wrestling with the Absolute, is about the type Hero, let's do the eternal Hero myth. I have been too much drawn into the Kafka hero, the frustrated pre-condemned struggler. That's not my bent; I'm not the stuff of which nihilists are made; I'm not even sympathetic toward the broken-winged; all that derived from a mimetic sympathetic admiration for the Kafka vision, perhaps merely for the Kafka art, the virtuosity with which he could present his maimed soul. I want to liberate myself from the Kafka hero—and can we call Hero the man who dies *"wie ein Hund"*?—while at the same time retaining that element in Kafka which is real to me, the seduction and the ambiguity and the terror of the Absolute?

So back to the Hero.

Let us bear in mind the eternal myth-patterns of the Hero—viewed not only as the Exceptional Man but as the potential in every man. His birth is surrounded with mystery. At first all he knows is the beatific, timeless, effortless floating in the womb. Then he is separated from that nirvana—the ego emerges as he becomes aware of an Outside which is not the self. He has two mothers: the benignant goddess of all living and the baleful enemy-mother who wishes to retain him in nirvana, to draw him back to the chaos of instinctual life. He has two fathers: the warrior-worker-creator to emulate; and the jealous old man who wishes to restrain and maim and kill him. He sets out on the quest for a treasure: the treasure is a virgin. He must win her through trials and perils.

At once I see that I have wasted time over the choice between Emporium and Craigie. (Yes, there is a play there, a theme there, but it is secondary to the more basic theme of the Hero's journey—and it has led me all this time into a resort to the tiresome moralizing side of my "formation.")

Let us say that our Hero does get into the Emporium at once, but at the ground floor: he is a package-wrapper in the basement.

The Girl is the daughter not of Craigie's but of the Emporium. She is guarded against young heroes, because even Excellence becomes tyrannical and conservative-petrified. The Emporium is old-fashioned and airless; the Hero wins the daughter of the Emporium and the power to refresh and renew it.

Now I can play with this business of the Older Actress playing the successive Good and Bad Mothers; and the Older Actor playing the Good and Bad Fathers. The Orphanage-Mother is Good, but against John's being sent away. The Orphanage-Father is Stern-Justice. The Farmer's Wife is in one scene both Good and Bad. (Can that be done?)

There is in the first Emporium Scene (this is just groping now) no Laurencia? John comes up at closing time from the bowels of the Emporium and inveighs against its airlessness, etc., and hears, again, about the Virgin-Princess.

It also sounds (1) excruciatingly schematized and (2) oriented toward a sunburst of a happy-ending; but let's see what can be done with it.

Now for some random ideas that accompany this new project:

In the Orphanage Scene: Mrs. Foster constantly asking the children have they eaten—dare I have her insisting that they each eat their mid-morning apple, and their mid-morning glass of milk. Their after-lunch nap.

In the Farmhouse Scene: John: "He's always swinging that scythe" (or sickle—Hell, you run into symbols at every turn). Mrs. Graham alternately urges him to stay and incites him to the Emporium. —There's no more about *not* seeing Gillespie or Schwingemeister—but isn't it run by an old woman?

Where on earth is our *Padre Nobile?* Can it be indicated (as I did rather well in *The Skin of Our Teeth*) that the repressive action of the fathers is a pure delusion in the young men's minds?

Now we can do the scene that was formerly the Craigie Annual Party with a whole new effect. It is the Emporium Annual Party. Old Mr. Gillespie—invalid, and fearful—is the Decrepit King. He no longer throws his daughter at the young Hero—he resists him at every turn.

It's now not so much a question as to whether it can be done, as one of whether I can catch fire from it. And whether the Opera-libretto cannot also be fed from some of these notions.

Where shall I begin to write on it? Not at the beginning, but at the (first) Emporium Scene. And here rises the question that if there's no Laurencia, how do I get that background-conversation in? Does Miss Gillespie visit the store at closing time to call for her father? Is Mr. Hobmeyer still with us? And can we now "work" the members of the audience who are seated on the [stage]?

PART
IV

The Alcestiad

WITH ITS SATYR PLAY

The Drunken Sisters

*T*he *Alcestiad*, directed by Tyrone Guthrie with Irene Worth playing Alcestis, and temporarily titled "A Life in the Sun," premiered at the 1955 Edinburgh Festival. Although well received by audiences, critics were less than kind, and Wilder withdrew the play's English rights. After revisions and the addition of a satyr play, in 1957 it was successfully staged in German at the Schauspielhaus in Zurich, the beginning of the successful career of *Die Alkestiade* before German-speaking audiences.

A revised English text, drawn from both the earlier English acting version and a German version published in 1960, did not appear in print until 1977, two years after the author's death. The English acting edition was first published in 1980. The Bibliographic and Production Notes of this volume contain additional information about this play as well as about the opera that the composer Louise Talma and Wilder (as librettist) adapted from it. The opera premiered in Frankfurt am Main in 1962.

The text of the play and Isabel Wilder's introduction to it appear here as they first appeared in the 1977 Harper & Row English edition. Wilder's program note for the Edinburgh production also appears in its entirety.

Befitting its audience, Isabel Wilder's introduction to the acting edition offers additional details about what she describes as the "near pageantry proportions" of the original and controversial Guthrie production:

> There is food for the ear but the primary objective is to feed the eye. *The Alcestiad* is a drama of ideas which challenges thoughtful responses in an audience. It should not have to compete with stunning processions and extraneous by-play no matter how handsome or clever. Spectators whose attention is drawn from the stage by victims of Thessaly's outbreak of plague clad in rags, crawling down the aisles of the auditorium, hideous with stage-putty sores exuding pus and blood from paint in the actors' makeup boxes, very easily lose track of what is being said and done on stage. The play was nearly lost.

FOREWORD

by Isabel Wilder

Isabel Wilder (1900–1995), Thornton Wilder's younger sister by three years, served as his personal agent for many years. In her own right she was the author of three novels published in the 1930s. She was also a member of the first graduating class of the Yale School of Drama in 1928. This introduction first appeared in the 1977 Harper & Row edition of *The Alcestiad*.

ON THE LAST PAGES of Thornton Wilder's novel *The Eighth Day*,* my brother has one of the leading characters refute the usual image of the life experience as a river flowing onward between defined banks. Instead, the human adventure is described as a tapestry with indeterminate breadth as well as length and the individual pattern visible on both sides of the fabric. The story is outlined in colored yarn, the design perhaps wildly asymmetrical but nevertheless clear, truthful, complete. A record and a portrait.

*[Wilder's sixth novel, which was published in 1967 and received the National Book Award.]

Thornton's tapestry was minute when at the age of seven or eight in Madison, Wisconsin, he first heard the name Alcestis while reading or being read to from Bulfinch's *The Age of Fable*. The story of the daughter of King Pelias, princess of princesses in the myth and the song of pre-Christian Greece, captured his imagination—and his heart. The thread of her white yarn was knotted into his bit of fabric and she became a benign insistence in his inner consciousness, that hidden storehouse which is an author's source and springboard. She was the haunting shadow of a play that would take years to write.

The knot in Alcestis's thread was tied when the Wilder family moved to Berkeley, California, where the magnificent Greek Theater built [in 1903] into the hillside of a eucalyptus grove was a new and lively part of the life of the university and the town. Several times a year the Classics Department mounted productions of plays by Sophocles, Aeschylus and Euripedes. Our mother joined the volunteer workers in the costume shop and stenciled furlongs of borders in the Greek-key or laurel-leaf patterns on gorgeously colored togas. She made a little blue one with shells around the hem for Thornton—and a green one for brother Amos—and sent them off to apply for roles as members of the Athenian mob. Thus Thornton discovered "total" theatre and the Golden Age of Antiquity. His experience until then had been a performance of *As You Like It* seen from the top gallery of a Milwaukee theatre. [In addition to crowd and chorus appearances in Greek dramas, a young Wilder also sang in several oratorios in this theatre.]

By now Thornton was ten; black-haired, blue-eyed, acquisitive and radiant. Even before this he had claimed his share of a writer's allotment of the twenty-six letters of the alphabet and had begun to tame them into a vocabulary that would allow him—in good time—to speak in his own way. He went to bed early and got up early to write, and the full range of his enlarging vocabulary was turned to inventing dialogue. He draped us and the neighbor's children in yards of begged or borrowed cheesecloth and coaxed us into declaiming his grandiloquent speeches.

Four years later he was a boarding pupil in the China Inland Mission School in Chefoo. Studies in the classics began early in a British school preparing its pupils for the Oxford-Cambridge Examinations.

The first half of his undergraduate years was spent at Oberlin College in Ohio, where he became a privileged student and friend of a great teacher who was also a distinguished classicist—Professor Charles H. A. Wager. Alcestis's thread wove a visibly increasing pattern during these years and later, following his graduation from Yale in 1920, when he spent eight months at the American Academy for Classical Studies in Rome. Not qualified as a Graduate Fellow, he nevertheless audited lectures, went on digs with the archaeologists and pored over fragile papyri. In the museums and art galleries of Italy he caught Alcestis's shadow.

In the decades of the twenties and the thirties the tapestry grew in size and density. The design was of teaching—first French at The Lawrenceville School and then comparative literature, including the Greek dramatists, at the University of Chicago*—and lecture tours and scriptwriting in Hollywood. He published two volumes of short plays and four novels. One novel, *The Bridge of San Luis Rey,* brought him the first of three Pulitzer prizes and, at the age of thirty, worldwide fame weighted with a cumbersome bag of perquisites: honors, privileges, dazzling opportunities balanced by loss of privacy and hazards to body, mind and spirit.

During these years the first of Thornton's long plays, *Our Town,* was produced to immediate success, and the second, *The Merchant of Yonkers,* to failure. André Obey's play, *Lucréce,* which Katharine Cornell had commissioned my brother to translate for her, opened and closed while

*[Wilder periodically taught courses in writing, and the Classics in Translation at the University of Chicago during the 1930s.]

Ibsen's *A Doll's House,* adapted by him for Ruth Gordon, was a conspicuous success. [The run lasted one hundred and forty-four performances—a Broadway record.]

In the summer of 1939 Thornton returned home wonderfully free at last of all outside commitments, with his head full of plans for his own work. He had the beginnings of two projects, both plays. One did not have a name yet. The other was *The Alcestiad.* September came and Hitler's armies flooded Holland and Belgium. Thornton had no choice: *The Alcestiad* was not a play for a war-torn world; the untitled project which became *The Skin of Our Teeth* was.

Soon after Pearl Harbor Thornton was commissioned a captain in the Air Force. By strange coincidence his final leave before going overseas came at the time of the previews and opening of *The Skin of Our Teeth* in New York. The morning that Mother and I said good-bye to him he patted his bulging duffle bag: "I have the manuscript of *The Alcestiad* in my kit. I've been thinking how I could make it into a good one-act. It's very possible by using just the big second act scene. I'd like to leave a finished piece of work . . . might come in handy, Mother. It's a toss-up if *The Skin of Our Teeth* will catch on . . ."

Two years later, while he was waiting in a camp near Boston to be separated from the Air Force (a lieutenant colonel now), his papers were lost. The commanding officer of the post offered a three-day pass. Thornton went straight from the Back Bay station to the Boston Public Library on Copley Square, where he drowned himself once more in the Golden Age of Greece. A few days later he was for the first time in more than three years seated at his own desk in Hamden, Connecticut.

A single sheet of paper from that time is before me now. Printed on one side in big block letters is:

THE ALCESTIAD

A PLAY OF QUESTIONS

On the reverse in his small careful penmanship is:

(Sketches up to and including the Teiresias scene of
    Act I had been made before the War and lost)
Draft One of the first act, May and July 1945
Draft Two, begun July 8, 1945
This Draft Three begun (after completion of Act II
    and half of Act III) on Dec

The unfinished date would be 1945.

The loss of the manuscript meant more to my brother than these few notes convey; his eagerness to get back to his peacetime profession fired his enthusiasm and carried him along for the seven months of work recorded here. But, like millions of other soldiers, he had returned home not only a disoriented and exhausted man but a changed one. He was not able easily to recapture his prewar vision of Alcestis and he did not have the reserve of physical and nervous energy to sustain the excitement and tension to finish his work. He found he was beginning to destroy rather than build. Fortunately he recognized this and put the manuscript away again before doing it injury.

Ancient literature is replete with warriors and battlefields, tyrants and heroes. My brother's thoughts were still lively with his own recent experiences of Hitler's and Mussolini's wars: one year spent on the North African coast among the ruins and ghosts of Hellenic and Roman conquest; another year in southern Italy, likewise haunted by dramatic legend, with Caesar's image triumphant. Thornton suddenly saw his next work plain. And so it happened that the novel *The Ides of March* was written and published in 1947. It opened the way for his return to civilian life, to teaching and lecturing again, to the theatre and to Alcestis.

Thornton was only one of many authors after Euripides to be inspired to retell in his own way the Alcestis fable. Among others Christoph Martin Wieland in Germany in 1773 wrote a libretto for an operetta on the subject. In the next century the poets Richard von Hofmannstahl in Austria and Robert Browning in England used the myth. T. S. Eliot borrowed from it for an aspect of his successful play, *The Cocktail Party*. And no wonder, for the theme of conjugal love and the willingness of a wife to die for her husband is an appealing and thought-provoking challenge to any author eager to explore and praise the capabilities of humankind.

After the success at the 1954 Edinburgh Festival of *The Matchmaker*—that happy invention which started its career as the New York failure *The Merchant of Yonkers* and went on to become the basis of the musical comedy hit *Hello, Dolly!*—the producers commissioned from my brother a new play for the next season. This gave him the impetus needed to finish *The Alcestiad*. He went into hiding at Aix-en-Provence for a long working period. At Christmas he joined a group of friends and me at Villars, Switzerland, for two weeks. During that time I typed from the manuscript the first two acts of the new text. He submitted them at once to the Festival Committee. They and Tyrone Guthrie accepted the play for their 1955 program. Before leaving Aix in the spring he sent in Act III.

A performance of the Classic Attic theatre consisted of a trilogy of more or less connected tragedies usually followed by a Satyr Play—a humorous or biting comment using characters and situations from the preceding dramas. Euripides, the youngest of the three major rival playwrights, sometimes broke with tradition by writing a single play that could stand alone or be grouped with others to complete the three-part pattern. His *Alcestis* is one of these. In fact, because of its "happy ending," with the heroine brought back from the underworld by Hercules, *Alcestis* was even used occasionally as a Satyr Play.

My brother's first idea for his version of the story was to commission a new translation of Euripides's text for a middle act and write a first and third to frame it. Soon he discarded the plan as not practical for his purposes.

In the Greek telling of the legend and Bulfinch's account centuries later, King Admetus knows that he can be saved from death if another will die for him. He goes begging the favor among his servants, former military colleagues, and friends to no avail. Next, he beseeches his parents relentlessly, pointing out that since they have so few years of living left, it is a little thing to ask. But neither the old father nor the old mother is willing to give up a breath for the son. The king does not request this sacrifice of his queen; when Alcestis offers her life with all her love his protests seem mild and unworthy.

Thornton, by having Admetus unaware that he can be saved by another's death, gains a very dramatic and human emotional peak in Act II, and deepens the characterizations and relationship of husband and wife, enriching the bare outlines of the legend for our twentieth century understanding. Concerning his version my brother has said:

> On one level my play recounts the life of a woman—
> of many women—from bewildered bride to sorely
> tested wife to overburdened old age. On another level
> it is a wildly romantic story of gods and men, of death
> and hell, of resurrection of great loves and great trials, of usurpation and revenge. On another level,
> however, it is a comedy . . . about the extreme difficulty of any dialogue between heaven and earth,
> about the misunderstandings that result from the
> incommensurability of things human and divine.*

Of Thornton's other works, his third novel, *The Woman of Andros*, published in 1930, comes closest in setting, feeling and ideas to *The Alcestiad*. Laid on a small Grecian island when Alcestis was already a legend, it is a nostalgic, quiet yet passionate prose-poem, a bridge with one end

*[See page 167 for the complete text of Wilder's program note for the Edinburgh production of *The Alcestiad*.]

mired in the mud of the cruel pagan world, the other straining toward a slowly rising dawn of release. The heroine, Chrysis, is beautiful, intelligent and has some education, but her profession as a *heitara* makes her an outcast. Nevertheless, she is spiritual sister to the Queen Alcestis.

In both these female characters Thornton pays his *hommage* to all women, giving them the burden of carrying his message. Chrysis in her living and her dying praises all life—"the bright and the dark"—and teaches others to do likewise. She is unknowingly a prophet, pointing ahead to a higher hope for humanity.

Alcestis, of course, had been entrusted with messages and heaped with laurel wreaths long before Thornton heard her name. In his play, brought back from hell to live again in the Golden Light of Apollo, she is not permitted a human end. The God steals her from Death and insists upon her perpetual life. He steals her from Admetus, thus denying her—and the king—a stela at his side in the royal tomb. Apollo leads her to His Evergreen Grove where she still wanders, a symbol, a myth, a truth for us all: one who escaped from darkness to be herself a light on the horizon comprehensible to the spirit of Christian humanism.

A play written in the form of ancient Greek drama should logically be performed in the traditional classic manner, in a setting of marble columns under a sun-lighted blue sky. Thornton wrote his *Alcestiad* so that it could be accommodated to the conventional theatre of the proscenium arch. At Edinburgh it was presented under still other circumstances, in the vast barn of a building known as The Church of Scotland Assembly Hall, box-shaped with rows and rows of uncomfortable seats facing three directions— a perfect setting for stormy sessions of factions warring over church politics and church dogma.

In this uncongenial place the simple storytelling script of *The Alcestiad* had to be blown up to near-pageantry proportions. There were not the words to cover the added action and the crowd scenes that filled the stage and trailed down the aisles under Tyrone Guthrie's exciting but over-dramatic direction. Good or bad the *play* was nearly lost.

Even the title was changed to *A Life in the Sun*, which the management thought would have "more box-office appeal." Thornton refers to this in a letter from Scotland to our brother Amos in Cambridge, Massachusetts:

> That's *The Alcestiad*, but the entrepreneurs hate that for a title . . . *A Life in the Sun* is a pretty cheery title for a play fraught with dire events, but it says that Alcestis's life is rooted in Apollo and there's a deal about his being the Sun, so there you are . . .

There were compensations for Thornton. He was not one to despair, nor even fret long. Guthrie's extraordinary talents lighted up some passages, the rare Irene Worth headed a strong cast, and most of the public seated in those uncomfortable rows were gratifyingly responsive and definite in their approval, although the critics, as they do more often than not, veered from appreciative interest and understanding to omniscient disdain.

Most important of all, the author saw his work as a living whole in three-dimensional form. He learned what he had or had not accomplished to his own satisfaction. He also received balm for having felt betrayed by The Church of Scotland Assembly Hall when Tyrone Guthrie very magnanimously confided to him, "I did not serve your play well."

There was much interest among theatrical producers in this country and elsewhere in obtaining the rights for a New York production. My brother had his own ideas as to what changes he wished to make in the text. He talked with a number of directors and listened to their suggestions. He began working on revisions. This always was difficult for him; he was at his best living in the present and looking into the future. Too many people were giving him advice, crowding him. "I need a longer perspective," he told them.

He withdrew the script from circulation, refusing acting rights to those who were willing to try it out as it stood.

When he was released from the unaccustomed pressure, fresh ideas began to come to him for both *The Alcestiad* and the Satyr Play he wanted to go with it in the proper tradition of Greek dramaturgy. He was soon enthralled with *The Drunken Sisters*. It was one of those works that the writer—or composer in any medium—experiences occasionally. It "came" to him all at once on a single direct line, unfolding from beginning to end. Few changes had to be made in the original manuscript for its appearance in the *Atlantic Monthly* in 1957.

With *The Drunken Sisters* demanding to be heard and seen on a stage, it was not difficult for my brother to be persuaded to sign a contract for the two plays to be presented at the Schauspielhaus in Zurich, Switzerland. It was in this theatre during the Second World War that *Our Town* and *The Skin of Our Teeth* had had their first European presentations; many of the most distinguished German and Austrian *regisseurs* and actors and actresses had sought refuge in Switzerland, and Thornton's works, fiction as well as drama, were well known to them and held in high regard.

Thornton worked with the translator, Herberth E. Herlitschka, a Viennese who had translated much of his earlier work into the German language. The revisions made at this time from the text performed at Edinburgh were not great, as he wanted to see the same play interpreted by another director and another cast. It was an exciting and stunning production in every way, the kind of evening in the theatre that has the audience alert, arguing between the acts, clapping hard at the curtains and leaving the theatre full of life.

The Zurich opening was followed by full-scale productions in most of the state-endowed theatres in the large and small cities throughout Germany. It was presented also at the Burg Theater in Vienna. During this period, Thornton made further revisions and, responding to the great demand in Germany, permitted publication of a German edition, by Fischer Verlag, in 1960.

The play was discussed in the literary sections of newspapers and magazines and in scholarly journals and books. Käte Hamburger, in her volume on classical figures in modern literature, *From Sophocles to Sartre*, wrote:

Wilder's work is the most significant interpretation of the [Alcestis] theme in modern world literature.[†]

Though Thornton did not continue to work on *The Alcestiad* as a playscript in English, he could not let it go. It seemed inevitable that when he started searching for a subject for an opera libretto for Louise Talma, whose musical compositions he admired greatly, the circle would be completed.

The opera, also entitled *The Alcestiad*, was six years in the making. It opened in the splendid, rebuilt opera house of Frankfurt, Germany, on March 2, 1962. It is opera on a grand scale requiring a large stage, a large orchestra, a large cast. The production, backed with a subsidy, was given all these elements, and Inge Borkh was a superb Alcestis. The final curtain came down to storybook, thunderous applause and cries of "bravo." There were over thirty curtain calls. Miss Talma, Thornton, everybody were called and recalled to take bows. The rejoicing was great at the dinner party after the performance. Yet the critics' reviews during the next few days and later in the weekly journals were very mixed. One veiled but definite complaint that came through in the most unsympathetic was that women should not write operas, another that the music was too modern.

For his part Thornton was completely satisfied with the score, and felt that any fault in the work came from his inexperience as a librettist. The opera has since been given in

[†]Ungar, New York, 1969. Translation of *Von Sophokles zu Sartre, Griechische Dramenfiguren Antik und Modern*, Stuttgart, 1962.

concert form, and arias from it have been sung in various recitals. Thornton never doubted that it was a work ahead of its time and would one day find full recognition.

Though my brother began writing early in life his list of accomplishments is not long: seven novels; some telling essays and introductions to books—his own and others; two volumes of short plays and four major long ones, counting *The Merchant of Yonkers* and *The Matchmaker* as one. In his work he was not afraid to repeat himself or to be influenced by the masters in the tradition of literature who had passed the torch from hand to hand. Of his theatre pieces he wrote in the preface to the collected *Three Plays* (Harper & Brothers, New York, 1957):

> I am not one of the new dramatists we are looking for. I wish I were. I hope I have played a part in preparing the way for them. I am not an innovator but a re-discoverer of forgotten goods and I hope a remover of obtrusive bric-a-brac.

But he experimented with form. He dared to play with chronological time, historical time, and literary time, plucking events from history, people from pedestals and picture frames, and characters from hallowed printed pages. He gave voice to death, angels, pagan gods, and animals.

In the Foreword to his collection of "three-minute" plays for reading, *The Angel That Troubled the Waters and Other Plays* (Coward-McCann, New York, 1928), my brother wrote of the problems of a young writer (he knew, for he had written some of these plays while he was still in his teens). He described moments of elation and discouragement, and the possibilities:

> How different the practice of writing would be if one did not permit oneself to be pretentious. Some hands

have no choice: they would rather fail with an oratorio than succeed with a ballad.

Thornton always believed firmly that a wastebasket was
a writer's best friend. Even so, his extant papers give evidence of some of his own failed oratorios, including the first
two acts—the third was never written—of *The Emporium,*
a play set in the largest, most alluring store in the world,
where you can find everything you need or think you want,
and *The Melting Pot,* an unfinished scenario for an epic film
on the growth of our country told through the lives of generations of people. But although he did not himself take
time from other projects to revise the English text of *The
Alcestiad* to agree with what he had authorized for publication in German, and would doubtless have made further
revisions, the play as printed is no failed oratorio. It is a
work that reflects successfully some of his most abiding
convictions about the verities of human experience.

Thornton Wilder's tapestry is finished. With the publication of *The Alcestiad* with *The Drunken Sisters* and the
telling of its story, the final design comes clear, revealing all
that he did with his portion of the alphabet, with his talents,
with the years given to him and, most of all, with what he
believed and tried to share. Now that the last length of
Alcestis's huge ball of yarn has been unwound and the last
stitch knotted there are no further mysteries on the subject
to be guarded at Delphi.

Isabel Wilder
Martha's Vineyard
July 1977

NOTES ON *THE ALCESTIAD*

by Thornton Wilder

With "box office appeal" in mind, *The Alcestiad* opened in Edinburgh with the name "A Place in the Sun." To further explain a play that seemed to stand on the other side of the world from a farce like *The Matchmaker*, Tyrone Guthrie prevailed on Wilder to write a note for the program. In it, Wilder highlights the influence of existentialism on the play, especially the contribution of Søren Kierkegaard. To his family in the same period, he put it differently: "It's a mixture of religious revival, mother-love-dynamite, and heroic daring-do. You can't beat that combination."

A LCESTIS chose to die for her husband. We are often told that soldiers die for their country, that reformers and men of science lay down their lives for us. Who commands them? Whence, and how do they receive the command?

The story of Alcestis has been retold many times. When her husband, Admetus, King of Thessaly, was mortally ill, a message came from Apollo saying that he would live if someone volunteered to die in his stead. Alcestis assumes the sacrifice and dies. The mighty Hercules happened to arrive at the palace during the funeral; he descended into the underworld, strove with Death, and brought her back to life. The second act of my play retells this story. There is, however, another legend involving King Admetus. Zeus, the father of gods and men, commanded Apollo to descend to earth and to live for one year as a man among men. Apollo chose to live as a herdsman in the fields of King Admetus. This story serves as the basis of my first act. My third act makes free use of the tradition that Admetus and Alcestis in their old age were supplanted by a tyrant and lived on as slaves in the palace where they had once been rulers.

On one level, my play recounts the life of a woman—of many women—from bewildered bride to sorely tested wife to overburdened old age. On another level it is a wildly romantic story of gods and men, of death and hell and resurrection, of great loves and great trials, of usurpation and revenge. On another level, however, it is a comedy about a very serious matter.

These old legends seem at first glance to be clear enough. One would say that they had been retold for our edification; they are exemplary. Yet on closer view many of them—the stories of Oedipus, of the sacrifice of Isaac, of Cassandra—give the impression of having been retained down the ages because they are ambiguous and puzzling. We are told that Apollo loved Admetus and Alcestis. If so, how strangely he exhibited it. It must make for considerable discomfort to have the god of the sun, of healing and song, housed among one's farm workers. And why should divine love impose on a devoted couple the decision as to which should die for the other? And why (though the question has been asked so many millions of times) should the omnipotent friend permit some noble human beings to end their days in humiliation and suffering?

Following some meditations of Søren Kierkegaard, I have written a comedy about the extreme difficulty of any dialogue between heaven and earth, about the misunderstandings that result from the "incommensurability of things human and divine." Kierkegaard described God under the image of "the unhappy lover." If He revealed Himself to us in His glory, we would fall down in abasement, but abasement is not love. If He divested Himself of the divine attributes in order to come nearer to us, that would be an act of condescension. This is a play about how Apollo searched for a language in which he could converse with Admetus and Alcestis and with their innumerable descendants; and about how Alcestis, through many a blunder, learned how to listen and interpret the things that Apollo was so urgently trying to say to her.

Yet I am aware of other levels, and perhaps deeper ones that will only become apparent to me later.

The Alcestiad

CHARACTERS

APOLLO

DEATH

FIRST WATCHMAN

ALCESTIS

AGLAIA

TEIRESIAS

BOY

ADMETUS

FIRST HERDSMAN

SECOND HERDSMAN

THIRD HERDSMAN

FOURTH HERDSMAN

RHODOPE

HERCULES

SECOND WATCHMAN

EPIMENES

CHERIANDER

AGIS

FIRST GUARD

SECOND GUARD

THIRD GUARD

FOURTH GUARD

SERVANTS

PEOPLE OF THESSALY

SETTING

The rear court of the palace of Admetus, King of Thessaly.

ACT I

No curtain, except at the end of Act III and after The Drunken
Sisters. *All three acts of* The Alcestiad *take place in the rear
court of the palace of Admetus, King of Thessaly, many centuries before the Great Age of Greece. Each act begins at dawn
and ends at sunset of the same day.*

*The palace is a low, squat house of roughly dressed stone,
with a flat roof. There is a suggestion of a portico, however, supported by sections of the trunks of great trees. The palace doors
are of wood and a gilded ox skull is affixed to each of them.
Before these doors is a platform with low steps leading down to
the soil floor of the courtyard.*

*The front of the palace fills the left three-quarters of the back
of the stage. The rest of the stage is enclosed by clay-brick walls.
In the wall to the right is a large wooden gate leading to the road
outside and to the city of Pherai. The wall on the left is less
high; a small door in it leads to the servants' quarters.*

*From the front center of the stage a path leads down (descend-
ing to the right) to what in a conventional theatre would be the
orchestra pit. At the bottom of this path is a "grotto"—a spring
with practical flowing water; a bronze door to the Underworld,*

overhung by vines, but large enough for actors to pass through.
Here is also (not seen, only assumed) the snake Pytho.

First streaks of dawn.

Gradually a light rises to brilliancy, revealing Apollo stand-
ing on the roof of the palace. He wears a costume of gold with
a long, dark blue mantle over his right shoulder. A blue light
begins to glow from the entrance to Hell, down by the spring.
Death—in a garment of large black patches, in which he looks
like a bat or a beetle—comes waddling up the path and sniffs
at the gate left and at the palace gate.

Throughout the scene Apollo gazes off toward the rising
sun—cool, measured, and with a faint smile on his lips.

APOLLO *(Like a "Good morning")*: Death!

DEATH: Aaah! You are here! The palace of Admetus has an
honored guest! We are to have a wedding here today.
What a guest! Or have you come to steal the bride away,
illustrious Apollo?

APOLLO: Death, you live in the dark.

DEATH: I do, I do. Have you come, Lord Apollo, to show us
some great sign, some wonder today?

(The Night Watchman, sounding his rattle and carrying a
waxed parchment lantern, comes around the palace, up
center.)

WATCHMAN *(Singsong)*: The watch before dawn, and all is
well in the palace of Admetus the Hospitable, King of
Thessaly, rich in horses. *(Starting to go off left)* Dawn.
The day of the wedding—of the greatest of all weddings. *(Exit left into the servants' quarters)*

DEATH: I was asking, Lord Apollo, if you had come to show
us some great wonder. *(Pause)* Yes? No? "Yes," I hope.
When the gods come near to men, sooner or later someone is killed. Am I to welcome some admired guest in my
kingdom today? Am I to have King Admetus or the
Princess Alcestis?

APOLLO: No.

DEATH: I shall watch and hope. *(He waddles to the center)* In which of your powers and capacities are you here today, may I ask? As healer? *(Pause)* As bringer of light and life? *(Pause)* As singer?

APOLLO *(Still gazing off; casually)*: They are all one and the same. I have come to set a song in motion—a story—

DEATH: —A story!

APOLLO: A story that will be told many times . . .

DEATH: Ah! A lesson! Will there be a lesson in it for me?

APOLLO: Yes.

DEATH *(Beating with his flippers on the ground)*: No!

APOLLO: Yes. You are to learn something.

DEATH *(Scuttling about in rage)*: No! There is no lesson you can teach me. I am here forever, and I do not change. It's you Gods of the Upper Air that need lessons. And I'll read you a lesson right now. *(Shrilly)* Leave these human beings alone. Stay up on Mount Olympus, where you belong, and enjoy yourselves. I've watched this foolishness coming over you for a long time. You made these creatures and then you became infatuated with them. You've thrown the whole world into confusion and it's getting worse every day. All you do is to torment them—who knows better than I? *(He waddles back to the top of the path, shaking himself furiously)* They will never understand your language. The more you try to say something, the more you drive them distraught.

APOLLO: They have begun to understand me. At first they were like the beasts—more savage, more fearful. Like beasts in a cage, themselves the cage to themselves. Then two things broke on their minds and they lifted their heads: my father's thunder, which raised their fears to awe; and my sunlight, for which they gave thanks. In thanks they discovered speech, and I gave them song. These were signs and they knew them. First one, then another, knew that I prompted their hearts and was speaking.

DEATH: Yes, they're not like they used to be: "Apollo *loves* Thessaly. Apollo *loves* the house of Pherai." Go back to Olympus, where you belong. All this loving . . . It's hard to tell which is the unhappier—you or these wretched creatures. When you try to come into their lives you're like a giant in a small room: with every movement you break something. And whom are you tormenting today? The king? Or his bride?

APOLLO: You.

DEATH: Me? Me? So you've decided to love me, too? No, thank you!

(*He flaps all his flippers, scrambles down the path, then scrambles up again; shrilly*) You can't trouble me, and you can't give me any lessons. I and my Kingdom were made to last forever. How could you possibly trouble me?

APOLLO: You live in the dark and you cannot see that all things change.

DEATH (*Screaming*): Change! There'll be no change.

(*He looks around in apprehension*) It's getting light. And this story you're starting today is about a change? A change for *me?*

APOLLO: For you and for me.

DEATH (*Disappearing into his cave, with one last sneering scream*): For *you!*

(*The light on Apollo fades and he disappears. The Watchman returns on his rounds. He shakes his rattle, then blows out the lamp.*)

WATCHMAN: Dawn. Dawn. And all is well in the palace of Admetus the Hospitable, King of Thessaly, rich in horses.

(*Descends toward audience*) It is the day of the wedding, the greatest of all weddings, and all is *not* well. Why can't she sleep—the princess, the bride, our future queen? Eight, ten times during the night, I've found her here—wandering about, looking at the sky. Sometimes she goes out into the road, as though she were waiting for a messenger. She stands here and raises her arms—whispers: "Apollo! A sign! One sign!" Sign of what? That she is right to marry King Admetus? Eh! Where will she find clearer signs than those written on his face? Oh, I have lived a long time. I know that a bride can be filled with fears on the night before her wedding. But to be afraid of our Admetus who has won her hand in such a wonderful way that all Greece is amazed. Oh, my friends, take an old watchman's advice. Don't meditate upon the issues of life at three in the morning. At that hour no warmth reaches your heart and mind. At that hour—huuu—you see your house in flames and your children stretched out dead at your feet. Wait until the sun rises. The facts are the same—the facts of a human life are the same—but the sunlight gives them a meaning. Take the advice of a night watchman. Now I want a drink of water. *(He descends to the spring and greets the snake Pytho)* Good day to you, Pytho, old friend. It will be a great day for you, too. You shall have a part in the marriage banquet—a great sheep, or half an ox. Now come! Leave my hands free to make the offering.

(He lets the water slip through his cupped hands. And mumbles the ritual: "You sources of life—earth, air, fire and water . . ." Then he scoops once more and drinks. He addresses the audience.)

Look, friends. Do you see this cave under the vines? This is one of the five entrances into Hell, and our good Pytho is here to guard it. No man has ever entered it, and no man has ever come out of it. That's what it is—merely one of the ten thousand things we do not understand.

(He drinks again. Shriek of a slain animal.)

Well, the great day has begun. They are slaughtering the animals for the feast. The cooks are building great fires. The meadows are filled with the tents of kings and of chiefs who have come to celebrate the wedding of King Admetus, and of the Princess Alcestis, daughter of Pelias, King of Iolcos.

(He starts up the path. Alcestis, in white, glides out of the palace doors. Animal cries.)

Hsst! There she is again!

(He hides on the path below the level of the stage. Alcestis comes to the center of the stage, raises her arms, and whispers:)

ALCESTIS: Apollo! A sign! One sign!

(She goes out the gate, right, leading to the road.)

WATCHMAN *(Softly to the audience, mimicking her)*: Apollo! One sign!

(Animal cries. Aglaia, the old nurse, comes out quickly from the palace. She looks about, sees the Watchman.)

AGLAIA *(Whispers)*: Where is the princess? *(He points)* All night—this restlessness, this unhappiness! "Apollo! One sign!"
WATCHMAN: "Apollo! One sign!"

(Alcestis comes in from the gate, in nervous decisiveness.)

ALCESTIS: Watchman!
WATCHMAN: Yes, Princess?
ALCESTIS: Find my drivers. Tell them to harness the horses for a journey. Aglaia, call together my maids; tell them to get everything ready.

AGLAIA: A journey, Princess—on your wedding day, a journey?

ALCESTIS *(Who has swept by her; from the palace steps)*: Aglaia, I have no choice in this. I must go. Forgive me. No, hate me; despise me—but finally forget me.

AGLAIA: Princess, the shame—and the insult to King Admetus.

ALCESTIS: I know all that, Aglaia. Aglaia, when I have gone, tell the king—tell Admetus—that I take all the shame; that I do not ask him to forgive me, but to despise me and forget me.

AGLAIA: Princess, I am an old woman. I am no ordinary slave in this house. I nursed the child Admetus and his father before him.

> *(To the Watchman)* Watchman, leave us alone. *(Exit Watchman)* You do not know King Admetus. In all Greece and the Islands you would not find a better husband.

ALCESTIS: I know this.

AGLAIA: You will find men who are more warlike, more adventurous, stronger perhaps—but not one more just, more . . . more beloved.

ALCESTIS: All this I know, Aglaia. I, too, love Admetus. Because of that I am doubly unhappy. But there is One I love more.

AGLAIA: Another? Another man? Above Admetus? Then go, Princess, and go quickly. We have been mistaken in you. You have no business here. If you have no eyes; if you have no mind; if you cannot see—*(Harshly)* —Watchman! Watchman! Everything will be ready for your journey, Princess. But go quickly.

ALCESTIS: No, Aglaia, not another man. The thing that I love more than Admetus is . . . is a God. Is Apollo.

AGLAIA: Apollo?

ALCESTIS: Yes. Since a young girl I have had only one wish—to be his priestess at Delphi.

> *(She despairs of expressing herself. Then suddenly cries, with passion:)* I wish to live in the real. With one

life to live, one life to give—not these lives we see about us: fever and pride and . . . and possessionship— but in the real; at Delphi, where the truth is.

AGLAIA: But the God has not called you? *(Pause)* The God has not sent for you?

ALCESTIS *(Low; in shame)*: No.

AGLAIA: And this real—it is not real enough to be the wife of Admetus, the mother of his children, and the Queen of Thessaly?

ALCESTIS: Any woman can be wife and mother; and hundreds have been queens. My husband. My children. To center your life upon these five or six, to be bound and shut in with everything that concerns them . . . each day filled—so filled—with the thousand occupations that help or comfort them, that finally one sinks into the grave loved and honored, but as ignorant as the day one was born—

AGLAIA: —Ignorant?

ALCESTIS: Knowing as little of why we live and why we die—of why the hundred thousand live and die—as the day we were born.

AGLAIA *(Dryly)*: And that you think you can learn at Delphi? But the God has not called you.

ALCESTIS *(In shame)*: I sent offerings . . . messages . . . offerings . . . *(Pause)* I was my father's favorite daughter. He wished me never to marry, but to remain with him until his death. But suitors came to seek my hand from all Greece. He imposed upon them an impossible task. He required of them that they yoke together a lion and a boar and drive them thrice about the walls of our city of Iolcos. They came from all Greece: Jason came, and Nestor; Hercules, son of Zeus, came; and Atreus. And all failed. Month after month the new suitors failed and barely escaped with their lives. My father and I sat at the city gates and my father laughed. And I smiled—not because I wished to live with my father, but because I wished for only this one thing: to live and die as a priestess of Apollo at Delphi.

AGLAIA: And then Admetus came. And he drove the lion and the boar—like mild oxen he drove them about the city; and won your hand, Princess.

ALCESTIS: But I loved Apollo more.

AGLAIA: Yes. But it was Apollo who made this marriage.

ALCESTIS: We cannot know that.

AGLAIA: The sign you are asking for, Princess, is before you—the clearest of signs. *(Drastically)* You have not been called to Delphi: you cannot read the simplest words of the God.

(Alcestis shields her face) Now listen to what I am telling you: were you not amazed that Admetus was able to yoke together the lion and the boar? Where Atreus failed, and Hercules, son of Zeus? I will tell you how he did it: in a dream, the God Apollo taught him how to yoke together a lion and a boar. *(Alcestis takes two steps backward)* First, he saw and loved you. Before he returned to Iolcos that second time—after his first failure—he fell ill. Love and despair brought him to the point of death—and I nursed him. Three nights he lay at the point of death. And the third night, I was sitting beside him—his agony and his delirium—and I heard, I *saw*, that in a dream Apollo was teaching him to yoke together a lion and a boar. *(Alcestis gazes at her)* This is true. I swear it is true.

ALCESTIS: True, yes—but we have heard enough of these deliriums and dreams, fevers and visions. Aglaia, it is time we asked for certainties. The clear open presence of the God—that is at Delphi.

AGLAIA: Clear? Open? Even at Delphi the sibyl is delirious; she raves; she is beside herself. Who ever heard of them speaking clearly?

ALCESTIS *(Turning with irresolute step toward the palace, in despair)*: I am alone, alone . . .

AGLAIA *(Firmly but affectionately)*: Now listen to me, Princess. Go to your room and sleep. *(Looking upward)*

It is two hours to noon. If, after a little rest, you are still of the same mind, you can go on any journey you want, and no one will try to stop you. *(Holding Alcestis's elbow, she guides her to the palace doors, prattling in maternal fashion)* You want the gods to speak to us clearly and openly, Princess? What can you be thinking they are, Princess? I hope you don't think of them as men!

(Both exit into the palace. For a moment the stage is empty. A sound of voices at the gate rises almost to clamor. Pounding and knocking at right. The Watchman comes around the palace up center.)

WATCHMAN: Well, now, what's that? What's all this noise? *(Opens the gate and talks through it, ajar)* The wedding guests enter at the gate in front of the palace. This is the rear gate. What? Don't everybody talk at once! What? Very well, very well. Let the old man in.

(Enter Teiresias, blind, unbelievably old, irascible, truculent, domineering, and very near to senile incoherence. One hand is on the shoulder of a Boy who guides him; the other ceaselessly brandishes a great stick. Townspeople follow him into the court; and some Servants come into the court both from the palace doors and from around the palace.)

TEIRESIAS *(Surprisingly loud and strong)*: Is this the palace of Minos, King of Crete?

(Laughter; the Boy starts pulling his sleeve and whispering into his ear.)

I mean, is this the palace of Oedipus, King of Thebes?
   (Striking the Boy with his stick) Stop pulling at me! I know what I'm saying.
   (Warding off those pressing about him) Bees, wasps, and hornets!

WATCHMAN: No, old man. This is the palace of Admetus, King of Thessaly.

TEIRESIAS *(Repeating his words)*: King of Thessaly. Well, that's what I said. That's what I meant. Call Admetus, King of Thessaly. I have a message for him.

WATCHMAN: Old man, the king is to be married today. He is busy with his guests. You sit here in the sun now; we shall wash your feet. The king will come and hear you later.

TEIRESIAS *(Threatening with his stick)*: Marrying ... washing. What have I got to do with marrying and washing? I'll not wait a minute. *(Stamping)* Call King What's-his-name.

(Enter Aglaia from the palace.)

AGLAIA: Who are you, old man? I shall tell the king—

TEIRESIAS: —Tell the king that I am Delphi, priest of Teiresias—Apollo, priest of Delphi ... Boy, what is this I'm saying? *(Boy whispers)* Tell the king I am Teiresias, priest of Apollo. That I come from Delphi with a message and that I am in a hurry to go back there.

AGLAIA: You are Teiresias? Teiresias!

WATCHMAN AND BYSTANDERS: Teiresias!

TEIRESIAS *(Beating with his stick on the ground)*: Call the king! Plague and pestilence! Call King What's-his-name.

AGLAIA: Coming, great Teiresias.

(She is hurrying to the palace door as it opens and Admetus comes out. More Servants gather.)

ADMETUS: What is it? Who is this, Aglaia?

AGLAIA *(Confidentially)*: It is Teiresias, come from Delphi.

ADMETUS: Teiresias!

AGLAIA *(Points to her forehead)*: As old as the mountains, King Admetus.

ADMETUS: Welcome, welcome, noble Teiresias, my father's old friend. Welcome to Pherai. I am Admetus, King of Thessaly.

TEIRESIAS *(Waving his stick)*: Back. Stand back. All this crowding and pushing . . . Have you ears, fellow?

ADMETUS: Yes, Teiresias.

TEIRESIAS: Then pull the wax out of them and listen to what the God says.

ADMETUS: They are open, Teiresias.

TEIRESIAS: Atreus, King of Mycenae, hear what the God says—

ADMETUS: —Atreus? Noble Teiresias, I am Admetus, King of—

TEIRESIAS: —Admetus? All right—Admetus, then. Hold your tongue and let me get my message out. I bring a message to you from Apollo's temple at Delphi. An honor, a great honor has come to Thessaly. Boy, is this Thessaly? *(He puts hands on the Boy's head; the Boy nods)* A great honor and a great peril has come to Thessaly.

ADMETUS: A peril, Teiresias?

TEIRESIAS: An honor and a peril. A peril is an honor, fool. No—an honor is a peril. Don't you know the first things up here in Thessaly?

ADMETUS: One moment, Teiresias. A message to me is also a message to my future queen. Aglaia, call the princess.

(Aglaia hurries into the palace.)

Today I am to be married to Alcestis, daughter of King Pelias of Iolcos. No guest is more to be honored than Teiresias. Rest first, Teiresias . . .

TEIRESIAS: There are ten thousand weddings. Let this queen make haste. Hear me, Minos, King of Crete . . . Boy, what is his name? *(Boy whispers)* Well, what does it matter? Is this queen here?

(Enter from the palace Alcestis, breathless with wonder.)

ADMETUS: She is here.

ALCESTIS: Noble Teiresias . . . great Teiresias! My father's old friend. I am Alcestis, daughter of King Pelias of Iolcos.

TEIRESIAS *(Waving his stick testily at those pressing around him)*: Back! Keep back! Geese and ducks and quacklings. Silence and hold your tongues. Zeus, father of gods and men, has commanded . . . has commanded . . . Boy, what has he commanded? *(Boy whispers. Teiresias strikes him)* Well, you don't have to run on . . . Has commanded that Apollo, my master—that Apollo come down from Olympus; and that he live on earth for one year, solstice to solstice . . . live as a man among men. I have given my message. Boy, lead me to the road. *(He turns to go)*

ALCESTIS *(While the Boy whispers into Teiresias's ear)*: Apollo is to live on the earth?

TEIRESIAS *(To the Boy)*: Yes, yes. Don't deafen me. And Apollo, my master, has chosen to live here—*(He strikes the ground with his stick)*—here as a servant of Admetus, King of Thessaly.

ADMETUS: Here? Here, noble Teiresias? *(Goes quickly to him)* One moment more, Teiresias. How do I understand this? You do not mean, divine Teiresias, that Apollo will be here, with us, as a servant, every day? With us, each day?

(As all watch him breathlessly, Teiresias, hand to brow, seems to fall into a deep sleep. Suddenly he awakes and says:)

TEIRESIAS: Outside the gate are four herdsmen. They are to be your servants for a year. Assign them their duties. One of them is Apollo.

ADMETUS *(Repeating)*: One of them is Apollo?

TEIRESIAS: Four herdsmen. One of them is Apollo. Do not try to know which one is the God. I do not know. You will never know. And ask me no more questions, for I have no more answers. Boy, call the herdsmen.

(The Boy goes out. Silence.)

ADMETUS: Teiresias, should we not . . . fall on our knees, on our faces?

TEIRESIAS: You do not listen to what's said to you. Apollo is here, *as a man.* As a man. As a common herdsman or shepherd . . . Do as I do!

(The Boy returns and presses close to Teiresias. Enter the Four Herdsmen. They are dusty, dirty, unshaven, common oafs. They are deeply abashed by the great folk before them, touch their forelocks obsequiously, shuffle into a line against the wall, and don't know what to do with their eyes. Two have great wineskins; all have big sticks. Teiresias speaks gruffly to them.)

TEIRESIAS: Come, don't be slow about it. Make your bow to your new master. Anyone can see you've been drinking. A nice way to begin your service. *(Waving his stick)* If I had eyes to see, I'd beat you. Forward; pick up your feet. Boy, are they all four here? Well, has the king lost his voice?

ADMETUS *(Pulling himself together)*: You are welcome to Thessaly. You are welcome to the wedding feast, for I am to be married today. Tomorrow I shall assign you your herds and flocks. You have made a long journey. You are welcome to Thessaly . . . Teiresias, you, too, have made a long journey. Will you not bathe and rest?

TEIRESIAS: I have a longer journey to go. My message has been delivered. Boy, lead me out the gate.

ALCESTIS *(Coming to a few steps before him; in a low voice)*: Divine Teiresias? Have you no message for Alcestis?

TEIRESIAS: Who's this woman?

ALCESTIS: I am Alcestis, daughter of King Pelias of Iolcos. I sent many messages and offerings to Delphi and—

TEIRESIAS: —Messages and offerings. There are mountains of them. Boy, lead me to the road.

(But the Boy keeps pulling at his sleeve and shoulder and trying to whisper to him.)

Oh, yes, I had a message for some girl or woman—for Jocasta, or Alcestis, or Dejaneira, or I care not whom, but I have forgotten it. Boy, stop dragging at me! *(He strikes the Boy with his stick)* Worthless! Impudent! *(The Boy falls. Teiresias continues to beat him)*

BOY *(Screaming)*: Teiresias! Help! Help! King Admetus!

ADMETUS: Surely, great Teiresias, the boy has not—

ALCESTIS: —It was a small fault, Teiresias. I beg you spare the boy. He will learn.

TEIRESIAS *(Suddenly stopping and peering at Alcestis)*: Whatever your name is: Jocasta, Leda, Hermione—

ALCESTIS: —Alcestis.

TEIRESIAS: I had a message for some girl, but I have forgotten it. Or else I've delivered it already. That's it: I've delivered it. By thunder and lightning, by the holy tripod—what use is Delphi if men and women cannot learn to listen?

(Teiresias is following the Boy out of the gate, when Admetus takes some steps forward.)

ADMETUS: You said . . . you said there was peril, Teiresias?

TEIRESIAS *(Half out of the gate)*: Of course there's peril, imbecile. When they *(Brusque gesture upward)* draw near it is always peril.

ADMETUS: But my father said that Apollo has always loved Thessaly . . .

TEIRESIAS: Yes—love, love, love. Let them keep their love
to themselves. Look at me: five-six hundred years old
and pretty well loved by the gods and I am not allowed
to die. If the gods didn't love men, we'd all be happy;
and the other way round is true, too: if we men didn't
love the gods, we'd all be happy. *(Exit, with the Boy)*

*(A bewildered pause. Admetus collects himself and says
in a more matter-of-fact, authoritative tone to the Four
Herdsmen:)*

ADMETUS: Again, you are welcome to Thessaly and to
Pherai.
   (To the Watchman) See that they are well provided
for.
   (Again to the Herdsmen) I am happy that you are to
be guests at my wedding today.

*(Admetus and all on the stage watch in confused awe as the
Watchman guides them down the path to the spring. They
pass Admetus with servile timidity; by the spring they
stretch out, pass the wineskin from one to another; one
promptly falls asleep. Admetus has not looked at Alcestis.
Partly to her and partly to himself, he says reflectively:)*

I do not know what to think of these things . . . I am a
mere herdsman myself. Alcestis, there is great need of
you in Pherai.

*(He stretches his hand out behind him. She, frozen in
thought, does not take it.)*

I must return to my guests.
   (With a last echo of his awe) I do not know what to
think of these things.
   (Then with a smile) Alcestis, there is an old custom
here in Thessaly that a bridegroom should not see the

face of his bride until the evening of his wedding day.
This has been said for many hundreds of years. Is there
also such a custom at Iolcos?

ALCESTIS *(Low)*: Yes, Admetus.

ADMETUS *(Passing her with youthful vigor, his hand shielding
his face)*: Hereafter—by the God's gift—I may look
upon your face until I die.

*(At the door of the palace, he is arrested by a thought. Still
shielding his face, he comes in slow deliberation to the point
of the stage, overhanging the Herdsmen by the spring.
After taking a deep breath of resolution, he says with
unemphatic directness:)*

Apollo, friend of my father and my ancestors and my
land, I am a simple man, devout. I am not learned in
piety. If, in ignorance, I blunder and fall short, may he
who has been the friend of my house and my people
forgive me. You have come on a day when I am the hap-
piest of all men. Continue your favor to me and to my
descendants . . . *(Slight pause)* I am not skilled in
speech. You can read all minds. Read what is in mine,
or rather . . . yourself plant in my mind those wishes
which only you can fulfill. *(He turns and goes quickly
into the palace)*

*(Alcestis has not ceased to keep her eyes on the Herdsmen,
half in longing and half in doubt and repulsion—though
they are now hidden from where she is standing, murmuring.)*

ALCESTIS: Is Apollo there?

AGLAIA: Princess!

ALCESTIS: One of those? And could that old man have been
Teiresias of Delphi—that broken, crazy old man?

AGLAIA *(Really shocked; firmly)*: Do not doubt these things,
Princess.

ALCESTIS *(After taking a few steps toward them; in sudden
resolve)*: Leave me alone with them.

(Aglaia makes a gesture to the Watchman and both go out. During the following speech, though one Herdsman is asleep and snoring, the others are embarrassed by her presence. The wineskin is being passed around; they scarcely dare to raise their eyes to her.)

Are you here? I have spoken to you a thousand times— to the sky and the stars and the sun. And I have sent messages to Delphi. Are you now, truly, within the hearing of my voice?

(Silence, broken by a snore and a grunt.)

Some say that you do not exist. Some say that the gods are far away; they are feasting on Olympus, or are asleep, or drunk. I have offered you my life. You know that I have wished to live only for you: to learn—to be taught by you—the meaning of our life.

(No answer.)

Are we human beings to be left without any sign, any word? Are we abandoned?

(She waits another second above the embarrassed silence of the Herdsmen, then turns toward the palace, and says to herself, bitterly:)

Then we must find our way by ourselves . . . and life is a meaningless grasping at this and that; it is a passionate nonsense . . .

(The First Herdsman—the dirtiest, most insignificant of the four—rises. He touches his cap in humble embarrassment and says:)

HERDSMAN: Princess, did that old man say that there was a god among us? Did I hear him say that? The God

Apollo? Then, lady, I am as surprised as you are. Lady, for thirty days we four have walked all across Greece. We have drunk from the same wineskin; we have put our hands in the same dish; we have slept by the same fire. If there had been a god among us, would I not have known it?

(Alcestis, in hope and revulsion, has taken several steps toward him.)

By all I value, lady, I swear we are just ordinary herdsmen. Ignorant herdsmen. But . . . but one thing I will say, lady: we are not quite ordinary herdsmen. Why, that fellow there—the one that's snoring: there's no illness he cannot cure. Snakebite or a broken back. Yet I know that he is not a god, Princess. And that fellow beside him, that one! *(He goes forward and kicks the Herdsman)* Can't you stop drinking while the princess is looking at you? He never loses his way. In the darkest night he knows his north from his south and his east from his west. Oh, it's wonderful. Yet I know well that he's not the god of the sun. *(Adding under his breath)* Besides, his habits are filthy, are filthy.

ALCESTIS *(Barely breathing it)*: And that one?

HERDSMAN: That man? He's our singer.

ALCESTIS: Ah!

HERDSMAN: Believe me, when he plays the lyre and sings— oh, Princess! It is true that at times I have said to myself, "Surely this is a god." He can fill us to the brim with joy or sadness when we have no reason at all to be joyful or sad. He can make the memory of love more sweet than love itself. But, Princess, he is no god. *(As though she had contradicted him; with sudden argumentative energy)* How can he be a god when he's in misery all the time and drinking himself to death? Killing himself, you might say, before our own eyes. The gods don't hate themselves, Princess.

ALCESTIS: And you?

HERDSMAN: I? *I*, Apollo? Not only am I not Apollo, but I'm not ready to believe that Apollo is here.

ALCESTIS: Teiresias . . . Teiresias said . . .

HERDSMAN: Was that Teiresias—that half-witted, crumbling old man? Can they find no better messenger than that? Can't they say what they have to say in any clearer way than this?

(Again Alcestis turns toward the palace; then turns toward the Herdsman and says, as though talking to herself:)

ALCESTIS: Then we are indeed miserable. Not only because we have no aid, but because we are cheated with the hope that we might have aid . . .

HERDSMAN *(Taking more steps onto the stage)*: But if they did exist, these gods, how would they speak to us? In what language would they talk to us? Compared to them, we are diseased and dying and deaf and blind and as busy as clowns. Why, there are some who even say that they love us. Could you understand that? What kind of love is that, Princess, when there is so great a gulf between the lovers? *(He starts to return to his place in the path)* That would be an unhappy love, no doubt about that.

ALCESTIS *(Earnestly and sharply)*: No, not unhappy!

HERDSMAN *(With equal spirit)*: Yes. For if they showed themselves to us in their glory, it would kill us.

(Pause) I did have an idea this morning: maybe there is another way—a way to bridge that gulf, I mean. Maybe they can find a way to bring those they love up—up nearer to them. If Teiresias is right, Apollo is here in Thessaly. Now, maybe that foolish old man got his message wrong. Maybe he was supposed to say that Apollo is here divided up among many people—us four herdsmen and others! Take Admetus, for example. I've only seen him for a few hours. I must confess,

Princess, at first I was very disappointed in Admetus. There's nothing very extraordinary about him. Did you ever see Hercules, Princess?

ALCESTIS *(Nods her head slightly)*: Yes.

HERDSMAN *(Suddenly recollecting)*: Ah, yes. He sought your hand. There's a man! Hercules, son of Zeus and Alcmene. And you can see it at once. I've seen a dozen better men than Admetus. But . . . slowly I began to see that King Admetus has something that all those other heroes haven't got. . . . The world changes; it changes slowly. What good would this world be, Princess, unless new kinds of men came into it—and new kinds of women?

(Enter Admetus, wearing on his right shoulder a light blue cloak like Apollo's. He stands watching from the top step.)

And wouldn't that be, maybe, the way those unhappy lovers *(He points upward)* would try to throw a bridge across the gulf I was talking about?

(He becomes aware of Admetus. Obsequiously bowing his head, and pulling his forelock, murmuring) We wish you all happiness . . . many years.

(He goes back to his place. The sun is setting. The sky behind the palace roof is filled with color.)

ADMETUS *(With set face)*: Aglaia has told me of your wish to leave, Princess Alcestis. You are, of course, free to go. There are no constraints here. There are no slaves in Thessaly, Princess—not even its queen. I have just given orders that your drivers and your maids be prepared for the journey. *(He takes one step down)* Before you leave, I wish to say one thing. I do not say this in order to win your pity, nor to dissuade you from what you have planned to do. I say this because you and I are not children; and we should not conceal from one another what is in our hearts.

(Slight pause) It is still a great wonder to me that I was able to yoke the lion and the boar. But I am in no doubt as to *why* I was able to do it: I loved you. I shall never see you again. I shall never marry. And I shall never be the same. From now on I shall know that there is something wrong and false in this world into which we have been born. I am an ordinary man, but the love that filled me is not an ordinary love. When such love is not met by a love in return, then life is itself a deception. And it is best that men live at random, as best they may. For justice . . . and honor . . . and love are just things we invent for a short time, as suits the moment. May you have a good journey, Princess Alcestis.

(Alcestis has been standing with raised head but lowered eyes. She now puts out her hand.)

ALCESTIS: Admetus. *(Slight pause)* Admetus, ask me again to marry you.

(He takes one quick step toward her; she again puts out her hand quickly to stop him.)

Ask me to love all the things that you love . . . and to be the queen of your Thessaly. Ask me in pain to bear you children. To walk beside you at the great festivals. To comfort you when you are despairing. To make sure that when you return from a journey the water for your bath will be hot, and that your house, Admetus, will be as well ordered as your mind. To live for you and for your children and for your people—to live for you as though every moment I were ready to die for you . . .

ADMETUS *(Joyously and loudly)*: No—no Alcestis! It is I . . . *(He takes her outstretched hand. They do not embrace)* Alcestis, will you be the wife of Admetus, King of Thessaly?

ALCESTIS: With my whole self, Admetus . . .

(They go into the palace.)

ACT II

The same scene, twelve years later.

Again first dawn. The same Watchman comes around the palace. He does not shake his rattle. He speaks softly, slowly and dejectedly.

WATCHMAN: The watch before dawn . . . the palace of
Admetus the Hospitable, King of Thessaly, rich in
horses. *(He stands a moment, his eyes on the ground; then
to the audience)* And all is as bad as it possibly could be
. . . as it possibly could be.

*(He goes to the gate, which is ajar, and talks to a whis-
pering crowd outside)* No, my friends. There is no news.
The king is still alive; he has lived through another
night. The queen is sitting by his bed. She is holding his
hand . . . No news. No change . . . Take that dog away;
we must have no barking. Yes, the king drank some ox
blood mixed with wine.

*(He returns to the center of the stage and addresses the
audience)* Our king is at the point of death, there is no
doubt about it. You remember those herdsmen, twelve

years ago, that Teiresias brought here, saying that one of them was Apollo—and that Apollo would live here as a servant for a year? You remember all that? Well, at the end of the year did they go away? No; all four of them are still here. Was Apollo in one of them? Nobody knows. Don't try to think about it; you'll lose your senses if you try to understand things like that. But, friends, that first year was a wonderful year. I cannot explain this to you: it was no more or less prosperous than other years. To a visitor, to a passerby, everything would have appeared the same. But to us who were living it, everything was different. The facts of our human life never change; it is our way of seeing them that changes. Apollo was certainly here.

(Pause) What? How did King Admetus come by his illness? Well, as I say, those four herdsmen stayed on. They were good fellows and good workers—though they talked south-country Greek. But two of them— eh!—drank their wine without water. And one evening at sunset time those two were sitting drinking—there, right there!—and a quarrel arose between them. There was shouting and chasing about, and King Admetus came out to put a stop to it. Then—oh, my friends— one of the herdsmen whipped out his knife and stabbed King Admetus by mistake, stabbed him from here *(Points to his throat)* right down his side to the waist. You could put your hand in it. That was weeks ago. The wound didn't heal. It got angry and boiled and watered and boiled and watered, and now the king must surely die. No one's wanted to punish the herdsman whose body held Apollo—you see? And the crime may have been Apollo's will—try to think that through! And that herdsman's outside the gate now—is always there— flat on the ground, flat on his face, wishing he were dead.

(There is a rising murmur of excited voices at the gate.)

Now what's all that noise about?

(Aglaia comes hurriedly out of the palace.)

AGLAIA: What's all that noise? Watchman, how can you
allow that noise?

WATCHMAN *(Hobbling to the gate)*: They've only just begun
it.

AGLAIA *(At the gate)*: What's all this cackling about? Don't
you know you must be quiet?

WATCHMAN: Have you no sense? Have you no hearts?
What? What?

AGLAIA: What? What messenger? Tell him to go around to
the front of the palace and to go quietly. What messenger? Where's he from?

(Enter Alcestis, from the palace.)

ALCESTIS: There must be no noise. There must be no noise.
Aglaia, how can you allow this noise?

AGLAIA: Queen Alcestis, they say that a messenger has come.

ALCESTIS: What messenger?

*(The Watchman has received through the gate a small rec-
tangular leaf of gold, which he gives to Alcestis.)*

WATCHMAN: They are saying that a messenger came during
the night and left this.

*(Alcestis stands looking at it in her hand. The Watchman
leans over and examines it in her hand and continues talking officiously.)*

It is of gold, lady. See, those are the signs—that is the
writing—of the Southland. There is the sun . . . and the
tripod . . . and the laurel . . . Queen Alcestis, it is from
Delphi. It is a message from Delphi!

(Alcestis suddenly performs the ritual: she places the leaf first to her forehead, then on her heart, then on her lips.)

ALCESTIS: Where is the messenger?

(The Watchman goes to the gate—now slightly open—and holds a whispered colloquy.)

WATCHMAN *(Turning back toward Alcestis)*: He went away—hours ago, they say.
ALCESTIS: Who can read this writing? Watchman, go call those four herdsmen!
WATCHMAN: They are here, lady—all four of them.

(Again a busy colloquy at the gate. It opens further to admit the four Herdsmen. The Herdsman who held the long conversation with Alcestis in Act I flings himself on the ground, face downward, holding his head in his hands.)

ALCESTIS: Can one of you read the writing of the Southland?
HERDSMAN *(Raising his head)*: I can . . . a little, Queen Alcestis.
ALCESTIS: Then stand. Stand up.

(He rises. She puts the leaf in his hand. He looks at it a moment, then puts it to his forehead, heart and lips; and says in awe:)

HERDSMAN: It is from the temple of Apollo at Delphi.

(Some Townspeople have pressed through the gate. The Herdsman starts reading with great difficulty.)

"Peace . . . and long life . . . to Admetus the Hospitable, King of Thessaly, rich in horses."
ALCESTIS: Long life?

HERDSMAN: "Peace and long life to Admetus the Hospitable—"

ALCESTIS: —Stop.

(*To the Watchman*) Close the gate.

(*The Watchman pushes the Townspeople off the stage, and after a glance at Alcestis, also drives off the three other Herdsmen. He closes the gate. Alcestis returns to the reader, who has been trying to decipher the text.*)

HERDSMAN: "King Admetus . . . *not* . . . will not . . . die."

AGLAIA: Great is Apollo! Great is Apollo!

HERDSMAN: "Will not die . . . if . . . if . . . because . . . no, if . . . another . . . if someone else . . . if a second person . . . desires . . . (*He points to his heart*) wishes . . . longs . . . desires to die . . ." Lady, I do not know this last word.

ALCESTIS: I know it.

HERDSMAN (*Struggling, finds it*): "In his place . . . in his stead." Great is Apollo!

AGLAIA: What does it say? What does it say?

WATCHMAN: I. I shall die. (*Starting left*) My sword, where is my sword?

AGLAIA (*Getting the idea*): No. (*Strongly to the Watchman*) No. This message is for me. I was there when he was born: I shall die for him. I shall throw myself in the river.

WATCHMAN (*Returning to Aglaia*): This is not for a woman to do.

HERDSMAN (*Kneeling, his fists pressed against his eyes in concentration*): I have begun to die already.

AGLAIA: Queen Alcestis, tell me . . . I must do it properly: how does one die for King Admetus?

WATCHMAN (*Self-importantly, placing himself between Aglaia and Alcestis*): Give your orders to me, Queen Alcestis. It is very clear that this message was meant for me.

HERDSMAN (*Again throwing himself full length on the ground*): I struck him. I am to blame for all!

ALCESTIS *(Who has waited, motionless, for silence)*: How would you die in his stead?

(Pause) Do you think it is enough to fling yourself into the river—or to run a sword through your heart?

(Pause) No—the gods do not ask what is easy for us, but what is difficult.

AGLAIA *(Sobbing)*: Queen Alcestis, how does one die for King Admetus?

HERDSMAN: I know. I know. *(He turns and starts to go to the gate)* Peace and long life to King Admetus!

ALCESTIS *(To the Herdsman)*: Wait!

(They all watch her. She says quietly:) Aglaia, go and lay out the dress in which I was married.

AGLAIA *(Stares at her in sudden realization; horrified whisper)*: No. No . . . you must not . . .

ALCESTIS: Tell the children I am coming to see them. Tell the king the sun is warm here. He must come out and sit in it.

(Sudden clamor from the others.)

AGLAIA: No. No, Queen Alcestis. We are old. Our lives are over.

WATCHMAN: Lady, look at me—I am an old man.

AGLAIA: You cannot do this. He would not wish it. You are queen; you are mother.

ALCESTIS *(Restraining their noise by voice and gesture)*: First! First I order you to say nothing of this to anyone. Aglaia, do you hear me?

AGLAIA: Yes, Queen Alcestis.

ALCESTIS: Watchman!

WATCHMAN: Yes, Queen Alcestis.

ALCESTIS: To no one—until tomorrow. No matter what takes place here, you will show no surprise, no grief. Now leave me alone with this man. *(Pointing to the Herdsman)*

(Aglaia goes into the palace; the Watchman out left. The Herdsman stands with one fist on his forehead in concentration, and suddenly cries:)

HERDSMAN: King Admetus—rise up! Rise up!

ALCESTIS: You cannot save him.

HERDSMAN: I have begun to die already.

ALCESTIS: Yes, maybe you could do it. But you would do it imperfectly. You wish to die, yes . . . not for love of Admetus, but to lift the burden of that crime from off your heart. This is work of love, Herdsman; not work of expiation, but of love.

HERDSMAN *(Almost angrily)*: I, too, love Admetus.

ALCESTIS: Who does not love Admetus? But your death would be a small death. You long to die: I dread, fear, hate to die. I must die from Admetus—*(She looks upward)* —from this sunlight. Only so will he be restored. Can you give him that? *(He is silent)*

(She continues, as though talking to herself) I know now what I have to do and how to do it. But I do not know why . . . why this has been asked of me. You . . . you can help me to understand why I must die.

HERDSMAN: I?

ALCESTIS: Yes, you—who came from Delphi; in whom Apollo—

HERDSMAN *(In sincere repudiation)*: —Lady . . . Princess, I told you—again and again. If Apollo was in us herdsmen, he was not in me!

ALCESTIS *(Softly and lightly)*: You made clear to me that Apollo willed my marriage.

HERDSMAN *(Still almost angrily)*: No. No. You asked me questions. I answered as any man would answer. You know well that I am an ordinary man.

(Alcestis turns in suffering frustration toward the palace door; then turns back again to the Herdsman.)

ALCESTIS: Then speak again as an ordinary man, and tell me why Apollo asks me to die.

HERDSMAN *(Still with a touch of anger)*: Then as an ordinary man I answer you—as many an ordinary man would: Delphi has said that one of us must die. I am ready to die. Why should I try to understand it?

ALCESTIS: But if we do not understand, our lives are little better than those of the animals.

HERDSMAN: No! Princess, to understand means to see the whole of a thing. Do we men ever see the whole of a story, the end of a story? If you let me die now for Admetus, I would not know what followed after my death, but I would die willingly. For I have always seen that there are two kinds of death: one which is an end; and one which is a going forward, which is big with what follows after it. And I would know that a death which had been laid on me by Delphi would be a death which led on to something. For if the gods exist, that is their sign: that whatever they do is an unfolding—a part of something larger than we can see. Let me die this death, Princess—for it would save me from that other death which I dread and which all men dread: the mere ceasing to be; the dust in the grave.

(Alcestis has received his words as full answer and solution. Her mood changes; she says lightly and quickly:)

ALCESTIS: No, Herdsman, live—live for Admetus, for me, and for my children. Are you not the friend of Epimenes—he who hates you now because you struck his father? You have almost broken his heart. He thought you were his friend—you who taught him to swim and to fish. Before I go I shall tell Epimenes that you have done me a great kindness.

(In silence the Herdsman goes out the gate. Alcestis again makes the ritual gesture with the gold leaf—forehead, heart, lips. Enter Aglaia from the palace.)

AGLAIA *(With lowered head)*: The dress is ready, Queen Alcestis.

ALCESTIS: Aglaia, for what I have to do now I cannot—I must not—see the children. Their heads smell so sweet. Do you understand?

AGLAIA: Yes, Queen Alcestis.

ALCESTIS: You are to tell Epimenes—from me—that he is to go to the herdsman who struck his father . . . that he is to forgive him, and to thank him for a great kindness which he has done me.

AGLAIA: I shall tell him.

ALCESTIS: You are to cut a lock of my hair. Say nothing to anyone, and place it on the altar *(Pointing to the gate)* in the grove of Apollo, across the road. Aglaia, after I am gone, you are to tell King Admetus that I have said that I wish him to marry again.

AGLAIA: Queen Alcestis!

ALCESTIS: A man must have that comfort. But oh, Aglaia! They say that stepmothers often bear ill will toward the children of the former wife. Stay by them! Stay near them! And oh, Aglaia—from time to time recall me to him. *(Her voice breaking)* Recall me to him!

(She rushes into the palace. Aglaia is about to follow when she is stopped by excited whispering and talking at the gate. Some Townspeople take a few steps into the court. Rhodope, a young girl of the palace servants, smothering her happy giggling, runs from the gate to the palace door.)

AGLAIA: What is this? What is this noise? Rhodope!

RHODOPE: He's coming along the road!

AGLAIA: Who?

RHODOPE AND TOWNSPEOPLE: Hercules is coming! He's down the valley! Hercules, son of Zeus!

AGLAIA: Hush, all of you. Go out of the court. Have you forgotten that there is sickness in this house! Rhodope, go in the house and hold your tongue!

(*Townspeople disappear. Rhodope slips through the palace door as it is opened by the Watchman, who enters, preceding two Servants, who are not yet seen with a day bed. Then to Aglaia, whose head is lowered in anxiety:*)

WATCHMAN: Hercules! Today of all days!

AGLAIA (*In a bad humor*): Yes. Yes. And every year. Why does he come every year? Do we know?

WATCHMAN: But . . . so great a friend!

AGLAIA: Yes, but great friends can sometimes make us a present of their absence.

WATCHMAN: Aglaia, I don't understand you!

AGLAIA (*Irritably*): I know what I know.

(*From the palace come two Servants. They are bearing a day bed and a low stool.*)

WATCHMAN (*To the Servants*): Come on . . . put them down here. You know where.

AGLAIA (*Taking over the ordering, while the Watchman turns back to help Admetus*): Here, right here! (*Getting her bearings by the sun*) Turn it so. (*She takes the cushions from them*) So. There. And the queen likes to sit here.

(*Enter Admetus, supported, his arms around the shoulders of the Watchman and a Guard.*)

ADMETUS: The sun is already halfway up the sky.
    (*To the Watchman*) You have watched all night. You should be asleep.

WATCHMAN: Oh, we old men, King Admetus, we sleep very little. Gently. Gently now.

ADMETUS: I don't know where the queen is, Aglaia.

AGLAIA (*Busies herself with the cushions*): She'll be here in a minute, King Admetus. You can be sure of that.

(*She goes quickly into the palace.*)

WATCHMAN: Now, sire, when you're comfortably settled on that couch, I have some news for you. You'll scarcely believe it.

(*He squints up at the sun*) Yes, sire, it will be a very hot day. We are in the solstice. The sailors say that the sun swings low, that he is very near us these days. That's what they say.

ADMETUS: What is your news?

WATCHMAN: A great friend, sire, is coming to see you—a very good friend.

ADMETUS: Hercules!

WATCHMAN: Yes, Hercules, son of Zeus!

ADMETUS: Today! Today of all days!

WATCHMAN: The whole town knows it. Oh, he comes slowly enough. At every village, every farm, they bring him wine; they put garlands on his head. He is very drunk . . . Oh, King Admetus, we must prevent his embracing you. You remember his embraces. He would surely kill you today.

ADMETUS: Does the queen know?

WATCHMAN: Oh, the maids will have told her all about it.

ADMETUS: I wish he could have come at another time.

WATCHMAN: Every time is a good time for Hercules. Your sons, sire, are beside themselves. Epimenes will ask him all over again how he killed the Nemean lion and how he cleaned the stables of King Augeas.

ADMETUS: Call Aglaia.

(*Enter Aglaia from the palace door.*)

WATCHMAN: Here she is now.

AGLAIA: Yes, King Admetus?

(*Behind the king's back, with her hand she directs the Watchman to leave. He exits left.*)

ADMETUS: Aglaia—come near to me. You have heard the news?

(The Watchman as he leaves gives Aglaia an anxious look and is relieved by her answer.)

AGLAIA: Yes, I have: the son of Zeus is coming to visit us.

ADMETUS *(Without pathos)*: Aglaia, this is my last day. I know it. I feel it.

AGLAIA: Sire, how would any of us know that? You must not talk now. You must save your strength.

ADMETUS: I shall die before sundown. Now, if it is possible—and you must make it possible—my death must be hidden from Hercules, for at least a day or two. You must say that one of the servants had died. And you must go about your life as though nothing had happened. The queen will show you the way of it. You know what Hercules's life is like—those great labors, one after another. When he comes to us as a happy visitor, we would not wish to show him a house of mourning. Especially Hercules, who is so often on the point of losing his life, and who has such an aversion to all that has to do with burial and mourning.

AGLAIA *(Again arranging his cushions)*: King Admetus, I am not a fool. All these things I understand very well. Now lie back and shut your eyes. This sunlight is going to give you strength.

ADMETUS: If it could only give me strength for one more day—to welcome Hercules! Go and see where the queen is.

AGLAIA: Here she is.

(Exit Aglaia left. Enter Alcestis from the palace door. She stands on the top step. She is wearing the dress of Act I. Admetus turns and gazes at her in silence.)

ADMETUS: Our wedding dress!

ALCESTIS *(Smiling, puts her finger on her lips to silence him; she goes to him and says lightly)*: Most wives save it for their burial. I wear it for life.

ADMETUS: Sit here, dearest. I was just saying to Aglaia—

(Alcestis sits on the stool beside Admetus and rests her hand beside his.)

ALCESTIS: Yes, yes, I know—when Hercules comes . . .

ADMETUS: He will soon be here.

ALCESTIS: Oh, he is being detained on the road. Hercules goes quickly only to danger. Perhaps he will be here tonight . . . perhaps not till tomorrow. We have time.
  (She rises and goes to the center of the stage and stands there listening) I hear shouts of joy in the valley.
  (She walks slowly back to her stool and repeats) We have time.
  (In the center of the stage, gazing at the sun as if for help) This is the healing sun—the sun of the summer solstice. Do you feel it?

ADMETUS: It is the healing sun, but for others. I have put all that behind me: I do not need hope. My life was short, but a single hour can hold the whole fullness of time. The fullness of time was given to me. A man who has been happy is no longer the subject of time . . . Come, we'll say to each other what is still to be said on this last day.

ALCESTIS *(Returning to her place beside him; with a gentle smile)*: This last day? You must rest and save your strength and breath. I shall talk. I shall talk for two— for you and for me. I do not know who gave me that second name: Alcestis the Silent. I think it was you, but also it was Hercules who carried it over Greece.

ADMETUS: Were you always silent?

ALCESTIS: I? No. As a girl—oh, I was a contentious and argumentative girl, as you know well. But there are times when I am impatient with my silence—this tiresome, silent Alcestis! There are times when I wish to be like other women, who can freely say what is in their hearts. What do other wives say? I think they must say something like this: Admetus . . . have I ever told you—let me look into your eyes again—have I ever told you that I have loved you more than life itself?

(Leaning over him, she is suddenly stricken with great pain. She rises, whirls about, one hand to her head, the other to her left side, where his wound is. Admetus has not noticed it. He has closed his eyes again, and starts to laugh in a low, long murmur.)

ADMETUS: That does not sound . . . no, that does not sound like my silent Alcestis. And if you were to speak for me, what would you say?

ALCESTIS *(The pain has slackened and she replies almost serenely)*: I would say that I—I, Admetus—have chosen neither the day of my birth not the day of my death. That having been born is a gift that fell to our lot—a wonderful gift—and that Alcestis's death—or my own—comes from the same hand.

ADMETUS *(Almost amused)*: Your death, Alcestis?

ALCESTIS: Were it to come from the same hand that gives life . . . Are you in pain, Admetus?

ADMETUS *(Puts his hand to his side wonderingly)*: No. I do not know why it is, but the pain seems to have . . .

ALCESTIS: Lift your hand!

(As he slowly raises his paralyzed left hand, the pain passes into her body; she clutches her side, bending in agony.)

ADMETUS: This lightness! *(He stares before him with hope)* No, I must not think of such things. I have put that behind me. We who have known what we have known . . . are not the subjects of time.

ALCESTIS *(The great pain has passed, but she moves guardedly; she has sat down again and speaks with her cheek pressed close to his)*: Yes, we, who were happy . . .

ADMETUS *(Suddenly grasping her hand, ardently)*: And you hated me once!

ALCESTIS *(Withdrawing her hand)*: No, never.

ADMETUS: That young man who kept coming back to that trial of the lion and the boar . . . There he is again—that young idiot from Thessaly.

(They are both laughing.)

ALCESTIS: Oh, what a road I have come!

ADMETUS: You didn't hate me, as I came around the corner straining over those damned beasts?

ALCESTIS: No. I suffered the more for it. I had begun to love that stern-faced young man from Thessaly. You were the only suitor who attempted that trial twice . . . Even Hercules gave up . . . To think that I could not see where life was carrying me!

ADMETUS *(Proudly, ardently)*: I, I saw.

ALCESTIS: Beloved Admetus . . . you saw. You married this self-willed, obstinate girl.

ADMETUS *(More ardently)*: Our love! Our love! . . . Our whisperings in the night! . . . The birth of Epimenes, when I almost lost you . . . *(She makes gestures of trying to silence him)* Alcestis! What we have known, what we have lived . . . Oh, to live forever—with you—beside you.

ALCESTIS: Ssh! There are things that we human beings are not permitted to say aloud.

ADMETUS *(Tentatively putting his foot on the ground)*: I do not understand . . . My knee does not tremble. *(With joyous hope)* Alcestis! It may be . . . it may be I shall live.

ALCESTIS *(Equally ecstatic, to the sky)*: Living or dead, we are watched; we are guided; we are understood. Oh, Admetus, lie quiet, lie still!

ADMETUS: I dare not . . . believe . . . hope . . .

ALCESTIS *(The pain returns; she is starting toward the palace door)*: Admetus, I would find it a natural thing, if a message came from Delphi to me, saying that I should give my life for my children or for Thessaly or . . . for my husband—

ADMETUS: —No. No. No man would wish another to die for him. Every man is ready to die his own death.

ALCESTIS *(Mastering her suffering)*: What are you saying, Admetus? Think of all the soldiers—thousands and thousands of them—who have died for others. And we women, poor cowardly soldiers, have died—a great many of us—for our husbands and children. *(She starts stumbling toward the palace door)*

ADMETUS: I would think less of the gods who could lay such a decision between husband and wife . . .

(Rising; in loud amazement) Look! This lightness!

ALCESTIS: Aglaia! Aglaia!

ADMETUS *(Springs up and rushes to her)*: Alcestis, you are in trouble! Aglaia! Aglaia!

(Aglaia hurries to her from the palace door.)

ALCESTIS: Take me to my bed.

ADMETUS: You are ill. Are you ill, Alcestis?

ALCESTIS *(Turning)*: Take my life. Be happy. Be happy.

(She collapses in their arms and is carried into the palace. From beyond the gate come sounds of an excited crowd, fragments of singing, etc., and the roar of Hercules's voice.)

HERCULES: Where is my old friend Ad-meeee-tus?

TOWNSPEOPLE: Hercules is here! Hercules is here!

HERCULES: Al-cess-s-stis! Where is the divine Al-cess-stis? Alcestis the Silent! Admetus the Hoss-s-spitable!

(The Watchman enters.)

TOWNSPEOPLE: Hercules is here! Hercules!

WATCHMAN: The gods preserve us! What can be done?

(More Townspeople pour in the gate, shouting, "Long live Hercules, son of Zeus!" Enter Hercules—drunk, happy, garlanded—a jug in his hand. Two Villagers laughingly carry Hercules's club as a great burden.)

HERCULES: Alcestis, fairest of the daughters of Iolcos! Admetus, crown of friends! Where are they?

TOWNSPEOPLE: Hercules, the destroyer of beasts! Hercules, the friend of man! Long live Hercules!

WATCHMAN: Welcome a thousand times to Pherai, great Hercules!

HERCULES: Where is my friend Epimenes—the mighty hunter, the mighty fisherman? Epimenes, I shall wrestle with you. By the God's thunder, you shall not throw me again!

WATCHMAN: All of them will be here in a minute, Hercules. They are beside themselves with joy.

(A wailing, a keening, is heard in the palace.)

HERCULES: That's weeping I hear. What is that wailing, old man?

WATCHMAN: Wailing, Hercules! The women and girls are rejoicing that Hercules has come.

(Enter Aglaia in haste from the palace.)

AGLAIA: A thousand times welcome, divine Hercules. The king and queen will be here in a moment. Happy, happy they are—you can be sure of that. Oh, son of Zeus, what a joy to see you!

HERCULES *(Loudly)*: I'm not the son of Zeus!

AGLAIA *(Covering her ears)*: Hercules, what are you saying?

HERCULES: I'm the son of Amphytrion and Alcmene. I'm a common man, Aglaia; and the work I do is as hard for me as for any other.

AGLAIA: Oh, may the gods prevent misfortune from coming to this house! You're very drunk, Hercules, to say such a wicked thing as that.

HERCULES: I'm a man, just an ordinary man, I tell you.

AGLAIA: God or man, Hercules, what do I see? Hercules, you are filthy! Is this the handsomest man in all Greece? By the immortal gods, I would never have known you! Now listen: you remember the baths that Aglaia prepares? They'd take the skin off an ordinary man. And the oil I have ready for you—you remember the oil, don't you?

HERCULES *(Confidentially)*: First, Aglaia—first! *(He makes a gesture of drinking)*

AGLAIA: You haven't forgotten our wine, is that it? You shall have some immediately!

HERCULES *(Suddenly roaring)*: On the road they told me that Admetus had been stabbed and wounded. Who struck him, Aglaia?

AGLAIA: Oh, that's all forgotten, Hercules. He's as well now as you or I!

(Rhodope and another girl come from the palace bearing a wine jar and some cups.)

Come, sit here and refresh yourself.

(Hercules tries to catch one of the girls, who eludes him. He then starts in pursuit of the other. He catches her.)

HERCULES: What's your name, little pigeon?

AGLAIA *(Angrily)*: Hercules!

(The girl escapes. Hercules runs after her, stumbles, and falls flat on the ground.)

HERCULES: Oh! I've hurt myself! Hell and confusion! My knee! My knee!

AGLAIA: Hercules! I haven't one bit of pity for you. Can you have forgotten where you are? Immortal heavens, what would Queen Alcestis think—you behaving like that!

HERCULES (*Who has slowly got up and sat down*): Twenty days I've walked. Where are they? Where are my friends, Admetus and Alcestis?

AGLAIA (*Confidentially*): Now, Hercules, you're an old friend of the house, aren't you?

HERCULES: I am!

AGLAIA: We can talk quite plainly to you, can't we? You're not one of those guests we have to conceal things from, thank the gods!

HERCULES: I'm their brother! Their brother!

AGLAIA: Now listen: one of the women in the house, an orphan . . . one of the women in the house . . .

HERCULES: What? Dead?

AGLAIA (*Finger on lips*): And you know how loyal and kind King Admetus and Queen Alcestis are to all of us who serve here . . .

HERCULES: Dead? An orphan?

AGLAIA: Yes, she'd lost both her father and mother. Now, they'll be here in just a minute—after you've had your bath. But now, just now—you know: they are by that poor girl, in friendship and piety. You understand everything, Hercules?

HERCULES: No. No, Aglaia, there are too many things I do not understand. But do you know who understands them all?

(*Pause*) Alcestis. Am I not right, Aglaia?

AGLAIA: Yes. Yes, Hercules.

HERCULES: Now I am going to talk frankly to you, Aglaia: I have come here—I have walked twenty days—to ask Alcestis one question.

AGLAIA: A question, Hercules?

(*For answer, Hercules twice points quickly and emphatically toward the zenith.*)

About the gods?

(He nods. Aglaia recovers herself and says briskly)
Well, first you must have that bath. You will come out
of it looking like a boy of seventeen. And I have such a
garland for you. And such perfumes!

(He rises and starts to follow her to the palace steps.)

HERCULES: And while I'm taking the bath you will sit beside
me and tell me again how Apollo came to Thessaly?

AGLAIA: Yes, I will. I'll tell you once more.

HERCULES *(Stopping her; with urgency)*: And no one knew
which was Apollo? *(She shakes her head)* A whole year,
and no one knew which was Apollo—not even Alcestis?
*(Again she shakes her head. Hercules clutches his fore-
head)* Aglaia, who can understand them? We shall
never understand them. When I try to think of them, I
start trembling; I get dizzy.

AGLAIA: Hercules! You are tired. Come . . .

*(Enter Admetus. He stands at the top of the stairs as
Hercules and Aglaia reach the bottom step.)*

ADMETUS *(Loudly)*: Welcome, Hercules, friend of all men;
Hercules, benefactor of all men!

HERCULES: Admetus! Old friend!

*(Admetus puts his hands on Hercules's shoulders. They
gaze into one another's eyes.)*

ADMETUS: From where have you come, Hercules?

HERCULES: From labors, Admetus . . . from labors.

AGLAIA: King Admetus, Hercules's bath is ready. You can
begin talking when he comes out. *(Looking up)* It will
be evening soon.

ADMETUS: No, first we will drink a bowl of wine together!
Come, sit down, Hercules. For a short time I was ill,

and this foolish womanish couch is where I used to sit in the sun. Now tell me—what has been your latest great labor?

(Aglaia and the girls have gone into the palace.)

HERCULES *(Hushed, wide-eyed)*: Admetus, Admetus—I killed the Hydra.

ADMETUS *(Rising, in awed astonishment)*: Great-hearted Hercules! You slew the Hydra! By the immortal gods, Hercules, you are the friend of man. Slew the Hydra! The Hydra!

HERCULES *(Beckoning to Admetus to draw his face nearer for a confidence)*: Admetus—*(Again beckoning)* It wasn't easy!

ADMETUS: I can well believe it!

HERCULES *(Almost bitterly; gazing into his face)*: It was not easy.
  (Abrupt change to urgent earnestness) Admetus, am I the son of Zeus?

ADMETUS: Hercules! Everyone knows that you are the son of Zeus and Alcmene.

HERCULES: One person can tell me. That is what I have come to ask Alcestis. Where is Alcestis, queen of women?

ADMETUS: But Aglaia told you!

HERCULES: Oh, yes. Who is this orphan girl that has died? Was she one of the first in the house?

ADMETUS: She called herself the servant of the servants.

HERCULES: But you were all fond of her?

ADMETUS: Yes. We all loved her.

HERCULES: You see, Admetus, everyone says I am the son of Zeus and therefore my labors must be easier for me than for another man. If I have the blood and the heart and the lungs of him *(Pointing upward)* in me, shouldn't they be easy? But, Admetus, they are not easy. The Hydra! *(He wraps his arms around Admetus in imitation of a snake and sets his face in extreme horror)* I was about to burst. The blood sprang out of my ears like fountains. If I am only a man—the son of Amphytrion and Alcmene—then, Admetus, *(Peering into Admetus's face with strained urgency)* then I'm a very good man!

ADMETUS: God or man, Hercules—god or man, all men honor and are grateful to you.

HERCULES: But I want to know. Some days I feel that I am the son of Zeus. Other days I am . . . I am a beast, Admetus, a beast and a brute. Every month messengers arrive from all over Greece, asking me to come and do this and do that. I'll do no more; I won't do a single thing until I've settled this matter. One of these days—yes, I foresee it—someone will come to me and ask me to . . . descend into the underworld . . . into Hell, Admetus, and bring back someone who has died. *(Rising, in terrified repudiation)* No! No! *That* I will not do. God or man, *no one* may ask that of me!

ADMETUS *(Sincerely shocked)*: No, Hercules—that has never been done, nor even thought of.

HERCULES: Every time I come here I look at that—that entrance to Hell—with great fear, Admetus.

ADMETUS: You must not think such thoughts!

HERCULES: Even a son of Zeus couldn't do that, could he? So—so you see the question? Isn't that an important question? And who can answer it? Who is wisest in just these matters where you and I are most ignorant? You know who: she who never speaks, or speaks so little. The Silent. She is silent, isn't she?

ADMETUS: Yes, she is silent.

HERCULES: But she'll speak to me . . . to her old friend Hercules? She'll speak for me, won't she? *(He pours himself more wine)* Do you know, Admetus—do you know what your Alcestis is?

(Admetus, in pain, rises, and sits down.)

No, you don't know. I journey from place to place—
from court to court. I've seen them all—the queens and
princesses of Greece. The daughters of the men we
knew and the girls we courted are growing up. Oedipus
of Thebes has a daughter, Antigone; and there is
Penelope, who's just married the son of Laertes of Ithaca.
Leda of Sparta has two daughters, Helen and Clytem-
nestra. I've seen 'em all, talked to 'em all. What are they
beside Alcestis? Dirt. Trash.

*(Aglaia comes from the palace bearing a garland of vine
leaves. The Watchman follows with a jar of oil. They stand
listening.*

   *Hercules rises and, in drunken energy close to violence,
turns Admetus about, shouting:)*

Do you know? Do you know to the full?

ADMETUS *(In agony, raising his arms)*: I know, Hercules.

HERCULES: Do you know all—her power to forgive, to
   pardon? No, you don't know a thing. Alcestis is the
   crown of Greece. The crown of women.

ADMETUS *(Taking three steps backward)*: Hercules! Alcestis
   is dead.

(Pause.)

The servants of servants. Forgive us, Hercules!

HERCULES *(Silence. A great rage rises in him. Then with savage bitterness)*: Admetus . . . you are no friend. By the
   immortal gods, you are my worst enemy!

*(He grasps him by the throat and, walking backward,
drags the unresisting Admetus with him.)*

If you were not Admetus, I would kill you now!

AGLAIA AND WATCHMAN: Hercules! Hercules, Queen Alcestis wished it! She wanted us not to tell you until later.

HERCULES: You have treated me as no friend. I thought I was your brother.

AGLAIA *(Pounding with her fists on his back)*: Hercules! Hercules!

HERCULES: Alcestis dead—and I was not worthy to be told! You let me boast and drink and revel . . .

AGLAIA: It was her wish, Hercules. Alcestis commanded it.

HERCULES *(Broodingly, holding Admetus bent far backward before him)*: You think I have no mind or heart or soul. What do I care for the thanks and praise of the world if I am not fit to share the grief of my friends?

(Pause.)

AGLAIA: It was for hospitality, Hercules. She wished it!

HERCULES: Hospitality is for guests, not brothers.

ADMETUS *(Quietly)*: Forgive us, Hercules.

HERCULES *(Releasing Admetus)*: Alcestis is dead. Alcestis is in the underworld.

(Suddenly struck by an idea; loudly) In Hell! Where is my club! My club! I shall go and get her!

AGLAIA: Hercules!

ADMETUS: No, Hercules. Live! She died in my place. She died for me. It is not right that still another die.

HERCULES: My club! My club! Admetus, now I shall tell you something—something that no man knows. Now all the world may know it. *(He has advanced to the top of the path)* I once came near to Alcestis in violence, in brutish violence. Yes, I, Hercules, son of Zeus, did that! A god—some god—intervened in time, to save her and to save me. Alcestis forgave me. How can that be? How can any man understand that? She spoke of it to no one in the world. And when I came to Pherai there was no sign in her face, in her eyes, that I had been the criminal. Only a god can understand that—only that loving smile. Forgiveness is not within our power—we commoner men. Only the strong and pure can forgive. I never wanted that she should forget that evil moment —no!—for in her remembering it lay my happiness; for her remembering and her forgiving were one.

ADMETUS: Hercules, I shall come with you.

HERCULES: Stay and rule, Admetus. Your labors I cannot do; you cannot do mine. What god shall I call on? Not my father—father and no father. Who is the god you mainly worship here?

AGLAIA: Have you forgotten, Hercules? This is Apollo's land.

HERCULES: Yes, now I remember. I have had little to do with him, but . . . *(Looking to heaven)* Apollo, I am Hercules, called the son of Zeus and Alcmene. All Greece says that you have loved these two—Admetus and Alcestis. You know what I'm about to do. You know I can't do it by myself. Put into my arm a strength that's never been there before. You do this—or let's say, you and I do this together. And if we can do it, let everybody see that a new knowledge has been given to us of what gods and men can do together.

ADMETUS: One moment, Hercules. *(He goes down the path)* Pytho! Pytho! This is Hercules, the loved friend of Alcestis and of me and of Epimenes. Let him pass, Pytho—going and coming.

HERCULES: Go into the palace, Admetus—all of you. I must work as I must live—alone.

(It is dark. The characters on the stage withdraw, except for Admetus, who stands by the palace door, covering his face with his cloak. A low beating on timpani, like distant thunder, grows louder, strikes a sharp blow, and jumps up a fourth. Hercules has disappeared into the door of the cave. Presently he returns, leading Alcestis. Over her white dress and head she wears a dark veil, which trails many yards

behind her. As they reach the stage, Hercules releases her hand. She sways, with groping steps, as though drugged with sleep. Hercules shoulders his club and goes off in his solitary way. Admetus, holding his cloak before him, as before a strong light, approaches, enfolds her. She rests her head on his breast. He leads her into the palace.)

ACT III

Twelve years later. Again, first streaks of dawn.
   Enter left, Alcestis—old, broken, in rags. She is carrying a water jar. She descends to the spring to fill it. Noise of a crowd on the road.

TOWNSPEOPLE *(Outside the palace gates)*: King Agis, help us! Save us! . . . King Agis must help us . . . We want to talk to King Agis!

   (Enter hurriedly, in horrified protest, a new and younger Night Watchman. He also carries a lighted lantern and a rattle. His face is smeared with ashes. He opens the gate a crack and speaks through it.)

WATCHMAN: You know the order: anyone who puts foot in these gates will be killed.
TOWNSPEOPLE *(Pressing in and overrunning the Watchman)*: Let him kill us! We're dying already! . . . The king must do something.

WATCHMAN *(Looking over his shoulder toward the palace, in terror)*: The king's doing everything he can. Pestilences and plagues come from the gods, he says, and only the gods can stop them. Bury your dead, he says, bury them the moment they fall. And smear your faces with ashes; rub your whole body with ashes and cinders. That way the plague can't see you, he says, and it will pass you by.

TOWNSPEOPLE: We've heard all that before. We want to see Queen Alcestis. Queen Alcestis! She can help us. Queen Alcestis!

WATCHMAN *(Indignantly)*: What do you mean—Queen Alcestis? There's no Queen Alcestis here. She's a slave, and the lowest of the slaves!

(Alcestis has come up the path, her jar on her shoulder. She stands and listens. The Watchman sees her.)

There she is! *(Violently)* Look at her! *She* brought the plague. She *is* the plague. It's she that's brought the curse on Thessaly!

TOWNSPEOPLE *(After a shocked silence, an outburst of contradictory cries)*: No, never! Not Queen Alcestis! What did he say? How did she bring it?

ALCESTIS *(Her head turning slowly as she looks into their faces; barely a question)*: I—brought the plague? I brought the plague?

WATCHMAN: She was dead, wasn't she? And Hercules brought her back from death, didn't he? She brought back death with her. Everybody belonging to her is dead. Her husband killed. Two of her children killed. One of her sons got away—but who's heard of him for a dozen years? The king will have her killed or driven from the country.

ALCESTIS: No, I did not bring this disease to Thessaly. Take me to these judges. If it is I who have brought misfortune to Thessaly, let them take my life and remove the disease from you and your children.

(Alcestis moves off to the left, into the servants' quarters. Light slowly comes up on Apollo, standing on the roof.)

TOWNSPEOPLE: No! She could not have brought evil to Thessaly! That is Alcestis the Wise!

WATCHMAN *(Amid contradictory cries from the crowd)*: Go to your homes! You'll all be killed here.

(To those in front) What do you know about it? Ignorant boors! Away, all of you! I've warned you. You know what kind of man King Agis is.

(Townspeople disappear, murmuring and grumbling, through the palace gate. The Watchman goes off left, shaking his rattle. As he goes:)

Dawn . . . dawn . . . and all is well in the palace of Agis, King of Thessaly, rich in horses . . .

(Death comes out of the cave, ascends the path, and sniffs at the doors.)

APOLLO: Death!

DEATH *(Who hasn't noticed him; taken unawares)*: Ah, you're here again!

APOLLO: It is getting light. You are shuddering.

DEATH: Yes. Yes, but I have some questions to ask you. Lord Apollo, I can't understand what you mean by this. So many dead! Down where I live there's such a crowding and trampling and waiting in line! And never have I seen so many children! But I confess to you, Lord Apollo, I don't know what you mean by it: you are the God of healing—of life and of healing—and here you are, the sender of plagues and pestilence. You loved Admetus, and his family, and his people; and all you do is kill them.

APOLLO *(A smile)*: I loved Alcestis, and I killed her—once.

DEATH: Contemptible, what you did!

APOLLO: Have you mended the wall—that wall through which Hercules broke?

DEATH: Broke? Hercules? *You* broke it. You broke the ancient law and order of the world: that the living are the living and the dead are the dead.

APOLLO: Yes—one small ray of light fell where light had never fallen before.

DEATH: You broke that law, and now you're caught up in its consequences. You're losing your happiness and your very wits because you can't make yourself known to them. And you're behaving like the rejected lover who dashes into the beloved's house and kills everyone there.

APOLLO: I *have* made myself known to them. I have set my story in motion.

DEATH: Your lesson.

APOLLO: Yes, my lesson—that I can bring back from the dead only those who have offered their lives for others.

DEATH: You brought back *one,* and now you are hurling thousands and thousands into my kingdom.

APOLLO: Yes, I must bring ruin and havoc, for only so will they remember the story. In the stories that are longest remembered, death plays a large role.

DEATH *(Shuddering)*: This light! This light! All these plague-stricken do not interest me. There is one mortal here that I am waiting for . . . she who escaped me once.

APOLLO: Alcestis? You will never have her.

DEATH: She is mortal!

APOLLO: Yes.

DEATH: She is *mortal!*

APOLLO: All mortal. Nothing but mortal.

DEATH: What are you going to do? You cannot steal her a second time?

APOLLO: Death, the sun is risen. You are shaking.

DEATH: Yes, but give me an answer. I am in a hurry.

APOLLO: Start accustoming yourself to a change.

DEATH: I?

APOLLO: One ray of light has already reached your kingdom.

DEATH *(In headlong flight to his cave, shrieking)*: There'll be no more. No second one. No more light. No more. No change!

(Exit. The light fades from Apollo, who disappears. Enter from the road—through the palace gate, left open—Epimenes, twenty-one, and Cheriander, also twenty-one. They are holding their cloaks about their noses. Under their cloaks they wear short swords. Cheriander comes forward eagerly and looks about him with awe. Epimenes follows him, morose and bitter.)

CHERIANDER: The Palace of Admetus and Alcestis! . . . And was Apollo here? Where did he place his feet—here, or here? *(Epimenes nods, scarcely raising his eyes from the ground)*

    And Hercules brought your mother back from the dead . . . where? *(Epimenes indicates the cave. Cheriander goes quickly down to it)*

    That I have lived to see this place! Look, Epimenes! There is your old friend Pytho guarding the door. Speak to him so that we can drink at the spring. This water, at least, is not poisoned.

EPIMENES: You remember me, Pytho? —He scarcely stirs.

CHERIANDER: Make the offering, and let us drink.

EPIMENES: "Sources of life—earth, air . . ." No, Cheriander, I cannot. How can I say the prayer we said here so many hundred times? In the morning my father and mother would bring us here. How could all this have happened? The God turned his face away. My father killed. My brother and sister killed. Myself sent away by night to live among strangers. My mother a slave—or dead. And the land under pestilence and the dead bodies lying unburied under the sun. To whom do I make a prayer?

CHERIANDER *(With quiet resolution)*: We are leaving Pherai. We are going out of that gate now. You are not ready to do what we came to do, and I will not help you.

EPIMENES: I can do what I have to do without prayer or offering. Justice and revenge speak for themselves. To strike! To strike into his throat. Yes, and to strike his daughter, Laodamia, too.

CHERIANDER: Epimenes, I will not help you. This is not the way we planned it. Kill or be killed, as you wish. I have not crossed Greece with you to take part in a mere butchery.

EPIMENES: You want me to make a prayer? To whom? To Apollo, who has blasted this house with his hatred?

CHERIANDER (*He descends, and putting his hands on Epimenes's shoulders, shakes him in solemn anger*): Are you the first man to have suffered? Cruelty, injustice, murder, and humiliation—is it only here that those things can be found? Have you forgotten that we came here to establish justice? That you yourself said that men of themselves could never have arrived at justice—that it was planted in their minds by the gods?

(*They gaze sternly at one another.*)

EPIMENES (*Quietly, looking down*): I do not deserve to have such a friend.

(*Enter Alcestis, left, carrying the water jar on her shoulder.*)

CHERIANDER: Are you ready to make the offering?

(*Epimenes recites the ritual, solemnly, but all but inaudibly. They both drink. Cheriander starts up the path, vigorously.*)

I am ready to knock at the palace doors.
(*He sees Alcestis. He hurries back to the spring, and says to Epimenes*) There is an old woman here. We will see what we can learn from her.

(Alcestis has taken a few steps down the path, but seeing the men, draws back. Cheriander comes up the path to her.)

Old woman, is this the palace of Agis, King of Thessaly?

(Her eyes go at once to the gate. Cheriander returns to Epimenes.)

She seems to be a slave. Perhaps it is your mother.

EPIMENES *(Goes quickly up the path, looks closely at Alcestis, then says brusquely)*: No.

CHERIANDER: You are sure?

EPIMENES *(Shortly)*: Sure. Certain.

CHERIANDER: Tell me, old woman, has this pestilence taken lives in the palace? *(She shakes her head)*

King Agis lives here with his family—with a young daughter, Laodamia? *(She nods)*

Tell me: the guards he has about him—did he bring them from Thrace, or are they of this country? *(No answer)*

EPIMENES: Perhaps she is deaf, or dumb.

(Louder) Does he often make journeys back to his own country—to Thrace?

ALCESTIS: You are in danger here. You must go—you must go at once.

EPIMENES: Oh, she can speak. Tell me, old mother, were you here in the days of King Admetus and Queen Alcestis?

ALCESTIS: Who are you? From where have you come?

EPIMENES: Did you know them? Had you talked with them? *(She nods)* King Admetus is dead? *(She nods)* Is Queen Alcestis alive? *(No sign)* Here in the palace? *(Her eyes return again to the gate)*

(He adds impatiently) By the immortal gods, since you can speak, speak!

ALCESTIS: You must go at once. But tell me . . . tell me: who are you?

CHERIANDER *(Staring at Alcestis, but urgently striking Epimenes's forearm)*: Look again. Look closely. Are you sure?

EPIMENES: Sure! These mountain women are all the same. They all have this silence, this slyness.

ALCESTIS: How did you come in at that gate? King Agis will certainly have you killed.

CHERIANDER: No. We bring a message to King Agis that he will be glad to hear.

ALCESTIS *(Repeatedly shaking her head)*: There is no message now that will save your lives, young man. Go. Take the road to the north and go quickly.

EPIMENES: The message we bring will make us very welcome. We have come to tell him of the death of an enemy—of his greatest enemy.

CHERIANDER: There is no need to tell it now.

EPIMENES: Whom he lives in dread of.

(Shaking her head, Alcestis passes him and starts down the path.)

We come to tell him of the death of Epimenes, the son of King Admetus and Queen Alcestis. He will be glad enough to hear of that.

(Alcestis is near the spring. She stops, lifts her head, and puts her hand to her heart, letting her jar slip.)

CHERIANDER *(Going to her and taking her jar)*: Let me carry your jar, old woman.

ALCESTIS *(Suddenly)*: You are Epimenes!

CHERIANDER *(Short laugh)*: No, old woman. Epimenes is dead.

ALCESTIS: You have proof of this?

CHERIANDER: Yes, proof.

(He has filled the jar and is starting up the path.)

ALCESTIS: We have always thought that he would return ... in secret, or disguise. My eyes are failing.

(Eagerly) You are Epimenes!

CHERIANDER: No, mother, no.

ALCESTIS: You knew him—you talked with him?

CHERIANDER: Yes, many times. Where can I carry this for you?

ALCESTIS *(At the top of the path, peers into Epimenes's face)*: Let me look at you.

(Then gazing into Cheriander's face) Do not tell lies to an old woman. He sent no message?

EPIMENES: None.

ALCESTIS: None?

EPIMENES: None but this. Can you see this belt? Queen Alcestis wove this for King Admetus before Epimenes was born.

ALCESTIS *(Peers at it, and gives a cry)*: What manner of young man was he who gave you this belt?

EPIMENES *(Mastering his impatience; as to a deaf person)*: Old woman, is Queen Alcestis near? Make some answer: yes or no. This is unendurable. Can you call Queen Alcestis, or can't you?

ALCESTIS: I am Alcestis.

CHERIANDER *(After amazed silence, falls on one knee; gazing into her face)*: You ... you are Alcestis?

EPIMENES *(Standing rigid, one fist on his forehead)*: I am ashamed to say my name. *(He also sinks to one knee)* I am Epimenes.

ALCESTIS: Yes—yes.

(Her eyes turning from palace to road) But in this danger ... this danger ...

EPIMENES: Forgive ... me.

ALCESTIS *(Touching his head)*: You are an impatient, self-willed young man, as I was an impatient, self-willed girl. It is time you were more like your father.

EPIMENES: You unhappy—

ALCESTIS *(Almost sharply)*: —No. No, Epimenes. Do not call me unhappy.

EPIMENES: This misery . . .

ALCESTIS: No! Learn to know unhappiness when you see it. There is only one misery, and that is ignorance—ignorance of what our lives are. That is misery and despair.

CHERIANDER *(Rising, intent)*: Ignorance?

ALCESTIS: Great happiness was given to me once, yes . . . but shall I forget that now? And forget the one who gave it to me? All that has happened since came from the same hands that gave me the happiness. I shall not doubt that it is good and has a part in something I cannot see . . . You must go now.

EPIMENES *(Rising)*: We have come to kill King Agis and to regain the throne.

(Alcestis starts turning her face from side to side and murmuring, "No. No.")

Our plans have been made in detail. This very night—

ALCESTIS: —No. No, Epimenes. The plague, the pestilence, has taken the place of all that. King Agis has only one thought, and one fear—not for himself, but for his child, Laodamia. The God is bringing things to pass in his own way.

CHERIANDER: We will do what she says, Epimenes, and go now.

ALCESTIS: Come back . . . in ten days. Go north. Hold your cloaks before your faces and go north.

CHERIANDER: Get your cloak, Epimenes.

(Epimenes descends to the spring.)

ALCESTIS: Where is your home, young man?

CHERIANDER: In Euboea—under Mount Dirphys.

ALCESTIS: Is your mother living?

CHERIANDER: Yes, Queen Alcestis.

ALCESTIS: Does she know my name?

CHERIANDER: Every child in Greece knows your name!

ALCESTIS: Tell her . . . Alcestis thanks her.

> (*Epimenes is beside her; she touches him lightly*)
> Remember, I have not been unhappy. I was once miserable and in despair: I was saved from that.
>
> (*Pointing*) Go through that grove . . . and follow the river.

> (*Sounds of Townspeople approaching. More breaking of gates. They come on to the edge of the stage, shouting. The Watchman and Guards come out of the palace in alarm. Alcestis beckons to the young men to descend and hide themselves by the spring. The Guards keep the people back by holding their spears horizontally before them.*)

TOWNSPEOPLE: Water! We want water from the palace spring! The water's been poisoned. King Agis, help us!

GUARDS: Back! Back and out—all of you!

> (*Enter from the palace King Agis. He is dressed in a barbaric, ornate costume. He is forty; a thick cap of black hair over a low forehead. His face is also streaked with ashes.*)

AGIS: How did these people get into the court?

TOWNSPEOPLE: King Agis, help us!

AGIS: This eternal "Help us!" I'm doing what I can. Which one of you let these people in?

GUARDS (*In confusion*): Sire—they've broken the gates. We can't hold them.

AGIS: Cowards! Do your duty. You're afraid to go near them, that's the trouble.

> (*To the Townspeople*) Stand back!
>
> (*To a Guard*) What is that they were saying about water?

FIRST GUARD: They say, Your Greatness, they think that the springs in the town have been poisoned, and they want some water from the springs in the palace.

AGIS: Very well, you shall have water from these springs.

(Holding a corner of his robe before his nose, he points to a man who has crawled far forward on his knees.)

Get back, you! People of Pherai, I have news for you. I thought I had done all a king could do; and now I find there is one more thing to be done. Where's this Alcestis?

WATCHMAN: She is here, Your Greatness.

AGIS *(Turns and looks at her in long, slow contempt, and s ays slowly)*: So . . . you . . . are . . . the bringer of all this evil! This is a great day, people of Pherai, for at last we have come to the heart of this matter. If it can be shown that this woman has brought this disease upon us, she will be stoned to death or driven from the country.

(To Alcestis) Woman, is it true that you were dead— dead and buried—and that you were brought back to life?

ALCESTIS: It is true.

AGIS: And that you and your husband believed that this was done by Hercules, with the aid of Apollo, and as a sign of Apollo's favor?

ALCESTIS: We believed it, and it is true.

AGIS: And is it true that you and your husband believed that Apollo was here for a year's time, out of love and favor for you and Thessaly?

ALCESTIS: We believed it, and it is true.

AGIS: And where is that love now? People of Pherai, this is Apollo's land. If Apollo formerly extended favor to this woman and to her family, is it not clear to you now that his favor has turned to hatred?

(The crowd is silent) Yes or no?

(Contradictory murmurs) What? You are of mixed mind? You dolts! Have you forgotten that this plague is raging among you? Watchman!

WATCHMAN: Yes, sire?

AGIS: Before the gates of the palace were closed, did you see the effects of the disease, and how it struck?

WATCHMAN: Yes, sire, I saw it.

AGIS: Describe it!

WATCHMAN: Your Greatness, it is not just one—there are three diseases. The first comes suddenly, like—

(A Guard has come from the palace, and presents himself before King Agis.)

AGIS *(Irritably)*: Well, what is it? What is it?

SECOND GUARD: Sire, your daughter is beating on her door. She says she wishes to be let out. She says she wishes to be where you are. Without stopping she is beating on her door.

AGIS *(With a reflection of his tenderness for her; urgently)*: Tell her that I shall be with her soon; that I have work to do here. Tell her to be patient; tell her that I shall come to her soon.

SECOND GUARD: Yes, sire.

(He starts toward the palace door.)

AGIS: Wait! *(Torn)* Tell her to be patient. I shall take her from her room for a walk in the garden later.

SECOND GUARD: Yes, sire.

(Exit.)

AGIS *(To the Watchman)*: Three? Three diseases, you say?

WATCHMAN: The first one strikes suddenly, Your Greatness, like lightning.

AGIS *(With a shudder, turning to Alcestis)*: *Your* work, old woman!

ALCESTIS: No! No!

WATCHMAN *(His hands on his stomach)*: Like fire. That's the one that strikes young people and children.

AGIS *(Beside himself)*: Children! Idiot! Don't you know better than to say words of ill omen here? I'll have your tongue torn out. Avert, you immortal gods, avert the omen! Hear not the omen!

(To the Watchman) I want no more of this.

(Turning to the palace in despairing frustration) Oh, go away—all of you! Who shall save us from this night . . . this swamp . . . this evil cloud?

(He turns his head from side to side in helplessness and revulsion; then suddenly pulls himself together; resolutely, pointing at Alcestis.)

Speak then! Apollo the God hates you, and through you has brought this curse upon Thessaly.

(Alcestis, in silence, looks at him with a level gaze.)

Is that not so? Speak!

ALCESTIS *(Taking her time)*: When Apollo came to this city, King Agis, his priest Teiresias said that that great honor brought with it a great peril.

AGIS: Peril?

ALCESTIS: You stand in that peril now. This floor is still warm—is hot—from the footprints of the God . . .

(As though to herself, almost dreamily) For a long time I did not understand this. It is solitude—and slavery—that have made it clear to me. Beware what you do here, King Agis.

AGIS *(Throws up his chin, curtly dismissing this warning)*: Answer my question.

ALCESTIS: The gods are not like you and me, King Agis— but at times we are like them. They do not love us for a day or a year and then hate what they have loved. Nor do you love your child Laodamia today and tomorrow drive her out upon the road.

AGIS *(Outraged)*: Do not name her, you . . . you bringer of death and destruction!

(He starts toward the palace door.)

ALCESTIS: We ask of them health . . . and riches . . . and our happiness. But they are trying to give us something else, and better: understanding. And we are so quick to refuse their gift . . . No! No! Apollo has not turned his face away from me . . . People of Pherai, had you ever been told that King Admetus was unjust to you?

TOWNSPEOPLE: No, Queen Alcestis.

ALCESTIS: Or I?

TOWNSPEOPLE: No-o-o-o, Queen Alcestis!

ALCESTIS: Do you believe that this disease has been sent to punish you for any wickedness of ours?

TOWNSPEOPLE: No! No!

ALCESTIS: If Hercules brought someone back from the dead, do you think he could have done it without the full approval of the gods?

TOWNSPEOPLE: No! No!

AGIS: Then what is the cause of this pestilence?

ALCESTIS: It has been sent . . . to call our attention to . . . to make us stop, to open our eyes . . .

AGIS: To call our attention to what, Alcestis?

ALCESTIS *(Lifted head, as though listening)*: I don't know. To some sign.

(There is a moment of suspended waiting. Then suddenly the First Guard, at the head of the path, sees the two Young Men and cries:)

FIRST GUARD: Sire, there are two strangers here.

AGIS *(Coming forward as near as he dares)*: How did they come here? Guards! Close in on them!

(Guards gather above and in front of them.)

Throw down your swords!

EPIMENES: Never, King Agis!

AGIS: What can you do—caught in that hole there? Throw down your swords!

(Alcestis has been shaking her head from side to side, and murmuring, "King Agis, King Agis . . .")

(To Alcestis) You brought them in. Neither you nor they have put ashes on your faces.

   (To the Guards) Kill them! Kill them!

(Two Guards start gingerly down the path.)

Cowards! Traitors! Do what I command!

(Suddenly a Third Guard on the stage is stricken with the plague. He throws down his spear and cries:)

THIRD GUARD: King Agis! Water! The plague! I'm on fire. Save me! Help me! I'm on fire!

(Intermittently he yawns.)

AGIS *(Recoiling, as all recoil)*: Drive him out! Strike his back with your spears.

THIRD GUARD *(Alternately lurching from side to side, and yawning, and crying out)*: Water! Water! Sleeeeep!

AGIS *(Holding his hands before his face)*: Push him out into the road.

(General tumult. The Third Guard tries to drag himself to the gate. Other Guards and Townspeople, averting their faces, try, with spears, with kicks, to hurry his departure. In these horrors, the Guards have removed their attention from

Epimenes and Cheriander. For a second all that can be heard is exhausted panting.)

(Screaming) My wagons! My horses! . . . To Thrace! To Thrace!
 (To Alcestis) Take back your Thessaly the Hospitable, Queen Alcestis! Rule over your dead and dying . . .
EPIMENES: Now, Cheriander!

(They rush upon the stage.)

CHERIANDER: Strike, Epimenes!
EPIMENES: Agis—I am Epimenes, son of King Admetus!
AGIS: Who? What is this? Guards!

(Alcestis, shaking her head, stands in front of King Agis, and with raised hands opposes Epimenes.)

ALCESTIS: No, Epimenes! No!
EPIMENES *(Outraged by Alcestis's attitude)*: Mother! The moment has come. He killed my father!
ALCESTIS: Don't do it!
AGIS: Guards! *(Taking distraught steps, right and left)* Coward! Guards!
CHERIANDER: Listen to your mother, Epimenes.
ALCESTIS *(Her back to Agis, but talking to him)*: Yes, King Agis, go back to your own kingdom.
AGIS: Is that your son? Alcestis, answer me: is this your son?

(In rage and frustration at seeing his revenge frustrated, Epimenes is on one knee, beating the floor with the hilt of his own sword.)

EPIMENES: Revenge! Revenge!
ALCESTIS: Epimenes, remember your father's words: that the murderer cuts the sinews of his own heart.

EPIMENES *(Sobbing, his forehead near the ground)*: He killed my father . . . my brother . . . my sister . . .

(The Second Guard rushes from the palace.)

SECOND GUARD: King Agis! Your daughter, the Princess Laodamia! She is beating on her door and calling for you—in pain, King Agis, in pain!

AGIS *(Arms upraised)*: The gods avert! Laodamia! Laodamia! Avert, you immortal gods!

(Agis rushes into the palace.)

ALCESTIS *(Standing over Epimenes and placing her hand on his shoulder)*: A man who has known the joys of revenge may never know any other joy. That is the voice of your father.

(She turns to the Townspeople and says calmly and impartially) Friends, go to your homes and get baskets and jars. Go to the quarries beyond the South Gate, where sulfur is. Epimenes, you remember the quarries where you played as a child? That yellow sulfur that the workers in iron used . . . Burn it in the streets. Spread it on the dead.

(To the Guards) Help them in this work; there is nothing more for you to do here. Epimenes, stand—stand up. Direct them in this.

EPIMENES *(Getting up)*: Yes, Mother.

(With quiet authority; to Guards and Townspeople) Come with me.

(They start off, but Cheriander returns and adds softly, in awe:)

CHERIANDER: Queen Alcestis . . . the sign you spoke of—from Apollo the God. Was this decision of King Agis—was that the sign?

ALCESTIS *(With lifted listening head)*: No . . . the sign has not come yet.

CHERIANDER *(With youthful ardor)*: You are the sign! You are message and sign, Queen Alcestis!

ALCESTIS *(Almost insensible, shaking her head; softly)*: No . . . no . . .

(Cheriander dashes out after Epimenes. Enter from the palace King Agis, howling with grief.)

AGIS: She is dead! Laodamia is dead! Twelve years old. She is dead . . . *(He beats his fists against columns and walls. He stamps down the stairs, then up them again)* Twelve years old. Her arms around my neck. In excruciating pain. "Father, help me . . . Father, help me!" . . . Her hair. Her mother's face. Her eyes, her eyes.

(He sees Alcestis) You—you brought this! You did this!

ALCESTIS *(Murmuring through his words, as if entreating)*: Agis . . . Agis . . . Agis . . .

AGIS *(Seizing her hand and touching it to his forehead and chest)*: Give me this plague. Let it destroy us all. "Father, help me!" She was everything to me. And she is dead—dead—dead!

ALCESTIS: Agis . . . Agis . . .

AGIS: You—whom Hercules brought back from the dead—you could do this.

(An idea strikes him) Hercules brought you back. Where was it? Was it here? *(He stumbles down the path)* There? *(He ascends the path quickly)* Tell me, Alcestis— how did Hercules do it? What happened below there? *(Alcestis shakes her head silently)* Show me what he did and I shall do it. Laodamia, I shall come for you. Answer me, Alcestis!

ALCESTIS: Agis, I saw nothing. I heard nothing.

AGIS: You are lying.

ALCESTIS: Agis, listen to me—I have something to say to you.

AGIS: Speak! Speak!

ALCESTIS: "Father, help me!"

AGIS: Do not mock me.

ALCESTIS: I am not mocking you. What was Laodamia saying, King Agis?

AGIS: She was in pain, pain, excruciating pain!

ALCESTIS: Yes, but that was not all. What more did she mean?

AGIS: What more?

ALCESTIS: The bitterness of death, King Agis, is part pain—but that is not all. The last bitterness of death is not parting—though that is great grief. I died . . . once. What is the last bitterness of death, King Agis?

AGIS: Tell me!

ALCESTIS: It is the despair that one has not lived. It is the despair that one's life has been without meaning. That it has been nonsense; happy or unhappy, that it has been senseless. "Father, help me."

AGIS: She loved me, Alcestis.

ALCESTIS: Yes.

AGIS: She *loved* me.

ALCESTIS: Yes, but love is not enough.

AGIS: It *was*. It was for her and it was for me. I will not listen to you.

ALCESTIS: Love is not the meaning. It is one of the signs that there is a meaning—it is only one of the signs that there is a meaning. Laodamia is in despair and asks that you help her. That is what death is—it is despair. Her life is vain and empty, until you give it a meaning.

AGIS: What meaning could I give it?

ALCESTIS *(Quietly)*: You are a brutal, cruel, and ignorant man. *(Brief silence)* You killed *my* Laodamia. Three times. Senselessly. Even you do not know how many times you have killed Laodamia.

AGIS: No!

ALCESTIS: You don't know. Go back to your kingdom. There, and only there, can you help Laodamia.

(Agis comes up the path and, passing her, goes toward the palace door.)

All the dead, King Agis . . . *(She points to the entrance to the underworld)* All those millions lie imploring us to show them that their lives were not empty and foolish.

AGIS: And what is this meaning that I can give to Laodamia's life?

ALCESTIS: Today you have begun to understand that.

AGIS *(His head against the post of the palace door)*: No.

ALCESTIS: I was taught these things. Even I. You will learn them, King Agis . . . Through Laodamia's suffering you will learn them.

(Broken, he goes through the palace door.
 During his slow exit, the light begins to fall on Apollo, entering from the palace doors. In his descent, he wears his cloak, but the hood has fallen back on his shoulders, showing a garland around his head. He first addresses Alcestis from the doors; then moves behind her.
 Left alone, Alcestis closes her eyes and takes a few steps left. Her head seems to bend with great weariness; she seems to shrink to a great age. She turns right and starts to move toward the gate to the road, her eyes half open.)

APOLLO: A few more steps, Alcestis. Through the gate . . . and across the road . . . and into my grove.

ALCESTIS: So far . . . and so high . . .

APOLLO: Now another step. It is not a hill. You do not have to raise your foot.

ALCESTIS: It is too far. Let me find my grave here.

APOLLO: You will not have that grave, Alcestis.

ALCESTIS: Oh, yes. I want my grave . . .

APOLLO: The grave means an end. You will not have that ending. You are the first of a great number that will not have that ending. Still another step, Alcestis.

ALCESTIS: And will there be grandchildren, and the grandchildren of grandchildren . . . ?

APOLLO: Beyond all counting.

ALCESTIS: Yes . . . What was his name?

APOLLO: Admetus.

ALCESTIS: Yes. And the shining one I wanted to serve?

APOLLO: Apollo.

ALCESTIS: Yes . . . *(Near the gate)* All the thousands of days
. . . and the world of cares . . . *(Raising her head, with
closed eyes)* And whom do I thank for all the happiness?

APOLLO: Friends do not ask one another that question.

(She goes out.
Apollo raises his voice, as though to ensure that she will
hear him beyond the wall.)

Those who have loved one another do not ask one
another that question . . . Alcestis.

END OF PLAY

The Alcestiad TO
The Drunken Sisters

At the close of the three acts of The Alcestiad *a curtain falls. Apollo comes before the curtain.*

APOLLO *(To the audience)*: Wait! Wait! We have still one more thing to do. We are in Greece, and here we do not believe that audiences should return to their homes immediately after watching stories that present what is difficult and painful in human life. Here we have this custom: we require that the poet write a short satyr play in the spirit of diversion—even of the comical. *(Confidentially)* We claim that the tragic insight cannot stand alone. It tends to its own excess. As one of you *(Pointing into the audience)* has said: neither Death nor the Sun permits itself to be gazed at fixedly. And further, we require that this satyr play deal with some element— some secondary aspect—of the preceding play. So— what shall we show you? Teiresias—the six hundred year old, the too-much-loved? How from time to time the gods made him young again; how from time to time they even changed him into a woman? And the quarrel between Zeus and Hera about that? *(He starts laughing but tries to control himself)* No, no—that's not suitable here. That play is too coarse. The Greeks have stomachs strong enough to endure such unseemly matters, but *(He is again overcome with laughter)* it is . . . No, no—not here. Or shall we show you the story about the sisters of Queen Alcestis? Her father, King Pelias, was an old fool and her two sisters were not very clever. That often happens in families—there is just one intelligent person. We could show you how the archcook Medea whispered into the sisters' ears, pretending to show them how they could make their dear father young again . . .

(Suddenly changing his tone) No! It is true that there are people who laugh only when they hear about something cruel. That play is a heap of cruelties, and when you went home you would be ashamed of yourselves for having been amused by it.

We have another: it is not very funny. Tonight did you ask yourselves how it was possible that the life of King Admetus was extended? Those great ladies the weird sisters, the Fates—can they be bribed? We shall show you how it happened.

(He starts taking off his outer robes, under which he is dressed as a kitchen boy, and calls into the wings: "My hat! My hat!")

In this little play I am again Apollo, in the disguise of a kitchen boy.

(From the wings are reached out to him a large cone-shaped straw hat and a belt, from which the effects of a kitchen boy—onions, etc.—hang. He calls into the wings: "My bottles!" sets his hat on his head, and puts on the belt.)

I hate disguises, I hate drunkenness—*(From the wings he receives a rope, from which three bottles hang)* —but see these bottles I have hanging around my neck? I hate lies and stratagems—but I've come to do crookedly what even All-Father Zeus could not do without guile: extend a human life.

(Calling through the curtain to the rear or into the wings: "All ready?" and then turning again to the audience.)

Yes, all is ready for the satyr play, to conclude the solemn trilogy of *The Alcestiad*.

(He remains standing at the proscenium pillar as the curtain rises.)

The Drunken Sisters

A SATYR PLAY

The Drunken Sisters, *The Alcestiad*'s satyr play, was first added to the text for the German production, which opened June 27, 1957 in Zurich.

In her introduction to *The Alcestiad* acting edition, Isabel Wilder paid special attention to the Fates' masks. Her brother learned "through experience that a mask should not be too ugly, not too grotesque, for then it distracts and alienates the viewer. If that happens its purpose is defeated." In addition to serving as satyr play for *The Alcestiad*, *The Drunken Sisters* also represents Gluttony in Wilder's cycle on "The Seven Deadly Sins" (published in *The Collected Short Plays of Thornton Wilder: Volume I*, TCG, 1997).

CHARACTERS

CLOTHO ⌉
LACHESIS │ *The Three Fates*
ATROPOS ⌋
APOLLO

SETTING

The time of Admetus, King of Thessaly.

The Three Fates are seated on a bench, which is largely hidden by their voluminous draperies. They wear the masks of old women, touched by the grotesque but with vestiges of nobility. Seated are Clotho with her spindle, Lachesis with the bulk of the thread of life on her lap, and Atropos with her scissors. They rock back and forth as they work, passing the threads from right to left. The audience watches them for a time in silence, broken only by a faint humming from Clotho.

CLOTHO: What is it that goes first on four legs, then on two legs? Don't tell me! Don't tell me!

LACHESIS *(Bored)*: You know it!

CLOTHO: Let me pretend that I don't know it.

ATROPOS: There are no new riddles. We know them all.

LACHESIS: How boring our life is without riddles! Clotho, make up a riddle.

CLOTHO: Be quiet, then, and give me a moment to think . . . What is it that . . . What is it that . . . ?

(Enter Apollo, disguised.)

APOLLO *(To the audience)*: These are the great sisters—the Fates. Clotho weaves the threads of life; Lachesis measures the length of each; Atropos cuts them short. In their monotonous work of deciding our lives they are terribly bored, and like so many people who are bored, they find great pleasure in games—in enigmas and riddles. Naturally they can't play cards, because their hands are always busy with the threads of life.

ATROPOS: Sister! Your elbow! Do your work without striking me.

LACHESIS: I can't help it—this thread is s-o-o l-o-o-ong! Never have I had to reach so far.

CLOTHO: Long and gray and dirty! All those years a slave!

LACHESIS: So it is! *(To Atropos)* Cut it, dear Sister. *(Atropos cuts it—click!)* And now this one; cut this. It's a blue one—blue for bravery: blue and short.

ATROPOS: So easy to see! *(Click)*

LACHESIS: You almost cut that purple one, Atropos.

ATROPOS: This one? Purple for a king?

LACHESIS: Yes; watch what you're doing, dear. It's the life of Admetus, King of Thessaly.

APOLLO *(Aside)*: Aie!

LACHESIS: I've marked it clearly. He's to die at sunset.

APOLLO *(To the audience)*: No! No!

LACHESIS: He's the favorite of Apollo, as was his father before him, and all that tiresome house of Thessaly. The queen Alcestis will be a widow tonight.

APOLLO *(To the audience)*: Alcestis! Alcestis! No!

LACHESIS: There'll be howling in Thessaly. There'll be rolling on the ground and tearing of garments . . . Not now dear; there's an hour yet.

APOLLO *(Aside)*: To work! To work, Apollo the Crooked! *(He starts the motions of running furiously while remaining in one place, but stops suddenly and addresses the audience)* Is there anyone here who does not know that old story—the reason why King Admetus and his Queen Alcestis are dear to me? *(He sits on the ground and continues talking with raised forefinger)* Was it ten years ago? I am little concerned with time. I am the god of the sun; it is always light where I am. Perhaps ten years ago. My father and the father of us all was filled up with anger against me. What had I done? *(He moves his finger back and forth)* Do not ask that now; let it be forgotten . . . He laid upon me a punishment. He ordered that I should descend to earth and live for a year among men—I, as a man among men, as a servant. Half hidden, known and not known, I chose to be a herdsman of King Admetus of Thessaly. I lived the life of a man, as close to them as I am to you now, as close to the just and to the unjust. Each day the king gave orders to the other herdsmen and myself; each day the queen gave thought to what went well or ill with us and our families. I came to love King Admetus and Queen Alcestis and through them I came to love all men. And now Admetus must die. *(Rising)* No! I have laid my plans. I shall prevent it. To work. To work, Apollo the Crooked. *(He again starts the motions of running furiously while remaining in one place. He complains noisily)* Oh, my back! Aie, aie. They beat me, but worst of all they've made me late. I'll be beaten again.

LACHESIS: Who's the sniveler?

APOLLO: Don't stop me now. I haven't a moment to talk. I'm late already. Besides, my errand's a terrible secret. I can't say a word.

ATROPOS: Throw your yarn around him, Lachesis. What's the fool doing with a secret? It's we who have all the secrets.

(The threads in the laps of the Sisters are invisible to the audience. Lachesis now rises and swings her hands three times in wide circles above her head as though she were about to fling a lasso, then hurls the noose across the stage. Apollo makes the gesture of being caught. With each strong pull by Lachesis, Apollo is dragged nearer to her. During the following speeches Lachesis lifts her end of the strands high in the air, alternately pulling Apollo up, almost strangling him, and flinging him again to the ground.)

APOLLO: Ladies, beautiful ladies, let me go. If I'm late all Olympus will be in an uproar. Aphrodite will be mad with fear—but oh, already I've said too much. My orders were to come immediately, and to say nothing—especially not to women. The thing's of no interest to men. Dear ladies, let me go.

ATROPOS: Pull on your yarn, Sister.

APOLLO: You're choking me. You're squeezing me to death.

LACHESIS *(Forcefully)*: Stop your whining and tell your secret at once.

APOLLO: I can't. I dare not.

ATROPOS: Pull harder, Sister. Boy, speak or strangle. *(She makes the gesture of choking him)*

APOLLO: Ow! Ow!—Wait! I'll tell the half of it, if you let me go.

ATROPOS: Tell the whole or we'll hang you up in the air in that noose.

APOLLO: I'll tell, I'll tell. But—*(He looks about him fearfully)*—promise me! Swear by the Styx that you'll not tell anyone, and swear by Lethe that you'll forget it.

LACHESIS: We have only one oath—by Acheron. And we never swear it—least of all to a sniveling slave. Tell us what you know, or you'll be by all three rivers in a minute.

APOLLO: I tremble at what I am about to say. I . . . ssh . . . I carry . . . here . . . in these bottles . . . Oh, ladies, let me go. Let me go.

CLOTHO AND ATROPOS: Pull, Sister.

APOLLO: No! No! I'll tell you. I am carrying the wine for . . . for Aphrodite. Once every ten days she renews her beauty . . . by . . . drinking this.

ATROPOS: Liar! Fool! She has nectar and ambrosia, as they all have.

APOLLO *(Confidentially)*: But is she not the fairest? . . . It is the love gift of Hephaistos; from the vineyards of Dionysos; from grapes ripened under the eye of Apollo—of Apollo who tells no lies.

SISTERS *(Confidentially to one another in blissful anticipation)*: Sisters!

ATROPOS *(Like sugar)*: Pass the bottles up, dear boy.

APOLLO *(In terror)*: Not that! Ladies! It is enough that I have told you the secret! Not that!

ATROPOS: Surely, Lachesis, you can find on your lap the thread of this worthless slave—a yellow one destined for a long life?

APOLLO *(Falling on his knees)*: Spare me!

ATROPOS *(To Lachesis)*: Look, that's it—the sallow one, with the tangle in it of dishonesty, and the stiffness of obstinacy, and the ravel-ravel of stupidity. Pass it over to me, dear.

APOLLO *(His forehead touching the floor)*: Oh, that I had never been born!

LACHESIS *(To Atropos)*: This is it. *(With a sigh)* I'd planned to give him five score.

APOLLO *(Rising and extending the bottles, sobbing)*: Here, take them! Take them! I'll be killed anyway. Aphrodite will kill me. My life's over.

ATROPOS *(Strongly, as the Sisters take the bottles)*: Not one more word out of you. Put your hand on your mouth. We're tired of listening to you.

(Apollo, released of the noose, flings himself facedown upon the ground, his shoulders heaving. The Sisters put the flagons to their lips. They drink and moan with pleasure.)

SISTERS: Sisters!

LACHESIS: Sister, how do I look?

ATROPOS: Oh, I could eat you. And I?

CLOTHO: Sister, how do I look?

LACHESIS: Beautiful! Beautiful! And I?

ATROPOS: And not a mirror on all the mountain, or a bit of still water, to tell us which of us is the fairest.

LACHESIS *(Dreamily, passing her hand over her face)*: I feel like . . . I feel as I did when Kronos followed me about, trying to catch me in a dark corner.

ATROPOS: Poseidon was beside himself—dashing across the plains trying to engulf me.

CLOTHO: My own father—who can blame him?—began to forget himself.

ATROPOS *(Whispering)*: This is not such a worthless fellow, after all. And he's not bad-looking. *(To Clotho)* Ask him what he sees.

LACHESIS: Ask him which of us is the fairest.

CLOTHO: Boy! Boy! You bay meek. I mean, you . . . you may thpeak. Thpeak to him, Lakethith; I've lotht my tongue.

LACHESIS: Boy, look at us well! You may tell us which is the fairest.

(Apollo has remained facedownward on the ground. He now rises and gazes at the Sisters. He acts as if blinded: he cowers and uncovers his eyes, gazing first at one and then at another.)

APOLLO: What have I done? This splendor! What have I done? You—and you—and you! Kill me if you will, but I cannot say which one is the fairest. *(Falling on his knees)* Oh, ladies—if so much beauty has not made you cruel, let me now go and hide myself. Aphrodite will hear of this. Let me escape to Crete and take up my old work.

ATROPOS: What was your former work, dear boy?

APOLLO: I helped my father in the marketplace; I was a teller of stories and riddles.

(The Sisters are transfixed. Then almost with a scream:)

SISTERS: What's that? What's that you said?

APOLLO: A teller of stories and riddles. Do the beautiful ladies enjoy riddles?

SISTERS *(Rocking from side to side and slapping one another)*: Sisters, do we enjoy riddles?

ATROPOS: Oh, he would only know the old ones. Puh! The blind horse . . . the big toe . . .

LACHESIS: The cloud . . . the eyelashes of Hera . . .

CLOTHO *(Harping on one string)*: What is it that first goes on four legs . . . ?

ATROPOS: The porpoise . . . Etna . . .

APOLLO: Everyone knows those! I have some new ones—

SISTERS *(Again, a scream)*: New ones!

APOLLO *(Slowly)*: What is it that is necessary to—*(He pauses. The Sisters are riveted)*

LACHESIS: Go on, boy, go on. What is it that is necessary to—

APOLLO: But—I only play for forfeits. See! If I lose . . .

CLOTHO: If you looth, you mutht tell uth which one ith the faireth.

APOLLO: No! No! I dare not!

LACHESIS *(Sharply)*: Yes!

APOLLO: And if I win?

ATROPOS: Win? Idiot! Stupid! Slave! No one has ever won from us.

APOLLO: But if I win?

LACHESIS: He doesn't know who we are!

APOLLO: But if I win?

CLOTHO: The fool talkth of winning!

APOLLO: If I win, you must grant me one wish. One wish, any wish.

LACHESIS: Yes, yes. Oh, what a tedious fellow! Go on with your riddle. What is it that is necessary to—

APOLLO: Swear by Acheron!

CLOTHO AND LACHESIS: We swear! By Acheron! By Acheron!

APOLLO *(To Atropos)*: You, too.

ATROPOS *(After a moment's brooding resistance, loudly)*: By Acheron!

APOLLO: Then: ready?

LACHESIS: Wait! One moment. *(Leaning toward Atropos, confidentially)* The sun is near setting. Do not forget the thread of Ad— You know, the thread of Ad—

ATROPOS: What? What Ad? What are you whispering about, silly?

LACHESIS *(Somewhat louder)*: Not to forget the thread of Admetus, King of Thessaly. At sundown. Have you lost your shears, Atropos?

ATROPOS: Oh, stop your buzzing and fussing and tend to your own business. Of course I haven't lost my shears. Go on with your riddle, boy!

APOLLO: So! I'll give you as much time as it takes to recite the names of the Muses and their mother.

LACHESIS: Hm! Nine and one. Well, begin!

APOLLO: What is it that is necessary to every life—and that can save only one?

(The Sisters rock back and forth with closed eyes, mumbling the words of the riddle.

Suddenly Apollo starts singing his invocation to the Muses:)

Mnemosyne, mother of the nine;
Polyhymnia, incense of the gods—

LACHESIS *(Shrieks)*: Don't sing! Unfair! How can we think?

CLOTHO: Stop your ears, Sister.

ATROPOS: Unfair! *(Murmuring)* What is it that can save every life—*(They put their fingers in their ears)*

APOLLO:

Erato, voice of love;
Euterpe, help me now.

Calliope, thief of our souls;
Urania, clothed of the stars;
Clio of the backward glances;
Euterpe, help me now.

Terpsichore of the beautiful ankles;
Thalia of long laughter;
Melpomene, dreaded and welcome;
Euterpe, help me now.

(Then in a loud voice) Forfeit! Forfeit!

(Clotho and Atropos bury their faces in Lachesis's neck, moaning.)

LACHESIS *(In a dying voice)*: What is the answer?

APOLLO *(Flinging away his hat, triumphantly)*: Myself! Apollo the sun.

SISTERS: Apollo! You?

LACHESIS *(Savagely)*: Pah! What life can you save?

APOLLO: My forfeit! One wish! One life! The life of Admetus, King of Thessaly.

(A horrified clamor arises from the Sisters.)

SISTERS: Fraud! Impossible! Not to be thought of!

APOLLO: By Acheron.

SISTERS: Against all law. Zeus will judge. Fraud.

APOLLO *(Warning)*: By Acheron.

SISTERS: Zeus! We will go to Zeus about it. He will decide.

APOLLO: Zeus swears by Acheron and keeps his oath.

(Sudden silence.)

ATROPOS *(Decisive but ominous)*: You will have your wish—the life of King Admetus. But—

APOLLO *(Triumphantly)*: I shall have the life of Admetus!

SISTERS: But—

APOLLO: I shall have the life of Admetus! What is your *but*?

ATROPOS: Someone else must die in his stead.

APOLLO *(Lightly)*: Oh—choose some slave. Some gray and greasy thread on your lap, divine Lachesis.

LACHESIS *(Outraged)*: What? You ask me to take a life?

ATROPOS: You ask us to murder?

CLOTHO: Apollo thinks that we are criminals?

APOLLO *(Beginning to be fearful)*: Then, great Sisters, how is this to be done?

LACHESIS: Me—an assassin? *(She spreads her arms wide and says solemnly)* Over my left hand is Chance; over my right hand is Necessity.

APOLLO: Then, gracious Sisters, how will this be done?

LACHESIS: Someone must *give* his life for Admetus—of free choice and will. Over such deaths we have no control. Neither Chance nor Necessity rules the free offering of the will. Someone must choose to die in the place of Admetus, King of Thessaly.

APOLLO *(Covering his face with his hands)*: No! No! I see it all! *(With a loud cry)* Alcestis! Alcestis! *(And he runs stumbling from the scene)*

END OF PLAY

Some Thoughts on Playwriting

"SOME THOUGHTS ON PLAYWRITING," published originally in 1941, was the work of an internationally acclaimed author who had won the Pulitzer Prize for fiction (*The Bridge of San Luis Rey*) and drama (*Our Town*), and was soon to win a third for his play, *The Skin of Our Teeth*. Something of the author's great success in the classroom and on the lecture circuit is also present in the essay's didacticism. Not long before writing this piece, Wilder had added still another level of theatrical experience to his résumé: for several weeks he had played the role of the Stage Manager in the original Broadway production of *Our Town*.

SOME THOUGHTS
ON PLAYWRITING

by Thornton Wilder

This essay first appeared as a contribution to *The Intent of the Artist,* Augusto Centeno, ed., Princeton University Press, Princeton, 1941. It was republished in *American Characteristics and Other Essays,* the collection of twenty-eight of Wilder's essays, tributes and research papers, edited by Donald Gallup, and published by Harper & Row in 1979.

F OUR FUNDAMENTAL CONDITIONS of the drama separate it from the other arts. Each of these conditions has its advantages and disadvantages, each requires a particular aptitude from the dramatist, and from each there are a number of instructive consequences to be derived. These conditions are:

    I. The theatre is an art which reposes upon the work of many collaborators;

   II. It is addressed to the group-mind;

 III. It is based upon a pretense and its very nature calls out a multiplication of pretenses;

 IV. Its action takes place in a perpetual present time.

I

THE THEATRE IS AN ART WHICH REPOSES
UPON THE WORK OF MANY COLLABORATORS

We have been accustomed to think that a work of art is by definition the product of one governing selecting will. A landscape by Cézanne consists of thousands of brushstrokes each commanded by one mind. *Paradise Lost* and *Pride and Prejudice*, even in cheap frayed copies, bear the immediate and exclusive message of one intelligence. It is true that in musical performance we meet with intervening executants, but the element of intervention is slight compared to that which takes place in drama. Illustrations:

1. One of the finest productions of *The Merchant of Venice* in our time showed Sir Henry Irving as Shylock, a noble, wronged, and indignant being, of such stature that the merchants of Venice dwindled before him into irresponsible schoolboys. He was confronted in court by a gracious, even queenly Portia, Miss Ellen Terry. At the Odéon in Paris, however, Gémier played Shylock as a vengeful and hysterical buffoon, confronted in court by a Portia who was a *gamine* from the Paris streets with a lawyer's quill three feet long over her ear; at the close of the trial scene Shylock was driven screaming about the auditorium, behind the spectators' backs and onto the stage again, in a wild Elizabethan revel. Yet for all their divergencies both were admirable productions of the play.
2. If there was ever a play in which fidelity to the author's requirements was essential in the representation of the principal role, it would seem to be Ibsen's *Hedda Gabler,* for the play is primarily an exposition of her character, Ibsen's directions read:

> Enter from the left Hedda Gabler. She is a
> woman of twenty-nine. Her face and figure
> show great refinement and distinction. Her
> complexion is pale and opaque. Her steel gray
> eyes express an unruffled calm. Her hair is of
> an attractive medium brown, but is not par-
> ticularly abundant; and she is dressed in a
> flowing loose-fitting morning gown.

I once saw Eleonora Duse in this role. She was a woman
of sixty and made no effort to conceal it. Her complexion
was pale and transparent. Her hair was white, and she was
dressed in a gown that suggested some medieval empress in
mourning. And the performance was very fine.

One may well ask: Why write for the theatre at all? Why
not work in the novel, where such deviations from one's
intentions cannot take place?

There are two answers:

1. The theatre presents certain vitalities of its own so
   inviting and stimulating that the writer is willing to
   receive them in compensation for this inevitable
   variation from an exact image.
2. The dramatist through working in the theatre gradually learns not merely to take account of the presence of the collaborators, but to derive advantage
   from them; and he learns, above all, to organize the
   play in such a way that its strength lies not in
   appearances beyond his control, but in the succession of events and in the unfolding of an idea, in
   narration.

The gathered audience sits in a darkened room, one end
of which is lighted. The nature of the transaction at which
it is gazing is a succession of events illustrating a general
idea—the stirring of the idea; the gradual feeding out of

information; the shock and countershock of circumstances; the flow of action; the interruption of action; the moments of allusion to earlier events; the preparation of surprise, dread or delight—all that is the author's and his alone.

For reasons to be discussed later—the expectancy of the group-mind, the problem of time on the stage, the absence of the narrator, the element of pretense—the theatre carries the art of narration to a higher power than the novel or the epic poem. The theatre is unfolding action and in the disposition of events the authors may exercise a governance so complete that the distortions effected by the physical appearance of actors, by the fancies of scene painters, and the misunderstandings of directors, fall into relative insignificance. It is just because the theatre is an art of many collaborators, with the constant danger of grave misinterpretation, that the dramatist learns to turn his attention to the laws of narration, its logic, and its deep necessity of presenting a unifying idea stronger than its mere collection of happenings. The dramatist must be by instinct a storyteller.

There is something mysterious about the endowment of the storyteller. Some very great writers possessed very little of it, and some others, lightly esteemed, possessed it in so large a measure that their books survive down the ages, to the confusion of severer critics. Alexandre Dumas had it to an extraordinary degree; while Melville, for all his splendid quality, had it barely sufficiently to raise his work from the realm of nonfiction. It springs, not, as some have said, from an aversion to general ideas, but from an instinctive coupling of idea and illustration; the idea, for a born storyteller, can only be expressed imbedded in its circumstantial illustration. The myth, the parable, the fable are the fountainhead of all fiction and in them is seen most clearly the didactic, moralizing employment of a story. Modern taste shrinks from emphasizing the central idea that hides behind the fiction, but it exists there nevertheless, supplying the unity to fantasizing, and offering a justification to what otherwise we would repudiate as mere arbitrary contrivance, pretentious lying, or individualistic emotional association-spinning. For all their magnificent intellectual endowment, George Meredith and George Eliot were not born story-tellers; they chose fiction as the vehicle for their reflections, and the passing of time is revealing their error in that choice. Jane Austen was pure storyteller and her works are outlasting those of apparently more formidable rivals. The theatre is more exacting than the novel in regard to this faculty and its presence constitutes a force which compensates the dramatist for the deviations which are introduced into his work by the presence of his collaborators.

The chief of these collaborators are the actors.

The actor's gift is a combination of three separate faculties or endowments. Their presence to a high degree in any one person is extremely rare, although the ambition to possess them is common. Those who rise to the height of the profession represent a selection and a struggle for survival in one of the most difficult and cruel of the artistic activities. The three endowments that compose the gift are observation, imagination and physical coordination.

1. An observant and analyzing eye for all modes of behavior about us, for dress and manner, and for the signs of thought and emotion in oneself and in others.

2. The strength of imagination and memory whereby the actor may, at the indication in the author's text, explore his store of observations and represent the details of appearance and the intensity of the emotions—joy, fear, surprise, grief, love and hatred—and through imagination extend them to intenser degrees and to differing characterizations.

3. A physical coordination whereby the force of these inner realizations may be communicated to voice, face and body.

An actor must *know* the appearances and the mental states; he must *apply* his knowledge to the role; and he must physically *express* his knowledge. Moreover, his concentration must be so great that he can effect this representation under conditions of peculiar difficulty—in abrupt transition from the nonimaginative conditions behind the stage; and in the presence of fellow actors who may be momentarily destroying the reality of the action.

A dramatist prepares the characterization of his personages in such a way that it will take advantage of the actor's gift.

Characterization in a novel is presented by the author's dogmatic assertion that the personage was such, and by an analysis of the personage with generally an account of his or her past. Since in the drama this is replaced by the actual presence of the personage before us and since there is no occasion for the intervening all-knowing author to instruct us as to his or her inner nature, a far greater share is given in a play to (1) highly characteristic utterances and (2) concrete occasions in which the character defines itself under action and (3) a conscious preparation of the text whereby the actor may build upon the suggestions in the role according to his own abilities.

Characterization in a play is like a blank check which the dramatist accords to the actor for him to fill in—not entirely blank, for a number of indications of individuality are already there, but to a far less definite and absolute degree than in the novel.

The dramatist's principal interest being the movement of the story, he is willing to resign the more detailed aspects of characterization to the actor and is often rewarded beyond his expectation.

The sleepwalking scene from *Macbeth* is a highly compressed selection of words whereby despair and remorse rise to the surface of indirect confession. It is to be assumed that had Shakespeare lived to see what the genius of Sarah Siddons could pour into the scene from that combination of observation, self-knowledge, imagination and representational skill, even he might have exclaimed, "I never knew I wrote so well!"

II
THE THEATRE IS AN ART ADDRESSED
TO A GROUP-MIND

Painting, sculpture and the literature of the book are certainly solitary experiences; and it is likely that most people would agree that the audience seated shoulder to shoulder in a concert hall is not an essential element in musical enjoyment.

But a play presupposes a crowd. The reasons for this go deeper than (1) the economic necessity for the support of the play and (2) the fact that the temperament of actors is proverbially dependent on group attention.

It rests on the fact that (1) the pretense, the fiction, on the stage would fall to pieces and absurdity without the support accorded to it by the crowd and (2) the excitement induced by pretending a fragment of life is such that it partakes of ritual and festival, and requires a throng.

Similarly, the fiction that royal personages are of a mysteriously different nature from other people requires audiences, levees and processions for its maintenance. Since the beginnings of society, satirists have occupied themselves with the descriptions of kings and queens in their intimacy and delighted in showing how the prerogatives of royalty become absurd when the crowd is not present to extend to them the enhancement of an imaginative awe.

The theatre partakes of the nature of festival. Life imitated is life raised to a higher power. In the case of comedy, the vitality of these pretended surprises, deceptions and *contretemps* becomes so lively that before a spectator, solitary or regarding himself as solitary, the structure of so much event would inevitably expose the artificiality of the attempt and ring hollow and unjustified; and in the case of tragedy, the accumulation of woe and apprehension would soon fall short of conviction. All actors know the disturbing sensation of playing before a handful of spectators at a dress rehearsal or performance where only their interest in pure craftsmanship can barely sustain them. During the last rehearsals the phrase is often heard: "This play is hungry for an audience."

Since the theatre is directed to a group-mind, a number of consequences follow:

1. A group-mind presupposes, if not a lowering of standards, a broadening of the fields of interest. The other arts may presuppose an audience of connoisseurs trained in leisure and capable of being interested in certain rarefied aspects of life. The dramatist may be prevented from exhibiting, for example, detailed representations of certain moments in history that require specialized knowledge in the audience, or psychological states in the personages which are of insufficient general interest to evoke self-identification in the majority. In the Second Part of Goethe's *Faust* there are long passages dealing with the theory of paper money. The exposition of the nature of misanthropy (so much more drastic than Molière's) in Shakespeare's *Timon of Athens* has never been a success. The dramatist accepts this limitation in subject matter and realizes that the group-mind imposes upon him the necessity of treating material understandable by the larger number.
2. It is the presence of the group-mind that brings another requirement to the theatre—forward movement.

Maeterlinck said that there was more drama in the spectacle of an old man seated by a table than in the majority of plays offered to the public. He was juggling with the various meanings in the word "drama." In the sense whereby drama means the intensified concentration of life's diversity and significance he may well have been right; if he meant drama as a theatrical representation before an audience, he was wrong. Drama on the stage is inseparable from forward movement, from action.

Many attempts have been made to present Plato's dialogues, Gobineau's fine series of dialogues, *La Renaissance*, and the *Imaginary Conversations* of Landor, but without success. Through some ingredient in the group-mind, and through the sheer weight of anticipation involved in the dressing-up and the assumption of fictional roles, an action is required, and an action that is more than a mere progress in argumentation and debate.

III

THE THEATRE IS A WORLD OF PRETENSE

It lives by conventions: a convention is an agreed-upon falsehood, a permitted lie.

Illustrations: Consider at the first performance of *Medea*, the passage where Medea meditates the murder of her children. An anecdote from antiquity tells us that the audience was so moved by this passage that considerable disturbance took place.

The following conventions were involved:

1. Medea was played by a man.
2. He wore a large mask on his face. In the lip of the mask was an acoustical device for projecting the voice. On his feet he wore shoes with soles and heels half a foot high.
3. His costume was so designed that it conveyed to the audience, by convention: woman of royal birth and Oriental origin.
4. The passage was in metric speech. All poetry is an "agreed-upon falsehood" in regard to speech.
5. The lines were sung in a kind of recitative. All opera involves this "permitted lie" in regard to speech.

Modern taste would say that the passage would convey much greater pathos if a woman "like Medea" had delivered it—with an uncovered face that exhibited all the emotions she was undergoing. For the Greeks, however, there was no pretense that Medea was on the stage. The mask, the costume, the mode of declamation were a series of signs which the spectator interpreted and reassembled in his own mind. Medea was being re-created within the imagination of each of the spectators.

The history of the theatre shows us that in its greatest ages the stage employed the greatest number of conventions. The stage is fundamental pretense and it thrives on the acceptance of that fact and in the multiplication of additional pretenses. When it tries to assert that the personages in the action "really are," really inhabit such and such rooms, really suffer such and such emotions, it loses rather than gains credibility. The modern world is inclined to laugh condescendingly at the fact that in the plays of Racine and Corneille the gods and heroes of antiquity were dressed like the courtiers under Louis XIV; that in the Elizabethan Age scenery was replaced by placards notifying the audience of the location; and that a whip in the hand and a jogging motion of the body indicated that a man was on horseback in the Chinese theatre; these devices did not spring from naïveté, however, but from the vitality of the public imagination in those days and from an instinctive feeling as to where the essential and where the inessential lay in drama.

The convention has two functions:

1. It provokes the collaborative activity of the spectator's imagination; and
2. It raises the action from the specific to the general.

This second aspect is of even greater importance than the first.

If Juliet is represented as a girl "very like Juliet"—it was not merely a deference to contemporary prejudices that assigned this role to a boy in the Elizabethan Age—moving about in a "real" house with marble staircases, rugs, lamps, and furniture, the impression is irresistibly conveyed that these events happened to this one girl, in one place, at one moment in time. When the play is staged as Shakespeare intended it, the bareness of the stage releases the events from the particular and the experience of Juliet partakes of that of all girls in love, in every time, place and language.

The stage continually strains to tell this generalized truth and it is the element of pretense that reinforces it. Out of the lie, the pretense, of the theatre proceeds a truth more compelling than the novel can attain, for the novel by its own laws is constrained to tell of an action that "once happened"—"once upon a time."

IV

THE ACTION ON THE STAGE TAKES PLACE IN PERPETUAL PRESENT TIME

Novels are written in the past tense. The characters in them, it is true, are represented as living moment by moment their present time, but the constant running commentary of the novelist ("Tess slowly descended into the valley"; "Anna Karenina laughed") inevitably conveys to the reader the fact that these events are long since past and over.

The novel is a past reported in the present. On the stage it is always now. This confers upon the action an increased vitality which the novelist longs in vain to incorporate into his work.

This condition in the theatre brings with it another important element:

In the theatre we are not aware of the intervening storyteller. The speeches arise from the characters in an apparently pure spontaneity.

A play is what takes place.

A novel is what one person tells us took place.

A play visibly represents pure existing. A novel is what one mind, claiming to omniscience, asserts to have existed.

Many dramatists have regretted this absence of the narrator from the stage, with his point of view, his powers of analyzing the behavior of the characters, his ability to interfere and supply further facts about the past, about simultaneous actions not visible on the stage, and, above *all,* his function of pointing the moral and emphasizing the significance of the action. In some periods of the theatre he has been present as chorus, or prologue and epilogue, or as *raisonneur.* But surely this absence constitutes an additional force to the form, as well as an additional tax upon the writer's skill. It is the task of the dramatist so to coordinate his play, through the selection of episodes and speeches, that though he is himself not visible, his point of view and his governing intention will impose themselves on the spectator's attention, not as dogmatic assertion or motto, but as self-evident truth and inevitable deduction.

Imaginative narration—the invention of souls and destinies—is to a philosopher an all but indefensible activity.

Its justification lies in the fact that the communication of ideas from one mind to another inevitably reaches the point where exposition passes into illustration, into parable, metaphor, allegory and myth.

It is no accident that when Plato arrived at the height of his argument and attempted to convey a theory of knowledge and a theory of the structure of man's nature, he passed over into storytelling, into the myths of the Cave and the Charioteer; and that the great religious teachers have constantly had recourse to the parable as a means of imparting their deepest intuitions.

The theatre offers to imaginative narration its highest possibilities. It has many pitfalls and its very vitality betrays it into service as mere diversion and the enhancement of significant matter; but it is well to remember that it was the theatre that rose to the highest place during those epochs that aftertime has chosen to call "great ages" and that the Athens of Pericles and the reigns of Elizabeth I, Philip II and Louis XIV were also the ages that gave to the world the greatest dramas it has known.

BIBLIOGRAPHIC AND PRODUCTION NOTES

Part I
The Angel That Troubled the Waters
and Other Plays
Three-Minute Plays for Three Persons
And
The Marriage We Deplore

The Angel That Troubled the Waters and Other Plays. First published 29 October 1928 in New York by Coward-McCann in a limited and author-signed edition of 750 copies and trade edition of 2,000 copies numbered and signed by the publishers. Also published in England (1928) and Germany (1954). Of the sixteen plays in this collection, twelve were first published as follows: *Nascuntur Poetae . . .* (as *The Walled City*) in *Yale Literary Magazine* (hereafter called *YLM*), New Haven, CT (Mar. 1918) 305–08; *Proserpina and the Devil* in *Oberlin Literary Magazine* (hereafter *OLM*), Oberlin, OH (Dec. 1916) 50–51; *Fanny Otcott* (as *That Other Fanny Otcott*) in *YLM* (Apr. 1918) 328–31; *Brother Fire* (as *Brother Fire: A Comedy for Saints*) in *OLM* (May 1916) 200–02; *The Penny*

That Beauty Spent in *YLM* (Mar. 1918) 303–05; *The Angel on the Ship* in *YLM* (Oct. 1917) 15–17, and reprinted and revised as the first of "Two Plays," in *Harper's Magazine*, New York (Oct. 1928) 564–65; *The Message and Jehanne* in *YLM* (Nov. 1917) 94–96, and reprinted and revised in *Theatre Guild Magazine* (Oct. 1928) 13–15; *Childe Roland to the Dark Tower Came* in *YLM* (June 1919) 238–40; *Centaurs* (as *The Death of the Centaur: A Footnote to Ibsen*) in *S 4 N*, Northampton, MA (Apr. 1920) 8–12; *Leviathan* (as *Not for Leviathan*) in *YLM* (Apr. 1919) 160–63; *And the Sea Shall Give Up Its Dead* in *S 4 N* (Jan./Feb. 1923) 9–13; *Mozart and the Gray Steward*, as the second of "Two Plays" in *Harper's Magazine* (Oct. 1928) 565–67.

Under the banners of "Wilder, Wilder" and "Producing the Unproducible," WHA-TV Public Television in Madison, Wisconsin, joined with the University of Wisconsin's Department of Theatre and Milwaukee Repertory Theater to air four of the plays—*The Penny That Beauty Spent, And the Sea Shall Give Up Its Dead, Now the Servant's Name Was Malchus* and *The Flight into Egypt*—on 21 March 1978.

The Marriage We Deplore. First printed here from the author's typescript/manuscript dated in his hand "June 10, [19]17," in the Thornton Wilder Archive of the Yale Collection of American Literature, Beinecke Rare Book and Manuscript Library (hereafter TWYCAL). Shown elsewhere as "Number 1" of a projected series of "Five-Minute Playlets for Five Persons" but for which no other plays exist or have survived.

PART II
THE UNERRING INSTINCT

"*The Unerring Instinct: A Play in One Act.*" Written for the National Conference of Christians and Jews (NCCJ) and first published in duplicated form in January 1948 in New

York by the Conference as one of its "NCCJ Scripts for Brotherhood." Distributed free to schools and dramatic clubs throughout the country and reproduction allowed "without permission except no radio performances may be given in 1948, and that credit be given to the National Conference of Christians and Jews and to Mr. Wilder."

PART III
"THE EMPORIUM"

Two scenes from an uncompleted play, "The Emporium." First published from the TWYCAL in November 1985 as Appendix I in *The Journals of Thornton Wilder: 1939–1961*, selected and edited by Donald Gallup, Yale University Press, New Haven and London, 1985, 297–314.

"Notes Toward the Emporium." First printed from the TWYCAL as Appendix II in *The Journals of Thornton Wilder: 1939–1961*, selected and edited by Donald Gallup, Yale University Press, New Haven and London, 1985, 315–336.

Readers interested in learning more about the writing of the "The Emporium" should refer to a number of other notes in *The Journals*.

PART IV
THE ALCESTIAD
With Its Satyr Play
THE DRUNKEN SISTERS

The Alcestiad (as *Die Alkestiade*). First published in German translation by Herberth E. Herlitschka on 10 April 1960 by S. Fischer Verlag in Frankfurt am Main, Germany, in an edition of 40,000 copies. This edition, including the satyr play *The Drunken Sisters* (*Die Beschwipsten Schwestern*), also translated by Herberth E. Herlitschka, has sold approximately 60,000 copies. The English text, edited by Donald Gallup from German and English sources with Foreword by Isabel Wilder, was published 16 November 1977 by Harper & Row, New York, Hagerstown, San Francisco & London with the title *The Alcestiad or A Life in the Sun: A Play in Three Acts—With a Satyr Play: The Drunken Sisters*, in an edition of some 5,000 copies. Subsequent editions include Avon Books (1979) and The Franklin Library (1977). An acting edition with revised introduction by Isabel Wilder was published March 1980 by Samuel French, Inc., New York, Hollywood, London and Toronto (hereafter SF).

This play, directed by Tyrone Guthrie, had its world premier with the title *A Life in the Sun* at The Church of Scotland Assembly Hall, The Mound, Edinburgh, on 22 August 1955. It was produced by the Edinburgh Festival Society in association with Tennent Productions Limited, and was directed by Tyrone Guthrie, with décor by Tanya Moiseiwitsch, and Irene Worth in the role of Alcestis. The first performance in the German language occurred on 27 June 1957 in the Schauspielhaus in Zurich, Switzerland. This production, including the satyr play *The Drunken Sisters* for the first time, was directed by Leopold Lindtberg with Maria Becker in the role of Alcestis. The play was produced professionally in Germany, Switzerland and Austria twenty-one times between 1957 and 1961, and ten times since. The U.S. premier, directed by Kent Paul, occurred on 21 July 1978 at the Pacific Conservatory of the Performing Arts in Santa Maria, California. The first U.S. professional production, directed by Vincent Dowling, occurred on 25 August 1984 in Cleveland at the Great Lakes Shakespeare Festival (with the title *Alcestis and Apollo*). In November 1986, John Reich directed the University of Wisconsin-Madison Theatre's production, "a tribute to its native son" (Thornton Wilder was born in Madison, Wisconsin on 17 April 1897). On 12 January 1998, The Stage Directors and Choreographers Foundation sponsored a Concert Reading in New York City directed by Robert Kalfin and read by professional actors. The play is performed occasionally by amateurs.

The opera version of *The Alcestiad*, with libretto by Wilder and music composed by Louise Talma (1906–1996), was published in 1978 by Carl Fischer as *The Alcestiad: An Opera in Three Acts*. The opera had its world premier in German translation, prepared by Herberth E. Herlitschka, on 2 March 1962, at the Frankfurt Opera House, Frankfurt am Main. The production was directed by Harry Buckwitz with Inge Borkh in the role of Alcestis. This was the first opera by an American woman to be produced by a major European opera house. It was first performed in English in this country (in excerpts) on 3 April 1976, at the Yale School of Music with Phyllis Curtin singing Alcestis. Inquiries about this work may be directed to Carl Fischer, Inc., 62 Cooper Square, New York, NY 10003.

For additional details about Wilder's last play, see Martin Blank, "*The Alcestiad*: The Play and Opera" in *Critical Essays on Thornton Wilder*, edited by Martin Blank, G. K. Hall & Co., New York, 1996, 88–98. For a discussion of Wilder's reception by critics with attention to the sources of his popularity in Germany, and a selected German bibliography, see Amos N. Wilder, *Thornton Wilder and His Public*, Fortress Press, Philadelphia, 1980.

The Drunken Sisters. First printed in the *Atlantic Monthly*, CC.5 (Nov. 1957) 92–95. A revised text was published in *The Alcestiad or A Life in the Sun: A Play in Three Acts—With a Satyr Play: The Drunken Sisters* by Harper & Row, New York, Hagerstown, San Francisco, London, in 1977. SF acting edition published in 1978. The play was published in *The Collected Short Plays of Thornton Wilder: Volume I*, by Theatre Communications Group, New York, 1997.

FEB 2005